CW00759749

ELIZABETHAN HOUSEHOLDS

ELIZABETHAN HOUSEHOLDS

An Anthology

by

LENA COWEN ORLIN

THE FOLGER SHAKESPEARE LIBRARY

WASHINGTON, D.C.

1995

This volume has been published in conjunction with the exhibition *Elizabethan Households*, presented at the Folger Library, Washington, D.C., from February 13 through May 20, 1995.

Major funding for the exhibition and publication comes from the Lila Wallace-Reader's Digest Fund and the Winton and Carolyn Blount Exhibitions Endowment. This publication is also supported by the Andrew W. Mellon Publication Endowment of the Folger Library.

Printed in the United States.

Distributed by
University of Washington Press, Seattle and London.

ISBN 0-295-97464-8

Photographs by Julie Ainsworth, except as follows: pp. 34, 54, 78, 95, 114, Katherine Wetzel for Agecroft Association; pp. 8, 95, 111, 114, Colonial Williamsburg Foundation; pp. 95, 96, 102, 114, 128, 134, 142, Metropolitan Museum of Art; pp. 36, 116, Philadelphia Museum of Art; pp. 94, 95, 98, Raymond Erickson for George Way.

COVER ILLUSTRATION:
Timber framing from Pierre Le Muet, *Maniere de Bastir pour Touttes Sortes de Personnes* (Paris, 1623).

TITLE-PAGE ILLUSTRATION:
"The parts of a house" from Johann Amos Comenius, *Orbis Sensualium Pictus* (Nuremberg, 1664).

Table of Contents

Foreword

Elizabethan Households grows out of an exhibition held at the Folger Shakespeare Library in 1995. Like the exhibition, this anthology has two aims: to open a fresh investigation of domestic life in Elizabethan England and to demonstrate some of the ways in which it is possible to pursue such an investigation in the rare book and manuscript collections of the Folger Shakespeare Library.

Our first object, then, is early English household life. The readings represent the varied activities and significances of the domestic life of the past: its material contexts, social practices, political hierarchies, economic enterprises, and religious offices. Attempts have been made to introduce not just noblemen and their great houses, but other Elizabethan men and women from a wide range of positions and stations, including servants, tradesmen, and farmers. While it is important to establish the guiding structures for domestic life by referring to contemporary ideological literature about how it *should* have been conducted, we can also find many points of access to how it actually *was* conducted. Private life was not as orderly in practice as it was in theory, and, around the edges of the didactic literature, we find evidence of debate and difference.

It should be pointed out here that the word "Elizabethan" is misleading, but there's no better term. It would be more appropriate to say "Tudor and Stuart," or "Elizabethan, Jacobean, and Caroline," or even "Late Sixteenth- and Early Seventeenth-Century English," but the first is still imprecise for our purposes and the second and third are awkward. "Early modern" is a phrase now much in vogue, but it, like "the Renaissance," covers too large a number of years in precisely the same way that "Elizabethan" covers too few. Those of us at the Folger who worked on this exhibition finally decided on "Elizabethan" as a term that has expanded so much in the popular imagination that perhaps it can accommodate this stretch, too. The period covered is basically 1570 to 1640, but we include materials from outside this chronological range when they seem to cast some light on it.

The second goal of this anthology is to represent the Folger collections as an archive in which this kind of materialist research into the history of private life can uniquely be pursued. All textual extracts are from materials held by the Folger; Folger shelf marks are provided in the index. The date given in each citation is that of the Folger volume consulted and does not always represent the first issue of a work (or even the Folger's earliest edition). Headnotes specify dates of first publication. Throughout, spelling has been modernized and capitalization and punctuation regularized. To retain a period flavor, titles are given in old spelling, though re-capitalized and often shortened. Of course, the illustrations offer a glimpse of the early printed texts and manuscripts in unedited form.

As always when embarking on a new project here, I have been astonished by the extraordinary riches of the Folger Library collections and overwhelmed by the knowledge and generosity of spirit represented in the Folger Library staff. It is not possible to do justice to either. For the latter, in particular, the list is so long that it will inevitably seem to obscure how invaluable were the contributions that each staff member made.

There is a first among equals, however: Rachel Doggett, Andrew W. Mellon Curator of Books and Exhibitions, who guided every step of this project from its first conceptualization. It advanced with the support of Werner Gundersheimer, Director; Janet Griffin, Director of Public Programs; Richard Kuhta, Librarian; and Barbara Mowat, Director of Academic Programs. J. Franklin Mowery, Head of Conservation; Julie Biggs, Senior Paper Conservator; and Linda Hohneke, Conservation Assistant, consulted on the selection of items, prepared them for exhibition, and mounted them. Julie Ainsworth produced the photographs of Folger materials. Special help was provided by Georgianna Ziegler, Louis B. Thalheimer Reference Librarian; Jean

Miller, Art Librarian; and Laetitia Yeandle, Curator of Manuscripts. Joan Morrison, Head Cataloger, and Betsy Walsh, Reading Room Supervisor, made unusual accommodations for the project. I would also like to thank Central Library staff members Harold Batie, LuEllen DeHaven, Jean Dunnington, Rosalind Larry, Henry Raine, Camille Seerattan, Kathleen Stewart, and Lafayette Seymore.

I am especially grateful to the members of the Department of Academic Programs. By keeping things going in the department, Kathleen Lynch, Program Administrator to the Folger Institute, and Amy Adler, Administrative Assistant, allowed me to disappear for a time into the rare book vaults. Rebecca Willson, Program Assistant to the Folger Institute, and Fredrik Jonsson, Program Intern, aided in research and fact checking. Carol Brobeck, Fellowships Administrator and Program Coordinator to the Folger Institute, read extracts against their originals with enormous care and sensitivity. Meanwhile, Gordon J. Schochet, in so many ways my inspiration in conducting this sort of historical investigation, was also kind enough to read this volume in draft.

Special thanks are due to the Agecroft Association, the Colonial Williamsburg Foundation, the Metropolitan Museum of Art, and the Philadelphia Museum of Art. One great pleasure of this exhibition has been meeting and working with curators at these lending institutions. Again, words fail to convey the generosity and grace with which they welcomed our requests. I would like to thank Mary Ann Caton at Agecroft; John Sands, Janine E. Skerry, and Kimberly Ivey at Colonial Williamsburg; Jessie McNab at the Metropolitan; and Dilys Blum at the Philadelphia Museum. Finally, it is a privilege to acknowledge private collector George Way. His special affinity for Elizabethan household objects added the zest that any long project like this should enjoy.

L. C. O.

SECTION ONE

THE GREAT REBUILDING

· THE GREAT REBUILDING ·

THE BARE OUTLINES OF WHAT HAS been called the "Great Rebuilding" of England can be seen most clearly in the transformation of the so-called "longhouses" of the countryside. Originally, these small buildings had two rooms, each with its own entrance. To one side was, effectively, the barn, where farm animals were sheltered and firewood and produce were stored. On that side of the building, the door was wide enough to allow cattle to pass in and out, and there was an opening low to the ground to flush out animal waste. To the other side, still under the same roof, was the dwelling, where the family of peasant farmers lived, ate, and slept. Dominating their domestic space was an open fire in the middle of the floor, with, above it, a hole in the peak of the roof to allow smoke to escape.

By the sixteenth and seventeenth centuries, most of these longhouses had been remodeled, and the lifestyle they supported had disappeared. First, a wall between the stable and the house might be erected or reinforced, making a clear demarcation of the two spaces. Second, a partial loft might be built in the domestic area, so that goods could be stored there and some members of the family could sleep separately. Third, a chimney might be installed, so that the hearth could be removed and the smoke vent in the roof closed in. Fourth, the upper level, originally defined by the loft, would now be completely floored over. With an additional opening in the chimney, this area, too, could serve for heated living space. For a while, the floorboards would be left loose, so they could be pulled aside and a ladder thrust upward at any point for easy access to storage. But then the floor would be nailed down and, fifth, a staircase would be built, in a lean-to if not within the original walls. Perhaps a window would be added in an upper-level gable to allow for natural light there. The final construction would be an outbuilding into which the animals and grains were moved. The family could then spread out, with one side of the building reserved for cooking and food storage, the other for living and sleeping.

In this thumbnail sketch can be seen many of the aspects of the architectural revolution of the early modern period: a higher standard of living, increased physical comfort, more individual privacy, the segregation of laboring and domestic life, and more household spaces, each with specialized functions. Changes that were the same in kind (if not in form) occurred all along the social scale. In great houses, for example, the new rooms might be private dining spaces, parlors, closets, studies, and long galleries, as well as bedchambers. But the effects for rich and poor were substantially the same, because experience is comparative. Most people were aware that their household life had improved over what they had known in the past.

The "Great Rebuilding" was a term proposed by W. G. Hoskins for all the architectural change that took place between 1570 and 1640. Some scholars have argued that the change was not as widespread and consistent as he believed, because regional variations and economic differences made for some irregular patterns across England as a whole. But these are minor adjustments to a thesis that seems true in its broadest aspects. The evidence is there in surviving buildings, in wills, in household inventories, and in reports like William Harrison's, which is included later in this section.

Advisedly, Hoskins called the phenomenon a *re*-building, not a "building," because, as was the case with the longhouses, much construction activity involved remodeling or redesigning rather than building from scratch. One impetus for change was the dissolution of the monasteries, following Henry VIII's break with Rome. Abandoned monastic buildings were repositories of worked stone and timber as well as of roof and paving tiles. The valuable tin and lead that lined their roofs was stripped first, and then other depredations followed, often with the consent of the crown, which sold off these reusable building materials. The sheer quantity of newly available resources was an impetus to construction.

In this period, building elements were endlessly movable and recyclable: not just shutters, doors, and wainscoting (or wall paneling), but also chimney pieces, staircases, window and door frames, and their fixtures. Therefore, many wills from the period had to designate that such items were to remain in place, because otherwise they would be removed or sold. One result of the Great Rebuilding was that, as people got more attached to the improvements they had made, these improvements themselves eventually came to seem more attached to their location. Elements that were thought of as furnishings early in the period, over the course of time came to seem like fixtures. The floorboards of the longhouse, first loose and movable, then nailed down, are a prime example.

Another illustration is window glass. When the earl of Northumberland visited his northern castles, for example, window glass, thought to be too fragile for regular use, was taken out of storage and put in place for his convenience. This was as late as 1567. In London, where improvements came earlier, the jurist Edward Coke decided in 1579 that "glass fixed by nails to windows or in any other manner cannot be moved, for without glass is no perfect house." But for some decades after his ruling, glass was evidently still being moved and removed. People had to dictate in their wills that they wanted the glass they had purchased and installed to remain, against custom, in their houses. The rebuilders were proud of what they had done, and they sought to leave these "fixtures" as their legacies, along with their movable goods and money.

Some of those who have quarreled with Hoskins would call this period the "Great Overbuilding." What they mean is that improvements in housing have been fairly steady throughout history, dating back to the medieval years. In their view, the change in the Renaissance was that work was *over*built, so that it outlasted the natural life of the domestic structure. In other words, builders were overcautious and, for instance, used three courses of brick where two would have done. According to this argument, our own perceptions of the period have been skewed by how many stately homes have survived and by the fact that even fairly modest houses were built in stone or with the unnecessary structural strength that means they are still standing. But surely it's too simple to suggest that these remarkable architectural monuments are merely the consequence of construction mistakes and anxieties. Builders at a variety of social levels were perfectly aware that they were leaving their marks on the landscape, as birthrights for their descendants and memorials to themselves.

After all, their projects had as much to do with aesthetics as with function. As they redesigned their lives in the wake of the classical revival, among other things, Englishmen looked to the Continent for inspiration. To remodel Hampton Court, Henry VIII brought in craftsmen from Germany (architectural and painted decoration), France (wainscoting), Italy (painting), and The Netherlands (window glazing). In 1550, John Shute was sent to Italy to collect building ideas for his patron. Eventually he published the first Renaissance architectural treatise in English, *The First and Chief Grounds of Architecture* (1563). Englishmen rediscovered Vitruvius and read Alberti; they were particularly influenced by Serlio and Palladio; they collected and shared among themselves site sketches and printed architectural treatises.

As Mark Girouard has pointed out, Elizabethans were pirates, not disciples, when it came to architecture. They liked to borrow ornamental details rather than whole floorplans. Among the great country houses, for example, Wollaton, Hardwick, Burghley, Blickling, Felbrigg, and Bolsover have only scattered bits of Serlio. But this shows again that much rebuilding was a matter of individual style, taste, self-representation, and freedom of choice.

Every great house required a small army for construction: stoneworkers, brickmakers, carpenters, coopers, sawyers, turners, joiners, plasterworkers, painters, and glaziers, as well as the carters who transported raw materials to the building site. Usually, all was not accomplished in a single build; there were continuing refinements and repairs. And even after the main construction was completed, there were the necessary domestic servants, including stewards, butlers, servingmen, cooks, kitchen boys, secretaries, attendants, chambermaids, laundresses, drudges, stableboys, and so on. All these workers were witnesses to the explosion of color, pattern, and ornament in Renaissance buildings: linenfold wainscoting, elaborate plaster ceilings, carved stone chimney pieces, wall paintings, and heraldic glass. Servants saw household goods and furnishings proliferate, and they observed a wider range of leisure activities and pursuits. These were models that they later took to their own establishments. The great houses were effective agents for disseminating the new standards of taste and, most of all, for inspiring new ambitions about household life.

This is the point about the Great Rebuilding of 1570 to 1640: not only that England produced buildings of great architectural distinction during this period, but, more, that the dramatic changes in domestic architecture reshaped private life. There are many points of intersection between our notions of comfort, privacy, luxury, and self-image and those that emerged during the architectural revolution of the Elizabethan years.

WILLIAM HARRISON

An Historicall Description of the Iland of Britaine (London, 1587)

☙ Written as an introduction to Holinshed's great *Chronicles of England, Scotland, and Ireland, The Description of England* is part gazetteer, part panegyric to Tudor England and its expanding economy. Harrison incorporates natural, social, economic, legal, ecclesiastical, folk, and architectural history. The second edition of 1587 is a third longer than that of 1577. In part, this reflects a desire to "improve" on a popular original. It also shows Harrison's continuing interest in demonstrating how much change he and his contemporaries had witnessed, including widespread building activity. An important symbol of change was the increasing use of glass in windows, which rendered houses "curious to the eye like paperwork."

It is a world to see, moreover, how divers men, being bent to building and having a delectable vein in spending of their goods by that trade, do daily imagine new devices of their own to guide their workmen withal, and those more curious and excellent always than the former. In the proceeding also of their works, how they set up, how they pull down, how they enlarge, how they restrain, how they add to, how they take from, whereby their heads are never idle, their purses never shut, nor their books of account never made perfect. . . . Many of our greatest houses have outwardly been very simple and plain to sight, which inwardly have been able to receive a duke with his whole train, and lodge them at their ease. Hereby moreover it is come to pass, that the fronts of our streets have not been so uniform and orderly builded as those of foreign cities, where (to say truth) the outerside of their mansions and dwellings have oft more cost bestowed upon them, than all the rest of the house, which are often very simple and uneasy within, as experience doth confirm. Of old time our country houses in stead of glass did use much lattice, and that made either of wicker or fine rifts of oak in checkerwise. I read also that some of the better sort, in and before the times of the Saxons (who notwithstanding used some glass also since the time of Benedict Biscop, the monk that brought the feat of glazing first into this land), did make panels of horn in stead of glass, and fix them in wooden calms [frames]. But as horn in windows is now quite laid down in every place, so our lattices are also grown into less use, because glass is come to be so plentiful, and within a very little so good cheap if not better than the other. . . . The ancient manors and houses of our gentlemen are yet and for the most

Brickmaker, from Hartmann Schopper, *Panoplia Omnium Illiberalium Mechanicarum* (Frankfurt, 1568). The builder of a great house might first have to establish a stoneworks, a brick kiln, an iron foundry, and a glass manufactory near his construction site. When his house was completed, these enterprises often remained as local resources for more modest building ventures. Brick was necessary for replacing open hearths with chimneys, an important aspect of the Great Rebuilding.

Paving Tile (London, 1600–1650), white tin glaze decorated in blue, green, yellow, and tan, 4¼ inches square. Because this tile is a kiln waster, found at a pottery site in Pickleherring, near London, we know that it is English work rather than a Netherlandish import. The Elizabethan fascination with exotic beasts is represented in this camel, shown standing among leaves. The Colonial Williamsburg Foundation.

Paving Tile (London, 1600–1650), white tin glaze decorated in blue, 5¼ inches square. Four tiles of this pattern together form the image of a Tudor rose encircled with a strapwork design. This is a Pickleherring kiln waster, but an identical tile with different colors has been found at the Royal Exchange in London. The Colonial Williamsburg Foundation.

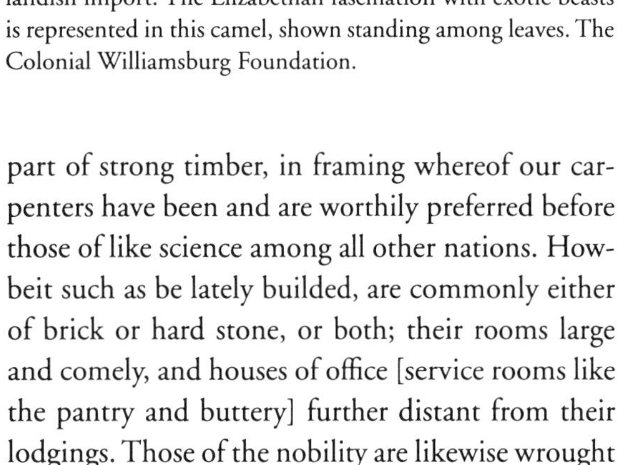

part of strong timber, in framing whereof our carpenters have been and are worthily preferred before those of like science among all other nations. Howbeit such as be lately builded, are commonly either of brick or hard stone, or both; their rooms large and comely, and houses of office [service rooms like the pantry and buttery] further distant from their lodgings. Those of the nobility are likewise wrought with brick and hard stone, as provision may best be made: but so magnificent and stately, as the basest house of a baron doth often match in our days with some honors of princes in old time. So that if ever curious building did flourish in England, it is in these our years, wherein our workmen excel, and are in manner comparable in skill with old Vitruvius, Leo Baptista [Alberti], and Serlio (vol. 1, sigs. $T3^{v}$, $R3^{r-v}$).

COMPANION TO GEORG VON SCHWARTZSTÄT, BARON VON OFFENBACH

Journal of Travels in The Netherlands, England, France, and Germany (1609)

❧ The only Tudor monarch to do much building was Henry VIII, but with Nonsuch, in particular, he set architectural standards for a century. This travel diary of 1609 makes clear that Nonsuch was not a "standing palace"; that is, furnishings (including tapestries) were put in place only when the court was in residence. The keeper of the diary, travel companion to the Baron von Offenbach, pasted in an illustration from John Speed's map of Surrey, and the first part of the description is copied from the 1607 edition of William Camden's *Britannia.* The motto reads: "Since they have not its like, the Britons / Often are wont to praise this, and call it Nonsuch by name." Translation from the Latin is by G.P.V. Akrigg.

Henry VIII chose this retreat for delights and his leisure, and he built it with such magnificence and elegance that you may deem the whole craft of architecture gathered together in this one building. There are so many lifelike statues, so many miracles of absolute art and works rivaling Roman antiquity, that Pleasantness herself, along with Health, seems to have chosen this seat for herself. . . . The main building is quadrilateral; it extends rather farther in length than in breadth. It has two courts. The outer court is set about with beautiful edifices. The courtyard itself is strewn with flint, while a walk made in the form of a cross from squared stone divides it. One passes into the inner court through a gate over which is set a tower, extremely ingeniously made as the accompanying picture shows. The court is elegantly paved with square stone. In the middle it has a square fountain; the facing is of white marble, statues carved most perfectly of shining white alabaster are set above. Roundabout are houses ornamented with very beautiful histories cast to the life in plaster; black stone, gilded in places, sets them off. We went up into the chambers of the King and Queen, of which the one looked in that direction, the other in this; in the middle is a junction of doors through which free passage is given in turn to each of them and descent into the garden. In the chambers we found nothing worth the seeing except in the King's Chamber a fountain, for washing the hands, of black marble and alabaster. The chambers were wanting in almost all ornament, though indeed they are always hung with tapestries when the King occupies them; and it is to be thoroughly understood that the whole magnificence of the chambers of the kings of England consists almost entirely in their tapestries, except that at Hampton Court we perceived that certain ones were ornamented in other fashion. It is to be noted also that almost all the royal houses are supplied with roofs suitable for

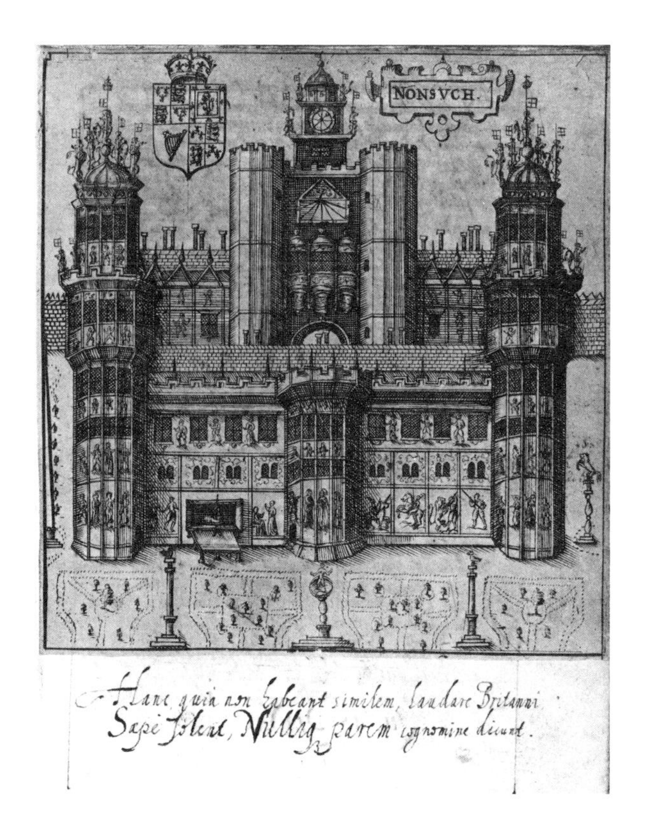

Nonsuch Palace, from *Journal of Travels in The Netherlands, England, France, and Germany* (1609), kept by a companion to Georg von Schwartzstät, Baron von Offenbach.

walking, and almost flat, so that here and elsewhere one can walk around on all the roofs. First, indeed, there are two towers placed in corners of the palace affording a pleasant prospect and walk. In each of them is a certain small chamber, placed so as to enjoy the summer breeze and air, absolutely open on all sides, with the windows taken away. Besides this, in each of the towers there are three round chambers, enviably fair. A smaller tower is placed between the other two and serves as a roof for the kings as they descend to the garden. At the foot of this tower is a fountain, carefully made of marble; to the right a marble table on which is set a column of marble and alabaster. The garden bounds the palace on three sides, although only half way on the left side. Again, this garden with the entire palace is enclosed by a most pleasant park. What fountains, what pyramids there are in the garden, the picture reveals; they are all royally made of marble and alabaster.

FRANCIS BACON

"Of Building," from *The Essayes or Counsels, Civill and Morall* (London, 1625)

❧ The earliest work on building in English, Andrew Boorde's *The Boke for to Lerne a Man to be Wyse in Buyldyng of his Howse for the Helth of Body & to Hold Quyetnes for the Helth of his Soule, and Body* (1540), emphasized the importance of siting a house for plentiful wood, clean water, and fresh air. Nearly a hundred years later, this is a principal theme for Sir Francis Bacon, too. His preference for function over form ("use before uniformity") is out of step with much of the grandest architecture of the period, in which an interior staircase or even a chimney might be built blocking a window to maintain symmetry on the external façade. The difference between Bacon's writing and others' practice gives evidence of architectural debate in the period.

Houses are built to live in, and not to look on: therefore let use be preferred before uniformity, except where both may be had. Leave the goodly fabrics of houses, for beauty only, to the enchanted palaces of the poets, who build them with small cost. He that builds a fair house upon an ill seat committeth himself to prison. Neither do I reckon it an ill seat only where the air is unwholesome, but likewise where the air is unequal, as you shall see many fine seats set upon a knap of ground, environed with higher hills 'round about it: whereby the heat of the sun is pent in, and the wind gathereth as in troughs, so as you shall have, and that suddenly, as great diversity of heat and cold, as if you dwelt in several places. Neither is it ill air only that maketh an ill seat, but ill ways, ill markets, and, if you will consult with Momus, ill neighbors. I speak not of many more: want of water; want of wood, shade, and shelter; want of fruitfulness, and mixture of grounds of several natures; want of prospect; want of level grounds; want of places, at some near distance, for sports of hunting, hawking, and races; too near the sea, too remote; having the commodity of navigable rivers, or the discommodity of their overflowing; too far off from great cities, which may hinder business; or too near them, which lurcheth [consumes or monopolizes] all provisions, and maketh every thing dear; where a man hath a great living laid together, and where he is scanted. All which, as it is impossible, perhaps, to find together, so it is good to know them and think of them, that a man may take as many as he can. And if he have several dwellings, that he sort them so, that what he wanteth in the one, he may find in the other (sigs. Ll1^r–Ll2^r).

ROBERT PLOT

The Natural History of Staffordshire (Oxford, 1686)

❧ Changing fashions in English domestic architecture are strongly marked in this illustration of Tixall Hall, with its irregular late-medieval house and symmetrical seventeenth-century gatehouse. Robert Plot, Keeper of the Ashmolean Museum and Professor of Chemistry at Oxford, clearly prefers the later style. In a description of notable buildings in Staffordshire, he also appreciates the fad for architectural emblems and puzzles.

One house indeed I past by 'twixt Cheadle and Oakamoore [in Staffordshire], built only of turf in a conical manner, much like the houses of the Indians near the straits of Magellan. But for the buildings of any note, they are either of brick or squared stone, whereof some are private, others public, and the latter either civil or ecclesiastical; and may all be considered either in the whole, or parts. Of the private structures, the most eminent in the county are those whose prospects the Reader has or will find engraven in this work. . . . The gatehouse of Tixall Hall, the seat of the right honorable Walter, Lord Aston, an eminent encourager of this design, is a curious piece of stonework, well worthy notice, and is here presented, together with the house, to the Reader's view, Table 29. It is remarkable also that the windows of the house, though very numerous, are scarce two alike; and so 'tis at Chillington, the seat of the ancient family of the Giffards. It is observable likewise that the tunnels of the chimneys in both these houses are very numerous, the hall chimney at Chillington having no less than eight tunnels to one hearth, the fretwork of the tunnels also in both these seats being so very various, that scarce two agree, whence 'tis easy to collect that the beauty of a structure in those days (which seems to be temp. Henry VIII) did not consist, as now, in uniformity, but in the greatest variety the artist could possibly show.

The stone rail upon the wall built about the

Tixall Hall, engraved by Nicolas Burghers for Robert Plot, *The Natural History of Staffordshire* (Oxford, 1686).

Green Court before Trentham House is a pretty piece of work, it being supported with Roman capital letters instead of ballisters, containing an inscription not only setting forth the name of the ancient proprietor and builder of this seat, but the time when it was done: the numeral letters put together making up the year of our Lord when it was finished, viz., Anno 1633, which will appear by the numerals set in Roman capitals in the inscription here annexed, the other capitals being all set in italic.

*CAROL*O *BRI*T*AN*I*AE REGE R*IC*ARD*V*S*
*L*E*VESON*
*EQ*V*ES BAL*N*E*I *AE*D*ES HAS*C*E H*IC
*F*I*ER*I V*OL*V*I*T*.*

There being two DDs, four CCCCs, four LLLLs, five VVVVVs, and eight IIIIIIIIs, which make up that date (sigs. Yy3v–Yy4v).

JOHN DEE

"Mathematical Preface" to Euclid's *Elements of Geometrie* (London, 1570)

❧ John Dee is perhaps best known for his conversations with angels and his experiments with alchemy, but earlier in his career, in 1550 at the College of Rheims in Paris, he introduced Euclid's geometry to an academic audience so large and avid that some had to look in at the windows. Under the umbrella of mathematics he included the practice of architecture. He holds up an ambitious, unrealized ideal for architecture, one derived from the classical and Continental authorities Vitruvius, Leo Baptista (whom we commonly call Alberti), and Plato.

An architect (sayeth [Vitruvius]) ought to understand languages, to be skillful of painting, well instructed in geometry, not ignorant of perspective, furnished with arithmetic, have knowledge of many histories, and diligently have heard philosophers, have skill of music, not ignorant of physic, know the answers of lawyers, and have astronomy, and the courses celestial, in good knowledge. He giveth reason, orderly, wherefore all these arts, doctrines, and instructions are requisite in an excellent architect.

. . . Now [sayeth Alberti], I think that I ought to express what man I would have to be allowed [allowed to be] an architect. For I will not bring in place a carpenter, as though you might compare him to the chief masters of other arts. For the hand of the carpenter is the architect's instrument. But I will appoint the architect to be that man who hath the skill (by a certain and marvelous means and way) both in mind and imagination, to determine, and also in work to finish, what works so ever, by motion of weight and coupling and framing together of bodies, may most aptly be commodious for the worthiest uses of man. And that he may be able to perform these things, he hath need of attaining and knowledge of the best and most worthy things. . . . And Plato affirmeth the architect to be master over all that make any work. Whereupon, he is neither smith, nor builder, nor, separately, any artificer: but the head, the provost, the director, and judge of all artificial works and all artificers. For the true architect is able to teach, demonstrate, distribute, describe, and judge all works wrought. And he only searcheth out the causes and reasons of all artificial things. Thus excellent is architecture, though few (in our days) attain thereto. Yet may not the art be otherwise thought on, than in very deed it is worthy. Nor we may not of ancient arts make new and imperfect definitions in our days, for scarcity of artificers: no more than we may pinch in the definitions of wisdom, or honesty, or of friendship, or of justice (sigs. d3r–d4v).

PIERRE LE MUET

Maniere de Bastir pour Touttes Sortes de Personnes (Paris, 1623)

❧ "Architecture" as we know it was not a profession in the sixteenth century; it was an avocation, principally for gentlemen. In the past, building had been a trade practice, with methods passed down from generation to generation of carpenters and masons. But as new ideas were imported from the Continent, new means of communication were required. It's not surprising that some men "set up" and "pulled down" repeatedly, as William Harrison complained. Building methods were difficult to describe in words, as this volume, once owned by John Evelyn, demonstrates. The excerpt is from an English translation of 1675, published in London by Robert Pricke.

Having hitherto largely discoursed of buildings of masons' and bricklayers' work, it seemeth also fitting for us to discourse likewise of carpenters' and plasterers' work, which may serve for the places where such building commonly is made and for other also in the which one may be compelled thereto, in respect of the small space that one may have. The carpenter's work, then, of a building shall be set upon the mason's or bricklayer's work, about two feet or two-and-an-half of height above the level of the street for to hinder the putrifying of the first mortering, the which shall be placed upon the stone or brickwork with an inch or an inch-and-an-half of setting off, with this observation in respect of the masonry, to set out with free-stone or hard grey stone, or the like, the places where gates close together. The summers [horizontal beams] shall be joined together upon the ends of the chief posts which divide the rooms, with half-an-inch of inbearing, and it is good that these chief posts have in thickness and breadth the double of others. Upon these chief posts shall meet the second, third, and fourth summers, whereof the second and third are placed about the planchers [planks], and within these summers the posts, as well of the doors' work as the crossbars of windows, shall meet by tenons and mortises, as the pieces and posts that fill up shall be in the midst, together with the parts of braces. And within, the posts of the crosses shall meet that which upholds underneath and the headpieces above; and underneath the said crosses shall meet, by tenons and mortises at the summer and prop of the crossbars, the small posts and quarters; and above, the said crosses do join, by tenons and mortises at the summer and lintel of the cross, three small posts or cross rafters. Now, the spaces which are between may be filled up three several ways: that

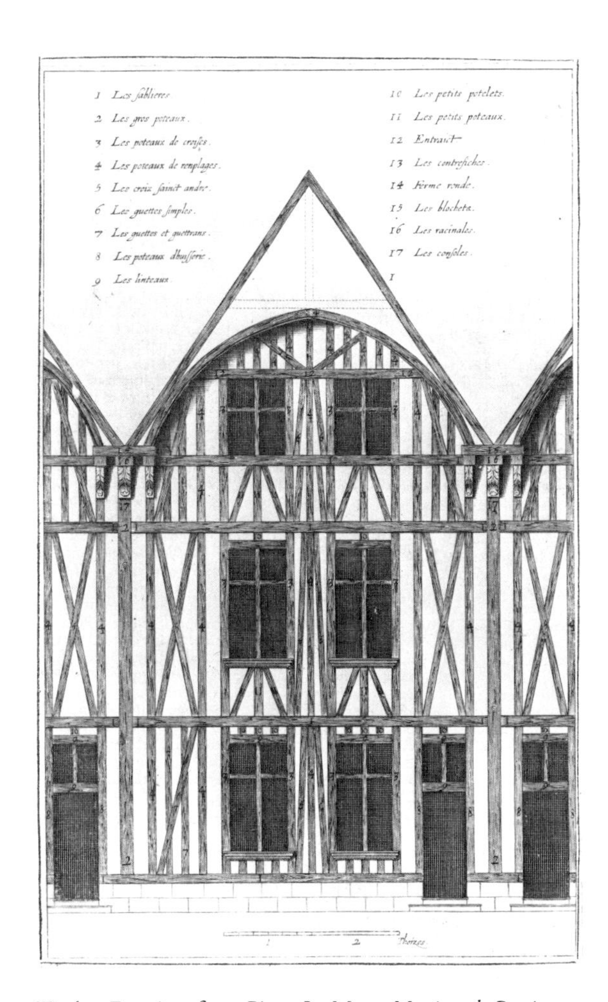

Timber Framing, from Pierre Le Muet, *Maniere de Bastir pour Touttes Sortes de Personnes* (Paris, 1623).

is, with single bars and a post in the midst; or else with crossbraces and posts by the side; the third with little bars and posts on the side. And above the doorworks shall meet three small posts within the summer, and above the boarding shall be made a small pinnacle of timberwork for covering of the tiles or slate, according to the manner set forth hereafter. The which pinnacle shall be made by the means of two rafters and spars above, the which rafters shall meet below, within the summer of the boarding, and above, within the king post, and within the said rafters shall be fixed with tenons and mortise upon the middle of the king post. Within the which wedge and within the summer below shall meet the posts of the crosses, and the spaces filled so as hath been said, and above the said wedge there shall meet two counterfixed pieces with the posts that fill up; and before the king post or small pinnacle and panel of wood shall be made a round shutter bearing out about two feet or two-feet-and-an-half, borne up below upon the raising-piece, and three stays with three cattoozes [cartouches] underneath (sig. H6^{v}).

HENRY WOTTON

The Elements of Architecture (London, 1624)

❧ It has been said that *The Elements of Architecture* was "written by an amateur and for amateurs." Wotton had illustrious epistolary and ambassadorial careers; he was not a builder. And yet, this product of his travels and his taste was extremely important for importing both Vitruvian and Palladian ideals to England. The selected passages show some ways in which architecture could be anthropomorphized in the period—and thus moralized and allegorized. As Wotton concludes, this tendency led to a close identification between the building and its owner.

In architecture, there may seem to be two opposite affectations, uniformity and variety, which yet will very well suffer a good reconcilement, as we may see in the great pattern of nature to which I must often resort. For surely there can be no structure more uniform than our bodies in the whole figuration: each side agreeing with the other, both in the number, in the quality, and in the measure of the parts. And yet some are round, as the arms; some flat, as the hands; some prominent, and some more retired. So as upon the matter, we see that diversity doth not destroy uniformity and that the limbs of a noble fabric may be correspondent enough, though they be various. . . .

Pillars, which we may likewise call columns (for the word among artificers is almost naturalized), I could distinguish into simple and compounded. But (to tread the beaten and plainest way), there are five orders of pillars, according to their dignity and perfection, thus marshalled. . . .

First, therefore, the Tuscan is a plain, massy, rural pillar, resembling some sturdy well-limbed laborer, homely clad. . . . The length thereof shall be six diameters of the grossest of the pillar below. Of all proportions, in truth, the most natural, for . . . the foot of a man is the sixth part of his body in ordinary measure. . . . The Tuscan is of all the rudest pillar, and his principal character simplicity.

The Doric order is the gravest that hath been received into civil use, preserving, in comparison of those that follow, a more masculine aspect, and little trimmer than the Tuscan that went before, save a sober garnishment now and then of lions' heads in the cornice, and of triglyphs and metopes always in the frieze. . . . To discern him will be a piece rather of good heraldry than of architecture, for he is best known by his place when he is in company and by the peculiar ornament of his frieze (before mentioned) when he is alone.

The Ionic order doth represent a kind of feminine slenderness, yet, saith Vitruvius, not like a light housewife but, in a decent dressing, hath much of the matron. . . . Best known by his trimmings, . . . the body of this column is perpetually channeled, like a thick plighted [pleated] gown. The capital dressed on each side, not much unlike women's wires, in a spiral wreathing which they call the *Ionian voluta*. . . .

The Corinthian is a column lasciviously decked like a courtesan, and therein much participating (as all inventions do) of the place where they were first born, Corinth having been without controversy one of the wantonest towns in the world. . . . In short, as plainness did characterize the Tuscan, so must delicacy and variety the Corinthian pillar. . . .

The last is the Compounded order: his name being a brief of his nature. For this pillar is nothing, in effect, but a medley or an amass of all the precedent ornaments, making a new kind, by stealth, and though the most richly tricked, yet the poorest in this, that he is a borrower of all his beauty. . . . To know him will be easy by the very mixture of his ornaments and clothing. . . .

Every man's proper mansion house and home, being the theater of his hospitality, the seat of self-fruition, the comfortablest part of his own life, the noblest of his son's inheritance, a kind of private princedom—nay, to the possessors thereof, an epitome of the whole world—may well deserve by these attributes, according to the degree of the master, to be decently and delightfully adorned. For which end, there are two arts attending on architecture like two of her principal gentlewomen, to dress and trim their mistress: picture and sculpture (sigs. C2^{v}–C3^{r}, D3$^{r–v}$, E1^{r}–E4^{r}, L1^{v}–L2^{r}).

JOHANN AMOS COMENIUS

Orbis Sensualium Pictus (Nuremberg, 1664)

❧ This little book for children illustrates different parts of the natural and material world as a means of conveying Latin vocabulary. In 1685 Charles Hoole translated the original Dutch into English, with the title *Visible World, Or A Picture and Nomenclature of all the Chief Things that are in the World; and of Mens Employments Therein.* Plate 66 shows the parts of a house, each numbered to correspond to the appropriate word. Only the English is given below.

"The Parts of a House," from Johann Amos Comenius, *Orbis Sensualium Pictus* (Nuremberg, 1664).

The Porch (1) is before the door of the house.

The door hath a Threshold (3) and a Lintel (2) and Posts (4) on both sides.

The Hinges (5) are on the right hand, upon which the Doors (6) hang; the Latch (7) and the Bolt (8) are on the left hand.

Before the house is a Fore-court (9) with a Pavement of square stones (10) borne up with Pillars (11), in which is the Chapiter [capital] (12) and the Base (13).

They go up into the upper stories by Greces [stairways] (14) and Winding-Stairs (15).

The Windows (16) appear on the outside, and the Grates (17), the Galleries (18), the Water-Tables (19), and Buttresses (20), to bear up the walls.

On the top is the Roof (21) covered with Tiles (22) or Shingles (23), which lie upon Laths (24), and these upon Rafters (25).

The Eaves (26) adhere to the roof.

The place without a roof is called an open Gallery (27).

In the roof are Juttings out (28) and Pinnacles or Knops (29) (sigs. K4^{v}–K5^{r}).

Mr Bagott, I thank you for your favor and indifferencie in the matter touching that lewde workman Cust whoe hath delt very badly and lewdly with me. he undertoke and covenanted to doe great worke for me and to finishe the same long since and hath receyved much more then reason for the same and by absenting himself before the performance thereof hath greatly disappoynted me and hindred my worke. by promise he is my hyred servant but I referr this matter to you and the rest of the Justice wherein what semeth best in your discretions I shalbe very well content withall. / so with my very harty commendacions I cease. / Hardwick this xixth of September 1594. /

Your assured loving frend

E Shrewsbury

Letter from Elizabeth, Countess of Shrewsbury, to Richard Bagott, 19 September 1594.

ELIZABETH, COUNTESS OF SHREWSBURY

Letter to Richard Bagott (19 September 1594)

❧ Hardwick Hall was so famous that it lent its name to a popular jingle ("Hardwick Hall, more glass than wall"), as well as to its builder, Elizabeth, Countess of Shrewsbury, better known as "Bess of Hardwick." She had built at Chatsworth and at Hardwick Old Hall before embarking on this ambitious venture in Renaissance architecture. But despite all her experience she confronted a familiar problem: a "lewd" workman who had not completed all the work he had promised and she had already paid for. She sought legal recourse from the county Justices of the Peace.

Master Bagott,
I thank you for your favor and indifferency in the matter touching that lewd workman Tuft, who hath dealt very badly and lewdly with me. He undertook and covenanted to do great works for me and to finish the same long since, and hath received much more than reason for the same, and by absenting himself before the performance thereof hath greatly disappointed me and hindered my works. By promise he is my hired servant, but I refer this matter to you and the rest of the Justices, wherein what seemeth best in your discretions I shall be very well content withall. So with my very hearty commendations I cease. Hardwick, this xixth of September 1594.

Your assured loving friend,
E. Shrowsbury

A Briefe Declaration for What Manner of Speciall Nusance Concerning Private Dwelling Houses, a Man May Have his Remedy by Assise (London, 1639)

❧ As in our time, so in the sixteenth and seventeenth centuries: building was not accomplished without difficulties. This tract, first published in 1636, represents the conflicting arguments of four lawyers in a case from over half a century earlier. One Master Hales had sued his neighbor, identified here only as J. S., for constructing a house that blocked his light. Among the legal issues are the nature and purpose of housing, the relative importance of light and air, and the necessity of setbacks in building.

Master [Robert] Mounson's Argument

The first and chief use of an house is to defend man from the extremity of the wind and weather. And by the receipt of comfortable light and wholesome air into the same, to preserve man's body in health.

Therefore, whoso taketh from man so great a commodity as that which preserveth man's health in his castle, or house, doth in a manner as great wrong as if he deseised [dispossessed] him altogether of his freehold [a tenure held in fee simple, as opposed to leasehold]. . . .

And though light and air be common, yet if by any man's own act they may be made private, they may not then be taken from him, and if they be, he shall not be without remedy. . . .

And therefore forasmuch as houses be necessary, and cannot be without light and air, their beginning was lawful, necessary, and reasonable. But that a man might stop up his neighbor's lights was never necessary, neither had lawful or reasonable beginning, neither had any time obtained the force of a law or custom.

Master [Edmund] Plowden's Argument

Albeit it hath been alleged that the windows have been time out of memory there, and the lights ancient, it is all one, as if the house had been built at this day. Put the case there is a pale [fence] betwixt your ground and mine, and you build to the uttermost [outermost] part of mine; by your first building I am bridled and stopped of my building. And in the country whoso maketh a hedge will make a dike in the uttermost part upon his own land. So he that maketh a park will leave ground out of the same compass without the pale for the keeper to walk about it, for there he may better hear if anybody be there within than if he were within himself, and this is called freebound [setback].

Master [Christopher] Wray's Argument

The nuisance which is supposed to be in stopping up of windows in the south part of an house, I conceive, is a nuisance by the common law, for by the common law one shall not hurt the freehold of another, and no greater hurt, grievance, or damage can be done to any man's freehold than to take away the light and air thereof, which is comfortable and commodious for him. For when this light and air are taken from him, his house remaineth as a dungeon. . . . This is no beautifying at all to the city. In our case, Master Hales his house is an ancient house, and therefore against reason that by later building, the commodity and use of the same should be taken away. You say also that it is a thing honorable to have buildings in cities; this I grant, and I think no man will deny it. But by building of one, to impair a better house, this is not any beautifying or honor at all to a city, but rather the contrary. . . . That a man should stop his neighbor's lights is altogether unlawful and unreasonable, and therefore the plaintiff ought not thereby to be barred of his action.

Master [Roger] Manwood's Argument

The air is not any element local, neither may any man miscarry it, for it suffereth nothing to be void. Also light and air be not things of necessity but of pleasure. . . . And the civil laws say that two lights on the former part and back of an house are sufficient. And if you make your windows into our garden, this is a wrong done unto us, for by this means I cannot talk with my friends in my garden but your servant may see what I do, and so the wrong first began in Master Hales. . . . J. S. hath not consumed or hurt any part of his house, but interrupted him of his pleasure only. But I further affirm that for every hurt a man may not have an action, but if a man be oftentimes hurt, he may very well have an action. . . . This city is the greatest city and most populous in this realm, and the more populous the more honorable, and the more buildings the more populous and honorable will it be. And therefore buildings is to be favored (sigs. $B2^{r–v}$, $B4^{r}$, $B4^{v}$–$C1^{r}$, $C3^{r}$, $D2^{r–v}$, $D3^{r}$, $D4^{r–v}$, $E1^{r–v}$).

SECTION TWO

MEMBERS OF THE HOUSEHOLD

❧

· MEMBERS OF THE HOUSEHOLD ·

IF *ROMEO AND JULIET* HADN'T BEEN so enormously important in our cultural history, we might have a very different sense of our social history. Juliet "hath not seen the change of fourteen years" when her mother advises her to "think on marriage." According to Lady Capulet, Veronese ladies younger than Juliet are already mothers; in fact, "I was your mother much upon these years." In consequence, we tend to think that in Shakespearean times couples married young.

This is our first misconception about the Elizabethan household. Speaking in statistical averages, twentieth-century couples marry younger and today's women become mothers earlier than they did at the time *Romeo and Juliet* was written. After all, Juliet, Lady Capulet, and the Capulet household are all fictional, and fiction has its own mandates. It's not hard to imagine that youth, and the seriousness of youth, and the impetuosity of youth, were deemed necessary to make credible this story of heat, passion, and suicide. So, too, the Italian setting. We willingly suspend disbelief when we watch or read *Romeo and Juliet* because it happened back in Elizabethan times, and we know that things were different then. But Elizabethans may have suspended disbelief when they watched or read *Romeo and Juliet*, too, because it took place in Italy, and they knew that things were different there. Just how different was demonstrated thirty years ago by Peter Laslett and the Cambridge (University) Group for the History of Population and Social Structure. They showed that, on average, Elizabethan men were twenty-five or twenty-six at first marriage, and women were twenty-three or so.

Our second misconception about the Elizabethan household is that it was multi-generational. In fact, a family was inaugurated when a man and wife moved into their own home, forming an independent social and economic unit. One of the principal reasons marriage occurred so late among Elizabethans was that men and women needed to gather the financial resources and locate the physical structure that would enable them to set themselves up in this fashion. Life expectancies were low enough that for many, the death of their parents provided the inheritance, the workshop, and/or the cottage that made it possible for them to establish themselves as householders and, thus, as fully enfranchised members of society.

If we understand that Elizabethan families were not, by and large, multi-generational, then we may hold a third misconception about the Elizabethan household: that it was nuclear. Instead, nearly all households included servants in some form or another, and even a poor farming family would have a field hand or two. This custom went hand-in-hand with the late age at marriage, for Elizabethans did not go out on their own until they had learned skills through service—as attendants in great households, for example, or as apprentices to tradesmen. This practice, in turn, took some pressure off the marriage market. Couples did not need to reproduce early in order to create for themselves a labor pool of their own children. Readily available were the men and women who expected to work for others through their late teens and early twenties. This is why it is more appropriate to use the term "household" than "family" in speaking of Elizabethan domestic arrangements.

If we take on board all these points, and particularly the last about servants, then we may leap to a fourth misconception, which is that the Elizabethan household was organized along the lines familiar to us from the term "upstairs, downstairs." The class structure was not nearly so finely tuned in the Renaissance, nor so rigid. Many servants were of a status, broadly speaking, with their employers. They were gentlemen who were learning courtly manners, estate management, or government or diplomatic service in noblemen's households. Or they were artisans learning technical skills and trade practices in small businessmen's shops. When they reached marriageable age, they were thoroughly prepared to move into the same social sphere as their former employers. For some in the expanding Tudor economy, there would even be movement further up the social ladder.

Household structures and practices further prevented strict segregation into classes. Life could not but be more communal when there were no private bedchambers, as was true of Elizabethan homes. Even in a household where the master and mistress shared a great curtained bedstead, there would have been in the same room a pallet or two for servants. This, too, militated against the clear articulation of master and servant classes. Difference was more often experienced in terms of wealth and status than "class" as we think of it today. Notably, marriage was an element of status. In 1602, defining matters of precedence, William Segar wrote that married men always preceded unmarried men if they were in other respects equal, because, in consequence of Elizabethan social practices, married men carried the civic authority of independent householding.

Elizabethan social thinkers recognized the place that households had to play in the public order of the period. It must also be remembered that there was no standing army in Elizabethan England, no state police, and, as a result of the Reformation, no church as authoritarian as the Roman church had been. Both the monarchy and the new church of England turned to the household as the institution in which order was to be created, modeled, and enforced, and they jointly took up the agenda of promulgating the responsibility of the household to serve these social ends. While every housewife, servant, and child was reminded of his or her role in maintaining a godly commonwealth, final responsibility for the household as a whole was loaded onto the householder or patriarch.

His central authority was essential to domestic structure as it was understood. A multi-generational household would not have functioned in this political scheme, as it would have had two competing heads (father and grandfather). Meanwhile, there were very few married servants in Renaissance England. They did not marry until they had their own place, where they could enact the prevailing hierarchical formula. To ask which came first, social and economic practice or political ideology, is a chicken-and-egg question. The fact is that there was a convergence between the single-family household as a unit of production and consumption and the single-family household as a political institution.

Our own notion that "a man's house is his castle" comes from the Renaissance. It was a legal precept originally, dating back to the fifteenth century, but gradually in the sixteenth century the phrase moved into public usage and became proverbial. It operated regardless of social status or individual situation. As the jurist Edward Coke used the phrase in court cases, it meant that the house was a safe haven from the clamor and complexity of the outside world. As schoolmaster Richard Mulcaster used it in writing of the home education of children, however, it meant that the householder had sovereign rights within his household.

Needless to say, there were exceptions to all these generalizations. The social rules were broken, for example, when it came to the houses of the great. There, economic independence was not at issue; instead, property and inheritance were. Children were often betrothed at a very young age to extend and secure the estate; they married young, as well; and their principal responsibility was the production of heirs to secure the family holdings. Such households were also more likely to be multi-generational. While younger sons would move out and daughters would be married off, elder sons remained in residence at the ancestral home. It was also in great houses, meanwhile, that the process of spatial differentiation initiated a social segregation which was eventually to result in an "upstairs" and a "downstairs," and all that implies. As the multiplying rooms of the Great Rebuilding became functionally more specialized, they could be (and increasingly were) classed and gendered, as well.

The political rules were broken, too, and these not just in great households. Despite all the efforts of ideology to enforce the lines of authority, there were rebellious wives, disobedient servants, and headstrong children. In order to understand what was at issue for the state, for the householder, and for these members of the household, we have to attend to the large orthodox literature that survives: homilies that were delivered by public decree in parish churches, puritan sermons that were preached and published, and myriad books of domestic advice. But if we take our picture of Elizabethan life from these sources, then we have as false a notion of the family as that we find in *Romeo and Juliet.* We must read these documents against the grain and we must look elsewhere for life as it was lived. After all, would these impassioned admonitions and exhortations have been necessary if every household was following the rules?

The Householder ❧

JOHN DOD AND ROBERT CLEAVER

A Godlie Forme of Householde Government: for the Ordering of Private Families, According to the Direction of Gods Word (London, 1598)

❧ The explosion of print culture produced manuals for the conduct of the householder as for the education of the prince. This was not the only parallel between the two. The household was thought of as a microcosm of the kingdom, with the householder sovereign within that "domestical kingdom" (as it was called). Just as it was presumed that the ideal political government was monarchic, so it was believed that the ideal household government was patriarchal. In order for the householder to assume his "proper" kingly role, others had to cede authority, including his children, his servants, and, most importantly of all, his wife. Of course, as Dod and Cleaver realized in this popular volume, authority was a double-edged sword. The husband carried a heavy burden of responsibility.

A household is as it were a little commonwealth, by the good government whereof, God's glory may be advanced; the commonwealth, which standeth of several families, benefited; and all that live in that family may receive much comfort and commodity. . . .

The husband his duty is, first, to love his wife as his own flesh. Then to govern her in all duties that properly concern the state of marriage, in knowledge, in wisdom, judgment, and justice. Thirdly, to dwell with her. Fourthly, to use her in all due benevolence, honestly, soberly, and chastely. . . .

The wife, her duty is, in all reverence and humility, to submit and subject herself to her husband in all such duties as properly belong to marriage. Secondly, therein to be an help unto him, according to God's ordinance. Thirdly, to obey his commandments in all things which he may command by the authority of an husband. Fourthly and lastly, to give him mutual benevolence. . . .

The husband ought not to be satisfied that he hath robbed his wife of her virginity, but in that he hath possession and use of her will, for it sufficeth not that they be married, but that they be well married, and live Christianly together, and very well contented. And therefore the husband that is not beloved of his wife, holdeth his goods in danger, his house in suspicion, his credit in balance, and also sometime his life in peril, because it is easy to believe that she desireth not long life unto her husband, with whom she passeth a time so tedious and irksome. . . . If she be not subject to her husband, to let him rule all household, especially outward affairs; if she will make head against him, and seek to have her own ways, there will be doing and undoing. Things will go backward, the house will come to ruin, for God will not bless where his ordinance is not obeyed. This is allowable, that she may in modest sort show her mind, and a wise husband will not disdain to hear her advice, and follow it also, if it be good. But when her way is not liked of, though it be the best way, she may not thereupon set all at six and seven, with "what should I labor and travail: I see my husband taketh such ways, that he will bring all to nothing." This were nothing else, but when she seeth the house falling, to help to pull it down faster. . . .

He is reckoned worthy to rule a commonwealth that with such wisdom, discretion, and judgment doth rule and govern his own house, and that he may easily conserve and keep his citizens in peace and concord, that hath so well established the same

The Householder and His Family, from *The Whole Booke of Psalmes* (London, 1563). William Harrison would have recognized lattice, rather than glass, in the window of the modest house represented here. Such a household might well have had only one chair, reserved for the head of the house, while the housewife and children would use stools or would share a form (or bench). The distinction conferred by the chair survives today in the title "chairman." The positioning of these figures is also telling of power relationships within the family, with the householder visibly exerting his dominance as against the housewife grouped with her children.

in his own house and family. And on the other side, none will think or believe that he is able to be ruler, or to keep peace and quietness in the town or city, who cannot live peaceably in his own house, where he is not only a ruler, but a King, and Lord of all. And in matrimonial debate and discord, the man is more to be blamed than is the woman, because that he being the chief ruler and head, doth not purge and remedy her of that vice (sigs. A8^{r}, I1^{v}, I2^{r}, M4^{r}, G1^{v}, N1^{r-v}).

R. R.

The House-holders Helpe, for Domesticall Discipline: Or, A Familiar Conference of Household Instruction and Correction, Fit for the Godly Government of Christian Families (London, 1615)

❧ The dialogue was a popular form for advice manuals. Generally there was a speaker offering wise counsel to a straw man, who was either ignorant or erring. In this dialogue between "father" and "son," the emphasis is upon the obligation of the householder to serve as a good model for those in his household. It was commonly understood that the head of the family was responsible for the moral and religious education of those in his household, including servants as well as children. Other manuals concur that the housewife was his deputy in these matters, so that in his absence she was to continue with Bible readings and ethical supervision. As with other duties, if she failed to conduct herself properly, the householder was ultimately accountable.

FATHER. I desire to have some religious conference with you and to admonish you concerning domestical discipline, for I have heard that your family is not catechized, admonished, nor corrected, according as formerly it was wont to be by your wife, when you are from home. And which more is, I hear that your self do ofttimes fail in the foresaid duties when you are at home. Is it so, my son, is it so?

SON. Good Father, with shame and sorrow for it, I do confess it to be so: we are much subject to spiritual idleness and to worldly carefulness. I pray God give us pardon of, and power against, these sins.

FATHER. I am sorry, my son, I am very sorry for you. I pray God forgive you and amend these evil manners in you. I perceive by your tears and speeches that you are humble-minded, and you do well to confess your sins, and to crave pardon of them, and power against them. . . .

[A] learned author counselleth such householders as know their own proneness to fall oft in the same offence, whatsoever open sin it be, to determine with themselves—yea, to resolve and vow—that as oft as they fall again into the same offence, to make open confession to the family of the first offence, if the fault be known to the family. For the second fault to use abstinence, and to eat but only bread, and to drink water only for one or two meals. For the third fault, to refrain all ordinary food for one or two meals, and to give it to the needy and hungry. For the fourth fault, to forfeit and to give away much money to many poor and needy men. . . .

I have seen a second example hereof showed by an honest-hearted householder, who upon some open show of discord betwixt his wife and him, before the family, was presently humbled for it, confessed it, et cetera. And compared himself and his wife to the couple pieces of the house, which if they fall asunder, they cause other timber of the house to shrink and to go out of order. So we, saith he, having fallen at variance and openly reproved one another (which reproof should have been in private), have caused all the family to go out of order and to imitate (as they are apt to do) our evil example, and thereupon will the[y] less reverence our counsels, our persons, or reproofs hereafter. We will therefore (say they) confess our faults and chastise our selves, et cetera, that thereby we may remove these stumbling blocks from our family and learn to wax wiser hereafter.

This caused their children and servants (they seeing them to rebuke and correct themselves and to reform their manners) to bear all rebukes and corrections with more humility, yea, both to be ready without gainsaying to yield, confess, and acknowledge a fault committed, with meekness and amendment ever afterwards. By all this that you have heard, you may evidently see the dignity and commodity of this domestical discipline, which should first be imposed by householders upon their own shoulders, before it be laid upon their servants (sigs. B1^{v}–B2^{r}, B6^{r}–B7^{r}, B8^{r}).

RICHARD BERNARD

Josuahs Godly Resolution in Conference with Caleb, Touching Houshold Governement for Well Ordering a Familie (London, 1612)

☙ In this fictitious dialogue, first published in 1609, Joshua makes the familiar connections between the householder and his house, the king and his kingdom, and also the head and the body. The idea of the household as a commonwealth takes an interesting turn here, where servants are viewed suspiciously as a kind of discontented populace. In his description of marital relations, Joshua draws on the popular notion that "love goeth downward" (that is, from husband to wife) and "duty cometh upward" (that is, from wife to husband). The husband is commanded to love his wife and she is ordered to be dutiful to him.

JOSHUA. I set my self before my household because the head leadeth first the body, before the body can move by the members to perform any office. So it is in the natural constitution of a body, so in the political government of the commonwealth. Let princes lead; the people will follow, for from the head cometh life and motion to the body. And the same order is to be observed in well guiding of a family. There is little hope to find a godly family where the master is either careless or prophane. He must set on and go before, if he intend to have the rest good. His life is of authority, his example draweth other to him, his words are of force, and in doing his duty may he expect a blessing. . . .
CALEB. What direction give you . . . to reform a disordered family?
JOSHUA. The governor must do as in making a new house, where an old stood: he must remove the old wholly as far forth as it is unprofitable and make the rest all new. The man and the wife must be sound; they be the two side posts. So their children, who are as the beams laid overthwart, if they be rotten, though all the rest be new, at the length the work will fall. . . .

Chiefly the husband and wife must love each other: if wrongs be between them, let themselves, between themselves, or with the good liking of a faithful secret friend to both, be ended. They must beware that the household become not partners in the matter, for servants by slander, flattery, and whisperings will kindle the contention and make a prey of them. The contending of man and wife must never want love, but if any smite either by the tongue, both must join in one against the smiter. . . . Complaints arise first upon neglect of duty, the performance whereof is the touchstone of profession: where the husband is loving, the wife learns obedience; where the wife is obedient, the husband is moved to be kind. By their well living the house is preserved in peace, and where they two do as they ought to themselves and their family, the children and servants learn to walk in subjection, and do in awful love discharge their duties (sigs. B4^{v}, B5^{v}, B7^{v}–B8^{r}).

[RICHARD DAY]

A Booke of Christian Praiers, Collected out of the Ancient Writers, and Best Learned in Our Time (London, 1608)

☙ Richard Day's father, John, assembled and printed a collection of prayers in 1569. The son's substantially revised edition of 1578, subsequently reprinted in 1581, 1590, and 1608, is generally known as "Queen Elizabeth's Prayer Book." As depicted here, home is a safe haven. It is very much in line with Edward Coke's legal definition of 1605: "the house of every one is to him his castle and fortress, as well for defense against injury and violence, as for his repose." According to the literature of the period, the householder aspired to peacefulness and quiet above all, and the advice manuals aimed to help him achieve that ideal.

A prayer to be said at our first going abroad

I must be fain to go abroad among the snares which the devil and his handservant, the world, have laid for me; and I carry with me besides the stings of mine own flesh. Guide me, therefore, O thou most sure guide: be thou my leader, thou God of my welfare. Defend me, O Captain, from the trains [snares] and stales [traps] that are laid for me, that whatsoever things I shall meet with, I may make no more account of them than they are worthy of, but keep on my way with mine eyes so fast fixed and settled upon thee alone, as I may not deal with any thing further forth then it hath respect unto thee. Lord, show me thy ways and lead me in thy paths for thy Son's sake. Amen.

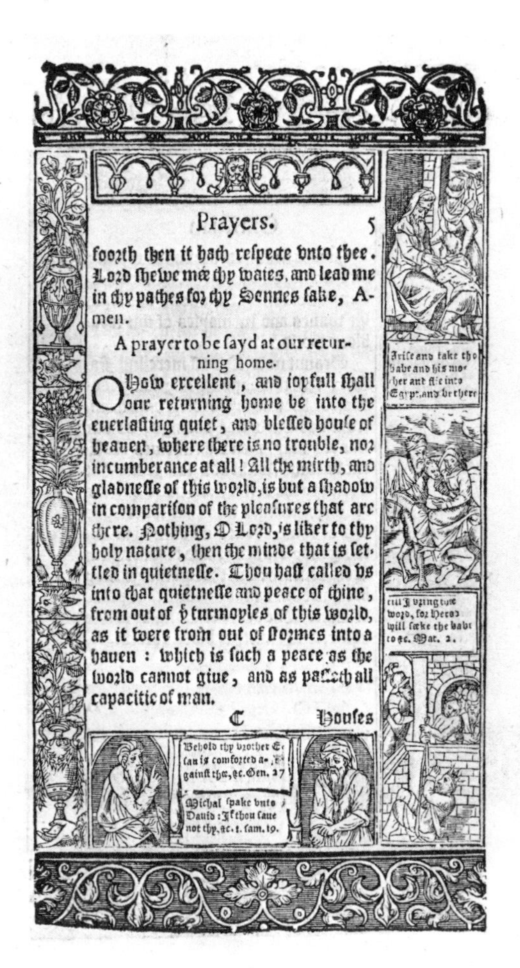

Prayers. 5

foorth then it hath reſpecte unto thee. Lord ſhewe mee thy waies, and lead me in thy pathes for thy Sonnes ſake, Amen.

A prayer to be ſayd at our returning home.

O How excellent, and ioyfull ſhall our returning home be into the euerlaſting quiet, and bleſſed houſe of heauen, where there is no trouble, nor incumberance at all! All the mirth, and gladneſſe of this world, is but a ſhadow in compariſon of the pleaſures that are there. Nothing, O Lord, is liker to thy holy nature, then the minde that is ſettled in quietneſſe. Thou haſt called vs into that quietneſſe and peace of thine, from out of ÿ turmoyles of this world, as it were from out of ſtormes into a hauen: which is ſuch a peace as the world cannot giue, and as paſſeth all capacitie of man.

C Houſes

A prayer to be said at our returning home

O, how excellent and joyful shall our returning home be into the everlasting quiet and blessed house of heaven, where there is no trouble nor encumbrance at all! All the mirth and gladness of this world is but a shadow in comparison of the pleasures that are there. Nothing, O Lord, is liker to thy holy nature than the mind that is settled in quietness. Thou hast called us into that quietness and peace of thine, from out of the turmoils of this world, as it were from out of storms into a haven: which is such a peace as the world cannot give, and as passeth all capacity of man.

Houses are builded for us to repair into, from the annoyance of the weather, from the cruelty of beasts, and from the waves and turmoils of this troublous world.

Grant now, O most merciful Father, that through thy singular goodness our bodies may so resort unto them from our outward doings, as our minds may yield themselves obedient unto thee without striving, and that they may the better and more quietly exalt themselves into that sovereign rest of thine above. Grant that nothing may disturb and disquiet them here beneath, but that all things may be quiet and calm through that peace of thine. The peace of Christ be to this house, and to all that dwell therein. Amen (sigs. B4v–C1v).

Prayers from *A Booke of Christian Praiers, Collected out of the Ancient Writers, and Best Learned in Our Time* (London, 1608), compiled by Richard Day.

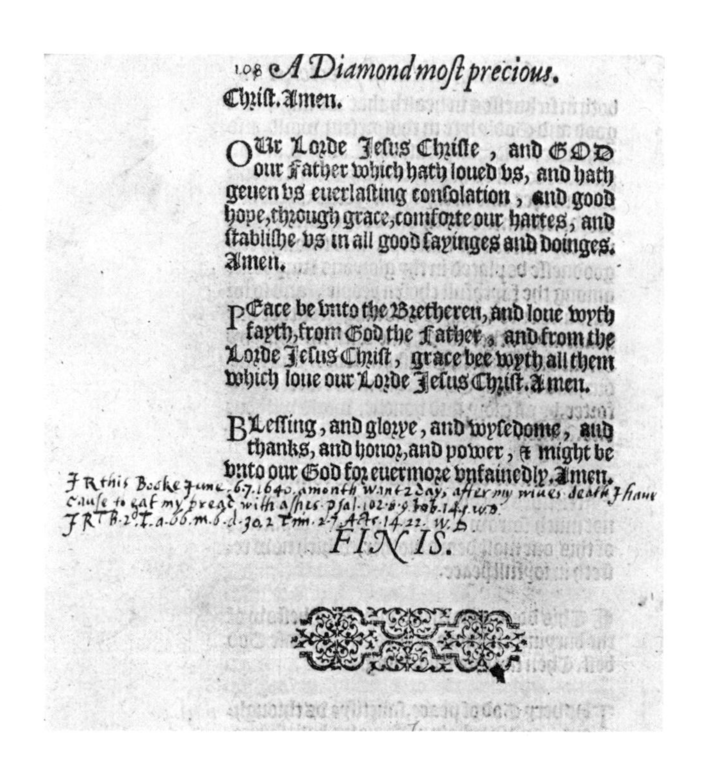
108 *A Diamond most precious.*

Christ. Amen.

OUr Lorde Jesus Christe, and GOD our Father which hath loued vs, and hath geuen vs euerlasting consolation, and good hope, through grace, comforte our hartes, and stablishe vs in all good sayinges and doinges. Amen.

PEace be vnto the Bretheren, and loue wyth fayth, from God the Father, and from the Lorde Jesus Christ, grace bee wyth all them which loue our Lorde Jesus Christ. Amen.

BLessing, and glorye, and wysedome, and thanks, and honor, and power, & might be vnto our God for euermore vnfainedly. Amen.

FINIS.

Annotations of William Dowsing (1640), in John Fit John, *A Diamonde Most Precious, Worthy to be Marked: Instructing all Maysters and Servauntes, How They Ought to Leade Their Lives* (London, 1577). There has been much discussion of whether there was room for love and affection in Elizabethan marital relations. Here, Dowsing displays strong emotion: "A month want[ing] two days after my wife's death I have cause to eat my bread with ashes."

WILLIAM WHATELY

A Care-Cloth, Or A Treatise of the Cumbers and Troubles of Marriage (London, 1624)

❦ Like John Dod and Robert Cleaver, Puritan divine William Whately recognized that the householder's absolute authority was a mixed blessing in terms of the burdens placed upon him. But this did not inspire Whately to rethink the gender hierarchy and the domestic power structure. A sacred premise of the Renaissance held that there could not be more than one head to a household. That was why families were not, by and large, multi-generational, and also why household servants were generally unmarried. When they wed, men and women went out of service to set up their own households, with the husband as the center of authority in the new establishment.

I will make bold to foretell those that will enter into marriage that they must make account in changing their estate, to change for the less easeful, and will advise him that will follow mine advice (if not, let him follow his own mind and say, ten years after, whether was the better counsel) to go into matrimony with fear of the worst, and to know beforehand that there grow briars and thorns in this way, whereon he must needs tread that will travail in it. Yet is not this written by me to make any man forbear marriage whom God calleth unto it, nor to make men hazard themselves to wickedness for fear of the cumbers of matrimony: but . . . to make men careful not to marry before God calls them to it and withall, being called, to fit themselves for it. . . . When doth God call a man to marriage? I answer: First, when he sets him in such a condition, that he may marry without wronging any other person, that is, when he is now become his own man, not bound by covenant to continue another man's servant: for God never crosseth himself. Whom he hath called for a certain time to be servant unto a master, him he doth not call, during that time, to break from that service, without his Master's liking, and to think of making himself a master before he have fulfilled the duty of a servant. Secondly, when God furnisheth a man with some convenient means to maintain a wife and family, and not before: for God calleth no man to any place until he have granted him some means of discharging the duties of that place; and it is one part of an householder's duty to provide for them of his household. The Lord sends not soldiers into the field to fight without some weapons—nor men to housekeeping with out some means to keep house (sigs. A3^{v}–A4^{v}).

NEHEMIAH WALLINGTON

Writing Book (1654)

Most diaries and letters from the early modern period were written by members of the clergy and the gentry. The remarkable Nehemiah Wallington was a London artisan, a "turner," or lathe-worker. He compiled fifty handwritten volumes of spiritual autobiography, copying in letters and sermons, recording examples of God's mercy, and authoring "An Extract of the Passages of My Life," from which these excerpts are taken. Written when he was fifty-six, the "extracts" describe his troubled puritanism, a series of suicide attempts, and a period of obsession with death. Perhaps because it was hoped that marriage would anchor the unstable young man, he wed earlier than was customary, at the age of twenty-three. These passages show his struggles with the responsibilities of householding and with the domestic ideals imposed by religion and ideology.

June the XVIII, 1621, being the Lord's day in the morning, I entered into this honorable estate of marriage (and a while after took an apprentice, one James Wells, which after his time was out he went into Ireland and was a good housekeeper till the beginning of the wars and then died). In this year 1621 I purposed to begin a new life, and I renewed my promises with my God but failed in keeping of them exceedingly, for which I was so perplexed in mind that now I was desirous to die and yet sometimes in fear of death. So then I was given to buy books concerning death: one book, *Learn to Die*, and *Death[’s] Advantage*, and funeral sermons, and many such-like book. And I took a great delight to buy pictures of death, but above all I was at great charge in buying *Anatomy of Death* and a little black coffin to put it in. And upon it written "Memento Mori." And this I had to stand upon a ginstool [joined stool] by my bedside every night, and some meals to stand upon or by my table. . . .

"An Extract of the Passage of My Life," from the Writing Book of London artisan Nehemiah Wallington (1654).

In the latter end of this year, 1621, I did come from the corner shop of Philpot Lane to keep shop in Leonard's Eastcheap, where now I have dwelt above this thirty yeers. . . .

This year, 1622, my family increasing and now having a wife, a child, a manservant, and a maidservant, and thus having the charge of so many souls, I then bought Mr. Goughe's book *Of Domestical Duties*, that so every one of us may learn and know our duties and honor God every one in his place where God had set them. For I was resolved with Joshua that I and my house will serve the Lord. And as I had drawn out 77 articles for myself, so a few years after I did draw out 31 articles for my family for the reforming of our lives, as followeth:

First, that we pray all together every morning and evening if we can convenient, or else by our selves. If not to pay to the poors' box a penny.

2 That when we hear of the troubles of the Church of God, that we sit some time apart for fasting and prayer, or else to pay to the poors' box two pence.

3 That we take not God's name in vain. If any do, then to pay to the poors' box a farthing.

4 That they that lie till six o'clock upon the Lord's day, then they pay a farthing.

[5] That we repeat what we heard or, if we miss, then to pay a half-penny.

[6] That every one read a chapter every day. If we miss on [one] time, then to double it another time or pay a farthing.

[7] If any quarrel or call one another out of their name, then to pay to the poors' box a farthing.

[8] If any counsel the faults of the ware, or use words of deceit, or take more for the ware than it is worth, then to pay to the poors' box a half-penny.

[9] If any tell a lie, then to pay one penny.

[10] If any eat or drink and not give thanks, or any break promise, and when they give the children anything to cause them to blessing and divers more such things, or else to pay to the poors' box.

To these laws we all set our hands: N[ehemiah] W[allington], G[race] W[allington], James Wells, Obediah Sely, Theophilus Ward, Susan Patie . . . .

In the beginning of the year 1625 the Lord did take away my maidservant Ann Exersail, which at her death praised God that ever she did come in my house and did see my face, for, saith she, if I had died in the country, I had died in ignorance and in my sin. But since I came to you I praise God I know more, and so this did yield to me some comfort to hear her say so (fols. 12ᵛ–14ᵛ, 29ᵛ).

A TABLE.

Particular Duties, from William Gouge, *Of Domesticall Duties* (London, 1622). Gouge charted 74 duties for the wife and 76 for the husband; each is crosslisted to fuller explanations and exhortations within the book. While the emphasis for the wife is on her duty to her husband, the accent for him is on his love for her. Gouge was Nehemiah Wallington's guide as he tried to master the range of his household responsibilities.

The Murder of Thomas Arden, from *The Lamentable and True Tragedy of Master Arden of Feversham in Kent* (London, 1633). In this illustration from the third edition of the stageplay based on Arden's murder, he is shown playing at "tables" (a game comparable to backgammon), with Mosby across the board from him, Black Will pulling his head back with a towel, his wife Alice advancing with a knife, and others of the assassins armed and at the ready.

RAPHAEL HOLINSHED

The Chronicles of England, Scotland, and Ireland (London, 1587)

Ten people were judged guilty of the 1551 murder of Kentish gentleman Thomas Arden. Even though it was a "private matter," Holinshed described the murder at length in his state history of Britain. The "horribleness," for Holinshed, for an anonymous playwright, and for a number of other authors, was the fact that the convicted ringleader was Arden's own wife, Alice. Her accomplices included her lover, Thomas Mosby; a manservant, Michael Sanderson; and a hired assassin, Black Will. Because, as the head of his household, Arden had a political status, the crime committed by the members of his household was petty treason rather than mere murder. Hanging wasn't good enough for Alice and Michael: she was burned at the stake and he was hanged in chains. A hundred years later, the case was still notorious as a signpost that family relations remained unsettled despite the widespread promulgation of domestic ideology.

About this time there was at Feversham in Kent a gentleman named Arden, most cruelly murdered and slain by the procurement of his own wife. The which murder, for the horribleness thereof, although otherwise it may seem to be but a private matter, and therefore as it were impertinent to this history, I have thought good to set it forth somewhat at large, having the instructions delivered to me by them that have used some diligence to gather the true understanding of the circumstances. This Arden was a man of tall and comely personage, and matched in marriage with a gentlewoman, young, tall, and well favored of shape and countenance, who, chancing to fall in familiarity with one Mosby a tailor by occupation . . . . and loathing her husband, wished and after practiced the means how to hasten his end. . . .

When they came into the parlor, Mosby sat down on the bench, having his face toward the place where Black Will stood. Then Michael, Master Arden's man, stood at his master's back, holding a candle in his hand, to shadow Black Will, that Arden might by no means perceive him coming forth. In their play [at the game of tables], Mosby said thus (which seemed to be the watchword for Black Will's coming forth), "Now may I take you, sir, if I will." "Take me?" quoth Master Arden, "Which way?" With that Black Will stepped forth, and cast a towel about his neck so to stop his breath and strangle him. . . . After that Black Will was gone, Mistress Arden came into the counting house, and with a knife gave him seven or eight picks into the breast. Then they made clean the parlor, took a clout [cloth], and wiped where it was bloody, and strewed again the rushes that were shuffled with struggling, and cast the clout with which they wiped the blood, and the knife that was bloody, wherewith she had wounded her husband, into a tub by the well's side, where afterwards both the same clout and knife were found. Thus this wicked woman, with her complices, most shamefully murdered her own husband, who most entirely loved her all his life time. . . .

Michael, Master Arden's man, was hanged in chains at Feversham, and one of the maids was burnt there, pitifully bewailing her case, and cried out on her mistress that had brought her to this end, for the which she would never forgive her. Mosby and his sister were hanged in Smithfield at London; Mistress Arden was burned at Canterbury the four and twentieth of March. Greene came again certain years after, was apprehended, condemned, and hanged in chains in the high way betwixt Ospring and Boughton-against-Feversham; Black Will was burnt on a scaffold at Flushing in Zeeland [Flanders] (vol. 2, sigs. Kkkkk1^{v}–Kkkkk3^{v}).

Ivory Shoehorn (English, 1613), engraved with stylized motifs, including a Tudor rose surmounted by a crown, 9 inches long. Robert Mindum, one of the earliest of the Master Horners working in London, Sheffield, and York, carved this shoehorn as a gift to his wife, Jane. Agecroft Association.

A Leather Wallet Containing Maps Drawn by Wenceslaus Hollar, *The Kingdome of England & Principalitie of Wales Exactly Described . . . Portable for Every Man's Pocket* (London, 1644). Barnabas Bainbr[idge] noted that this handy collection of maps was "his book" in 1650. The wallet continued in the family at least until 4 June 1667, when it was inscribed, "my son Bainbrigg gave me this book."

The Housewife ❧

THOMAS GATAKER

A Good Wife Gods Gift: and, A Wife Indeed. Two Marriage Sermons (London, 1623)

❧ Thomas Gataker maintains that a wife is not made simply through marriage; she has to earn the name. He argues with such rhetorical flourish that one can almost hear him delivering his message from the pulpit. To prepare the sermon for publication, however, he added dense marginal notes citing his sources; he was learned in Hebrew, Greek, and Latin. This extract deals with the wife's role, but Gataker also anticipates a possible response from the man married to a woman, not a wife: "May not a man forbear to do the duty of an husband to such an one?" His answer is "no." Because duty goes upward, the husband's duty is owed to God rather than to the wife, and "no default of duty on her part . . . can discharge thee of thy debt to Him."

Many have good skill in choosing of wares, in valuing of lands, in beating a bargain, in making a purchase, that are yet but blind buzzards in the choice of a wife. . . .

Every wife should be then as a part of her husband, as a limb of him that hath her. But the woman that beareth the name, and standeth in the room of a wife, but doth not the office and duty of a wife, is but as an eye of glass, or a silver nose, or an ivory tooth, or an iron hand, or a wooden leg, that occupieth the place indeed, and beareth the name of a limb or a member, but is not truly or properly any part of that body whereunto it is fastened; it is but equivocally so called.

Yea, those artificial and equivocal limbs, though they be not properly parts, nor stand the body in much stead, yet are they rather helpful than hurtful or harmful any way to it; they help to supply a place defective that would otherwise stand vacant and, by supplying it, to conceal in part such blemishes as would otherwise lie more open to the eye of others.

But with a bad wife, an undiscreet woman, it is far worse. She not only standeth her husband in no stead, but she is a sore burden, and a foul blemish, and not an eye-sore only, but even an heart-sore to him that hath her. . . . And she may therefore be compared rather to a wart or a wen, and that sited and seated in some conspicuous part (for she is as ointment in one's hand that cannot be concealed) which, as it is no benefit, so it is a burden and a blemish to the body; or to a wolf, or a cancer, that consumeth the flesh, wasteth the vital parts, and eateth even to the very heart. . . .

Though thou wert contracted before a thousand witnesses, and married publicly in the frequentest and most solemn assembly, not by the hand of an ordinary minister but of a bishop or an archbishop, no rite or ceremony omitted, either the wedding ring (that Tertullian more than once mentioneth, and freeth from taint of superstition) or any other: Yet are thou no wife, if thou doest not the duty of a wife, if thine husband have not that good of thee that God's spirit here speaketh of. . . .

She is a wife then, indeed, and none but she, in whom these two concur: that she is both a good housewife and a good wife too to him that hath her. But how many married women are there, in whom neither of these are? How many in whom they meet not? How many are there not housewives, but drones rather? Living wholly on the sweat of their husbands' brows, as the drone doth on the honey that the bee maketh and bringeth in? How many though not drones, yet droils [menial drudges] rather than wives? That will toil and moil indeed about the house, as we say, like horses, but are withall of so crooked and crabbed a nature, of so currish, unquiet, and contentious a disposition, that their husbands can have no joy nor comfort at all of them. There can be no comfortable cohabitation or conversing with them.

There may be good cause therefore even for married women to examine themselves whether they be wives or no: since that if they answer not that which God's word and will, yea, which the very name giveth them, requireth of them, they are as no wives in God's account (sigs. C1^{r}, F2^{r-v}, F4^{v}–G1^{r}).

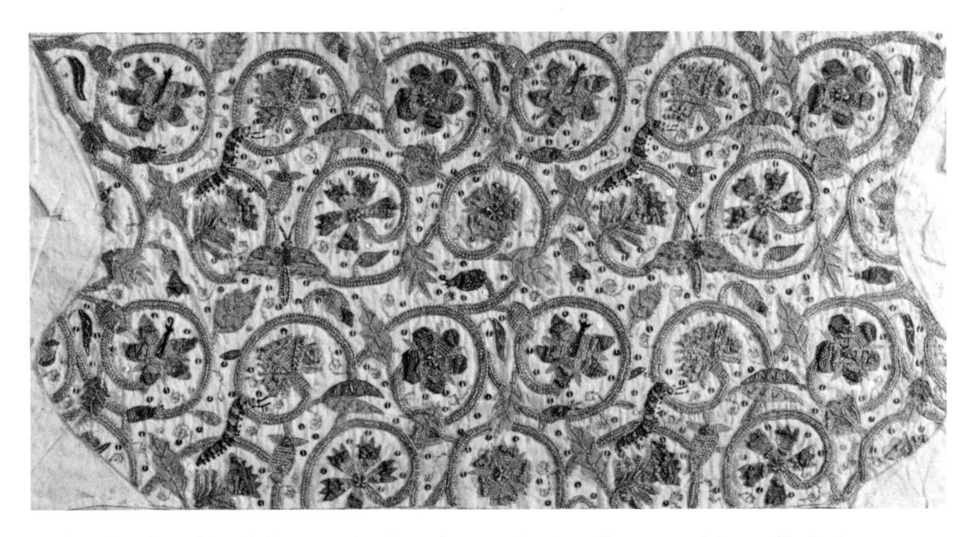

Embroidered Coif (English, c. 1580), silk on linen with vines, flowers, and bees. Elizabethan women wore coifs inside the house. This beautiful example has not been cut out and assembled for wearing. Instead, it remains as when its embroiderer finished the delicate work. The Philadelphia Museum of Art.

PHILIP STUBBS

A Christal Glasse for Christian Women. Containing, A Most Excellent Discourse, of the Godly Life and Christian Death of Mistresse Katherine Stubs (London, 1592)

❧ Two years after publishing the notorious *Anatomy of Abuses* (1583), with its attack on stage plays and other contemporary "vices," Philip Stubbs took a six-year sabbatical from writing, and married. In 1591 he reappeared on the literary scene with this tribute to his young wife, who had died six weeks after giving birth. The woman he describes conforms so strictly to the ideals of the advice manuals that it is an open question whether Stubbs succeeded in finding a wife who shared his own rigorous puritanism, or whether this memorial was an act of fictionalization—or, perhaps, a bit of both. The book was so popular that it was reprinted thirty times between 1591 and 1669, with two additional undated editions in the 1680s and '90s.

You could seldom or never have come into her house and have found her without a Bible or some other good book in her hands. And when she was not reading, she would spend the time in conferring, talking, and reasoning with her husband, of the word of God and of religion, asking him, what is the sense of this place, and what is the sense of that? How expound you this place, and how expound you that? What observe you of this place, and what observe you of that? So that she seemed to be, as it were, ravished with the same spirit that David was, when he said: "The zeal of thy house hath eaten me up." She followed the commandment of our savior Christ, who biddeth us to search the scriptures, for in them ye hope to have eternal life. She obeyed the commandment of the Apostle, who biddeth women to be silent, and to learn of their husbands at home. She would suffer no disorder or abuse in her house to be either unreproved, or unreformed. And so gentle was she and courteous of nature, that she was never heard to give any the lie in all her life, nor so much as to "thou" any [speak accusatively] in anger. She was never known to fall out with any of her neighbors, nor with the least child that lived, much less to scold or brawl, as many will nowadays for every trifle, or rather for no cause at all. . . .

When her husband was abroad in London or elsewhere, there was not the dearest friend she had in the world that could get her abroad to dinner or supper, or to any disports, plays, interludes, or pastimes whatsoever. Neither was she given to pamper her body with delicate meats, wines, or strong drinks, but rather refrained them altogether, saying that we should eat to live and not live to eat. And as she excelled in the gift of sobriety, so she surpassed in the virtue of humility. For it is well known to divers yet living, that she utterly abhorred all kind of pride both in apparel and otherwise. She could never abide to hear any filthy or unseemly talk of scurrility, bawdry, or uncleanness, neither swearing or blaspheming, cursing or banning [damning], but would reprove them sharply, showing them the vengeance of God due for such defects . . . . There was never any man or woman that ever opened their mouths against her, or that ever either did or could once accuse her of the least shadow of dishonesty, so continently she lived, and so circumspectly she walked, eschewing even the very outward appearance or show of evil.

Again, for true love and loyalty to her husband and his friends, she was (let me speak it without offence), I think, the rarest paragon in the world, for she was so far of[f] from dissuading her husband to be beneficial to his friends that she would rather persuade him to be more beneficial to them. If she saw her husband merry, then she was merry; if he were sad, she was sad; if he were heavy or passionate, she would endeavor to make him glad; if he were angry, she would quickly please him, so wisely she demeaned herself towards him. She would never contrary him in anything, but by wise counsel and sage advice, with all humility and submission, seek to persuade him (sigs. A2^{v}–A3^{r}).

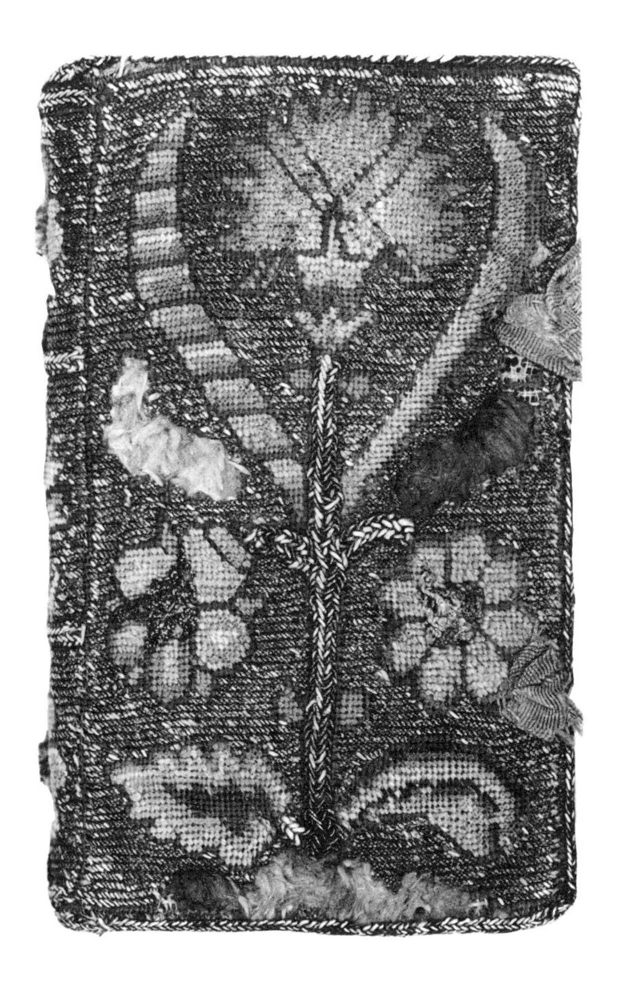

Embroidered Binding, *The Whole Booke of Psalmes* (London, 1635). Women stitched decorative bindings and then carried these small volumes about the house with them. According to her husband, Katherine Stubbs was rarely found "without a Bible or some other good book in her hands."

[THOMAS HEYWOOD]

A Curtaine Lecture (London, 1637)

☙ In *A Godly Form of Household Government* (1598), John Dod and Robert Cleaver warned the potential husband that he should "take heed when thou choosest a wife," for she "must continually be conversant with thee, at thy table, in thy chamber, in bed, in thy secrets, and finally, in thy heart and breast." Thomas Heywood's collection of anecdotes and observations about women takes as its dominant conceit the moments "in bed," where the wife could have her say. (The "curtain" of the title refers to bed curtains, which enclosed the couple for the night.) The motto reads: "When wives preach, 'tis not in the husband's power / To have their lectures end within an hour: / If he with patience stay till she have done, / She'll not conclude till twice the glass [hourglass] be run."

A question being asked, why our first and great grandmother Eve was rather in her formation taken out of the side of Adam than any other part of his body? It was thus learnedly answered: because the side is the middle of the body, to signify that the woman is of equal dignity with the man. And therefore she was taken not from the head, nor the foot, for she must not be superior or inferior unto him. It is probable also that she was taken out of the left side, for the heart of man inclineth that way rather than to the other, to denote unto us that man and woman should embrace each other with an hearty and entire love. And as the left side is the weakest, so the woman made from thence is the weaker vessel. Also all male children are conceived in the right side, and the females in the left, and as the sides are defended by the arms, so ought a woman to be by her husband.

Another demanding a question, why women are more apt to talk and, for the most part, make a greater and louder noise than men? Answer was returned that for that there was very great reason to be given: for, saith he, we know that Adam the first man was created from the dust of the earth, which is of its own nature soft, pliant, and tractable, and in the handling yieldeth no noise or sound at all. But the woman was made of a rib (a bone taken out of Adam's side) which is of a much harder temper. Now, for example, take a bushel bag or a quarter sack, and fill it with dust or with flesh, and tumble it or toss it which way you please: no echo ariseth from thence at all. But empty them and fill them with bones, and so shake and bolt [sift] them together, and you shall then hear what a rattling they will keep. . . .

An esquire's wife, being an excellent housewife

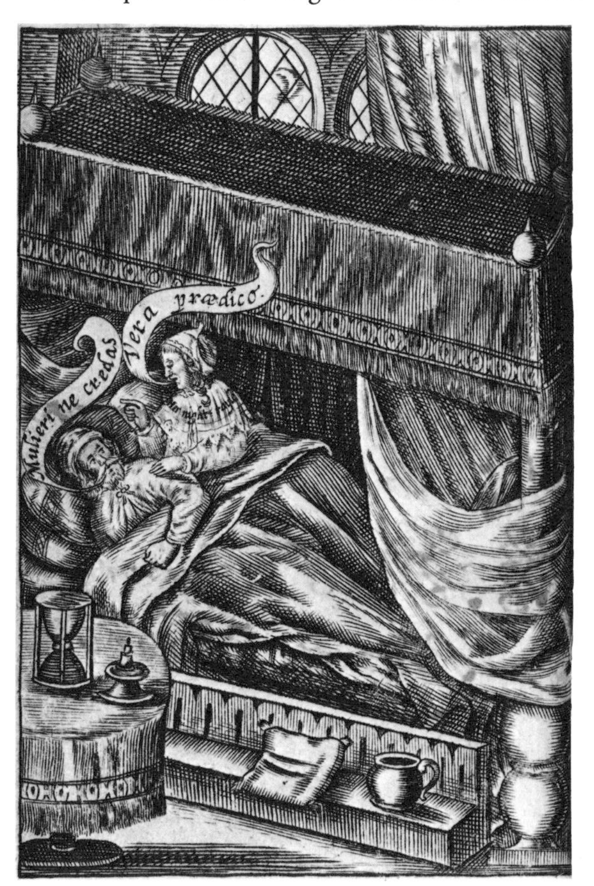

Frontispiece to *A Curtaine Lecture* (London, 1637), attributed to Thomas Heywood. The picture is cluttered with bedroom furnishings: the bedstead with its valance, curtain, sheets, blanket, and stacked pillows; a table with its cover, hourglass, and candle; a cushion and a chamber pot.

but of a very loud tongue withal, used to tax him for being too free in his kitchen, cellar, and at his table; for keeping too many impertinent servants, too many horses and dogs, hounds, greyhounds and spaniels, hawks, et cetera, which drew him to unnecessary charges. Then laid the law to him, what he might save in the year, which he vainly and profusely wasted, with divers other things to the like purpose. With so often iteration (as preaching still upon one text), both at board and in bed, that, tired with her continual clamors, and withal she often forbearing his embraces unless he would reform all things according to her mind and leave all his estate to her sole management, he grew not to love her so well as at the first, and, casting his eye upon a pretty slut, his gardener's wife, he, neglecting his own, grew very much enamored of her. . . . It was then concluded that they should meet in a lodge some half a mile from the manor house. . . . the gentlewoman follows, and before [in the presence of] her husband discovers the woman. The cause was at first somewhat bitterly debated betwixt them. But all the choler being vented, they fell to a more mild atonement, in which it was concluded he would ever after forsake his lust, so long as she would forbear her lecture (sigs. I1^{v}–I3^{r}, L3^{v}–L6^{r}).

WILLIAM WHATELY

A Bride-Bush, Or A Wedding Sermon (London, 1617)

❧ Political ideology and economic necessity do not always go hand in hand. Elizabethan life was complicated enough that the householder had to rely on his wife to run things in his absence, and this was as true for the powerful aristocrat as for the poor laborer. Whately tried to make a virtue of this necessity by finding a political justification for shared authority. He may have succeeded in theory, but there was no way to win in practice. Everyone had difficulty drawing the lines: which activities was the wife to supervise? which purchases? which servants? which servants at some times and not others?

Again, in commanding, it must be regarded that authority descend not unto low, mean, and trivial things, which are not of any moment or importance in the family. The life of the head must be derived even unto the feet. So the husband's authority doth indeed guide all, even the meanest things in the family, but the head is not always actually stooping unto the foot, for then the body would grow crooked and ill-shapen. So must not the husband be charging, bidding, and intermeddling by strict commandments in the small matters of the family, putting his hand (as it were) to every matter. For that garment which is much worn, must needs become threadbare. And this power of commanding is like a vesture for high days, to be put on for some special and needful occasions. When the husband will be housewife and all, and be dealing with brewing, baking, washing, and the particulars of these and the like businesses, it comes to pass that his wife can help in nothing, because he will do all things. When the man will bid and charge so eagerly in a thing of nothing, as if his whole estate did depend upon serving the swine or washing the buck, et cetera, this devalues his word, and makes his charge of no regard. In such things he should let his wife rule under him, and give her leave to know more than himself, which hath greater matters and more nearly concerning the family to exercise his knowledge. And if he see any thing in these and the like matters done disorderly, it were his part to advise and counsel, rather than command. He that will be drawing out his commandments for every light thing shall find it at length regarded in nothing. See then that the matter be so much worth, before thou lay a charge concerning it (sigs. D2^{r-v}).

HENRY SMITH

A Preparative to Mariage (London, 1591)

❧ Much has been made of the concept of "companionate marriage" that developed during the Renaissance. As has been seen, however, marital friendship was notionally enjoyed only within a strictly hierarchical relationship: love goes downward, duty comes upward. Even Henry Smith's argument against wife-beating is made in terms of the inferiority and dependence of the wife. This was a sufficiently frequent topic in the marital advice manuals that it was probably a fairly common problem. Smith's remarks also cast a chilling light on the fate of household servants.

He must tender her as much as all her friends, because he hath taken her from her friends, and covenanted to tender her for them all. To show how he should tender her, Peter saith, "Honor the woman as the weaker vessel." As we do not handle glasses like pots, because they are weaker vessels, but touch the[m] nicely and softly for fear of cracks, so a man must entreat his wife with gentleness and softness, not expecting that wisdom, nor that faith, nor that patience, nor that strength in the weaker vessel, which should be in the stronger. . . .

This is far from civil wars between man and wife; in all his offices is found no office to fight. . . . Then weigh and judge how harsh and bitter a thing it is for man and wife to live together in enmity. For the first year after marriage, God would not have the husband go to war with his enemies, but no year would he have him war with his wife. And therefore God gave him that year to stay at home and settle his love, that he might not war nor jar after. For the God of peace dwelleth not in the house of war. As a kingdom cannot stand if it be divided, so a house cannot stand if it be divided, for strife is like fire which leaves nothing but dust and smoke and ashes behind it. We read in the scripture of masters that struck their servants, but never of any that struck his wife, but rebuked her. Lot was drunk when he lay with his daughters instead of a wife; and is he

A Husband Beating His Wife, engraved by Abraham Bosse (Paris, c. 1640).

sober which striketh his wife instead of his servants? . . . She is come to thee as to a sanctuary, to defend her from hurt, and canst thou hurt her thyself? . . . So then, if a man ask whether he may strike his wife? God saith nay, thou mayest not hate thy wife, for no man hateth his own flesh, showing that he should not come near blows, but think his wrath too much. For Paul saith, "Be not bitter to your wives," noting that anger in a husband is a vice. Every man is ashamed to lay hands on a woman, because she cannot match him, therefore he is a shameless man which layeth hands on his wife (sigs. E8v–F3r).

ANNE SOUTHWELL

Commonplace Book (c. 1588–1636)

❧ Lady Anne Southwell's manuscript compilation includes rental records, inventories, some prose descriptions of fabulous beasts, and poems she wrote, including sonnets, elegies, epitaphs, and witty verses like the example below. After her death in 1636 her husband Captain Henry Sibthorpe added a list of her books. We know that most or all of them were hers because in 1631 she owned three trunks full of books, according to an inventory of her personal possessions. Evidently the interests of women were not always as predictable and as limited as advice writers would have us believe. Here, the classical authors are represented, as are contemporary political texts, and there is an impressive collection on the arts of war. The catalogue lists ninety-eight books; twelve more are added in a separate sequence, to bring the total to 110. The size of each volume is specified: folio (two leaves from each sheet of paper), quarto (four per sheet), octavo (eight per sheet), and duodecimo (twelve per sheet).

All married men desire to have good wives:
but few give good example by their lives.
They are our head; they would have us their heels.
This makes the good wife kick; the good man reels.
When God brought Eve to Adam for a bride,
The text says she was ta'en from out man's side.
A symbol of that side whose sacred blood
Flowed for his Spouse, the Church's saving good.
This is a mystery, perhaps too deep
For blockish Adam that was fallen asleep.

. . .

A List of my Books

1. Calvin's *Institutions*, in Folio.
2. Calvin's *Sermons upon Job*, in Folio.
3. *Synopsis Papismi, or A General View of Papistry*, by Andrew Willet, in Quarto.
4. Hooker's *Ecclesiastical Polity*, in Folio.
5. Pliny's *Natural History*, in Folio.
6. *General History of The Netherlands*, in Folio.
7. *History of the Roman Emperors*, in Folio.
8. Camerarius' *Historical Meditations*, in Folio.
9. *Triumph of God's Revenge against Murder*, in Folio.
10. *Orlando Furioso*, in Folio.
11. Sallust his *History*, in English, in Folio.
12. Eusebius' *Ecclesiastical History*, in Folio.
13. Spenser's *Faerie Queene*, in Folio.
14. *Purchas his Pilgrimage*, in Folio.
15. Gerard's *Herbal*, in Folio.
16. An old Dictionary in Folio.
17. Markham's *Book of Honor*, in Folio.
18. Montaigne's *Essays*, in Folio.
19. Moryson's *Travels*, in Folio.
20. *The Siege of Breda*, in Folio.
21. Suetonius, *Of the 12 Caesars*, in Folio.
22. Sir Christopher Sibthorp's book against Popery, in Quarto.
23. Doctor Donne's *Poems*, in Quarto.
24. Machiavelli's *Art of War*, in Quarto.

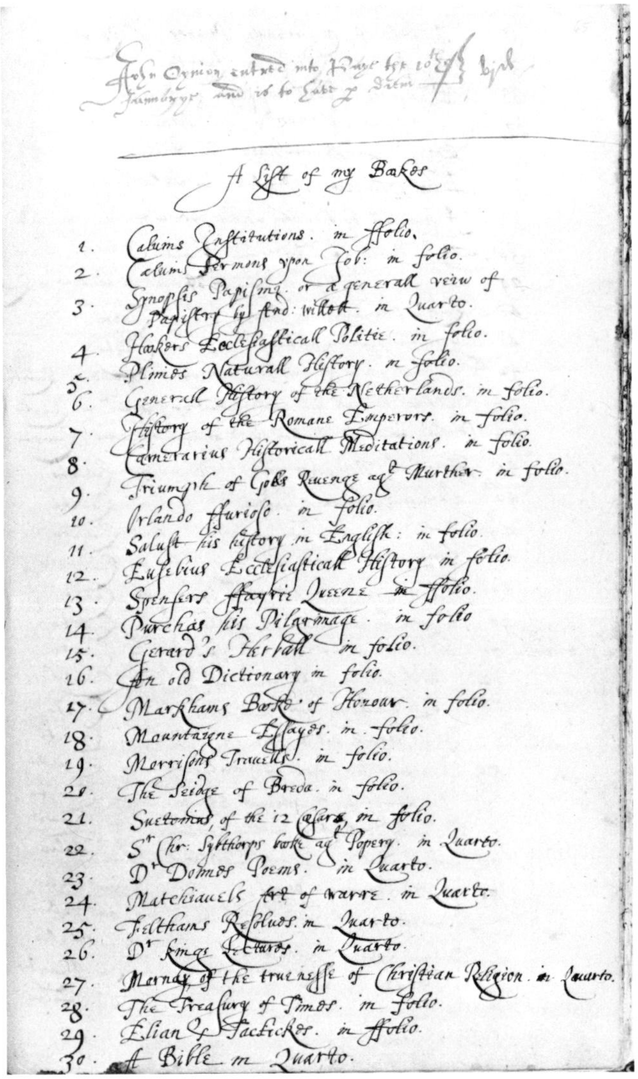

"A List of My Books," from Anne Southwell's Commonplace Book (c. 1588–1636).

25. Feltham's *Resolves,* in Quarto.
26. Dr. King's *Lectures,* in Quarto.
27. Mornay, *Of the Trueness of Christian Religion,* in Quarto.
28. *The Treasury of Times,* in Folio.
29. Aelian's *Tactics,* in Folio.
30. A Bible in Quarto.

. . .

These are likewise books belonging to me

99. *Private Devotions,* in Duodecimo.
100. *The Crumbs of Comfort,* in Duodecimo.
101. *Meditations and Vows,* in Octavo.
102. *A New and Admirable Invention,* et cetera, in Duodecimo.
103. *The Truth of our Times,* in Octavo.
104. *Select Cases of Conscience,* et cetera, in Octavo.
105. *The Temple* in *Sacred Poems,* in Octavo.
106. *The Practice of Piety,* in Octavo.
107. The English Dictionary, in Octavo.
108. *The Christian Warfare,* in Quarto.
109. *The Dippers Dipt* by Doctor Featley, in Quarto.
110. A Great Bible in Folio.

(fols. 16^{r}, 64^{v}, 65^{r})

WILLIAM GOUGE

Of Domesticall Duties (London, 1622)

❧ Puritan divine William Gouge dedicated the *Domestical Duties* to his parishioners in the Blackfriars precinct in London. They had heard preliminary versions in his weekly sermons, one on Wednesdays and two on Sundays. Just because a thesis was preached or printed, however, doesn't mean it was believed. Gouge himself lets us see that the responses of his audience—and especially its female members—were more complicated than that. Evidently, the Puritan authors repeatedly reminded women that they were to be obedient and submissive because many weren't.

I remember that when these Domestical Duties were first uttered out of the pulpit, much exception was taken against the application of a wife's subjection to the restraining of her from disposing the common goods of the family without or against her husband's consent. . . . Many that can patiently enough hear their duties declared in general terms cannot endure to hear those generals exemplified in their particular branches. This cometh too near to the quick and pierceth too deep. But (to interpret all according to the rule of love, in the better part) I take the main reason of the many exceptions which were taken to be this: that wives' duties (according to the Apostle's method) being in the first place handled, there was taught (as must have been taught, except the truth should have been betrayed) what a wife, in the uttermost extent of that subjection under which God hath put her, is bound unto, in case her husband will stand upon the uttermost of his authority. Which was so taken as if I had taught that an husband might and ought to exact the uttermost, and that a wife was bound in that uttermost extent to do all that was delivered as duty, whether her husband exact it or no. But when I came to deliver husband's duties, I showed that he ought not to exact whatsoever his wife was bound unto (in case it were exacted by him), but that he ought to make her a joint governor of the family with himself, and refer the ordering of many things to her discretion, and with all honorable and kind respect to carry himself towards her. In a word, I so set down an husband's duties, as if he be wise and conscionable in observing them, his wife can have no just cause to complain of her subjection. That which maketh a wife's yoke heavy and hard is an husband's abuse of his authority, and more pressing his wife's duty than performing his own, which is directly contrary to the Apostle's rule. This just apology I have been forced to make, that I might not ever be judged (as some have censured me) an hater of women (sigs. *3^{v}–*4^{r}).

Servingmen ❧

J. M.

A Health to the Gentlemanly Profession of Servingmen; Or, The Servingmans Comfort (London, 1598)

❧ "Service" encompassed an enormous range of social level and of labor, from stableboys and manual workers to stewards and secretaries. Until they married, many gentlemen's sons continued their education and acculturation through attendance in great households. The unidentified author of this tract distinguishes "servingmen" of this sort from mere "servants" such as "Dick to droil [drudge], Ralph to run, Kit the caterer." He remembers and laments a lost golden age of service built on loyalty and largeness of spirit, in sharp contrast to the more contractual and currency-based relationships of a post-feudal age.

Another, in the same time of persecution and trial of friends, having a fair shadowed vineyard and in it a goodly cave, deep and large (for the which peradventure he was condemned), by chance refreshing himself in the said cave, one of his servants perceiving the questers yet afar off, which came to finish

Watercolor Illustration (English, early seventeenth century), from a collection of royal, military, and court costumes of the time of James I. As the principals of the household and their guests play cards, a servingman brings in dishes.

his master's tragedy, for the pure love and sincere affection that he bore to his master hid him safely, as he thought, in the secret place of the den, and furnished himself with his master's apparel, feigning to be he, even offering himself to the death for his master's safety. O rare examples, worthy of everlasting memory: what greater goodwill? what purer love, or more sincere affection can be found amongst any consort of creatures than this? O happy servants, that had your being in those golden days, when masters would merit such marvels at your hands: and thrice happy masters, that passed your pilgrimage in those blessed hours, when by your love and liberality, you tied your servants with this undissolvable bond of assured friendship, even to deserve and merit the full measure of your good will towards them. . . . long is it since this love and affection was thus in the highest degree made manifest, and the trial of friendship thus exercised. . . .

I have told you before, that servingmen's only maintenance consisteth upon liberality, for their wages was never (in any age) able to defray their necessary charges and expenses. But I would not have you to misconstrue my meaning in this liberality, that it was bestowed upon them in mere commiseration, pity, and charity, as them of ability do upon impotent beggars. But the servant by his duty and diligence did merit and deserve it before he had it, though it was over and above his covenant and bargain. . . .

The liberal master is a rare phoenix. . . . There is none, no, not one in this age that beareth that love in liberality towards his servants, that he in goodwill ought, or they by duty do daily merit. . . . Pity it is, that Liberality, that honest fellow, should, dying, be buried without his rites and ceremonies, his funerals and obsequies, to be duly solemnized. I fear me that none was so charitable as to ring his soul knell or bestow on him a winding sheet. O, that I had lived when he died, or had been at the making of his will. Though I had been none of his executors, nor had had any legacy bestowed upon me, yet would I, at my own charges, have seen him honestly brought forth to his long home [his grave] (as the saying is) but sure he died intestate, and for heirs apparent I think he had none, for since his death I never heard of any his successors. Notwithstanding though he were before my time, yet have I heard so much good of him, as loath I am that his fame should be buried in oblivion: wherefore I will (though I be no professed poet) frame some epitaph of his life and death. . . .

The courtly crew, of noble minds,
Would give reward for every leg.
To crouch and kneel now duty binds,
Though suitor nought but right doth beg.
Weep, therefore, weep, and wail with me
For dead is Liberality.

(sigs. $C2^{v}$–$C3^{r}$, $D2^{v}$, $E1^{r}$–$E2^{v}$)

THOMAS FOSSET

The Servants Dutie. Or, The Calling and Condition of Servants (London, 1613)

❧ The lines of authority between masters and servants were much clearer than those between husbands and wives. If householders were domestical kings, housewives constituted an aristocracy. Servants were mere commoners. Still, the wife and the servant shared one potential dilemma that the ideological literature could not equip them to resolve. Both were enjoined to submit and obey, but both were instructed to resist if the householder's directive conflicted with moral authority. This sounded clear enough in the abstract, especially in works like Thomas Fosset's *Servant's Duty*, but it was a delicate and hazardous matter in practice.

Every creature is called to some one thing wherein his calling doth consist, as the bird to fly, the fish to swim; and man (saith Job) is called to travail and labor, as the sparks fly upwards. Yea, men being all of one and the same nature, have divers callings: the king to rule, the master to teach and command, and the servant to obey. Yea, the servant is called to three things: to labor, to suffer, and to serve. . . .

The third thing whereunto a servant is called is to serve, that is, to obey and to be in subjection, to have no will of his own nor power over himself, but wholly to resign himself to the will of his Master, and this is to obey. For what is obedience, but as it is defined by the learned . . . a voluntary and reasonable sacrificing of a man's own will: voluntarily, freely, and without any constraint, and reasonably, that is, according to reason and religion, in the obedience and fear of God, to deny his own will, his own affections, and to submit himself altogether to the will of God, and his superiors in God. . . . Here then servants may see and learn how they must serve and obey. They must be obedient at a word, at a call, and at a beck. . . .

All obedience must be subordinate unto the divine obedience due unto God. If thy Master bid thee do evil, hurt thy neighbor's cattle, or steal his goods; if he command thee, or give thee example to cog [cheat] and lie, to steal or use any fraud or deceit in buying or selling, to sell that which is evil for good, to exact more than a thing is worth, to do anything which you would not be content should be done to you, then say, as Christ the Master of us all said, when one told him that his mother and his brethren stood without to speak with him: "Who," saith he, "is my mother, and who are my brethren, et cetera?" (sigs. B2^{v}, B7^{v}, C6^{r}).

[JOHN FIT JOHN]

A Diamonde Most Precious, Worthy to be Marked: Instructing all Maysters and Servauntes, How They Ought to Leade Their Lyves (London, 1577)

❧ In this treatise, set in dialogue form, Civis, a citizen, gives advice to Puer, a boy. Puer is determined to leave the country and go to London, where he imagines that he will wait on a gentleman, dress finely, and accompany his master in gentlemanly pursuits. Given his background in farming, however, service of this type is not in his future. More likely, he will be apprenticed in a craft or trade. Civis professes to give him a more realistic picture of the life of the apprentice in London. As is to be expected, given the homiletic purpose of the treatise, he paints a grim picture.

CIVIS. No, what wilt thou do then?

PUER. What will I do? I will tell you: I will be a servingman, and wait on a gentleman, and then I shall go a hawking and hunting and have my delight as gentlemen hath. I shall have two new coats a year; I will have my suits of hose, my hats with feathers, and be all in the bravery, after the new fashion. And sometime I shall wait upon a gentlewoman, who would desire to live a merrier life. . . .

CIVIS. Can you not live by taking pains with husbandry [farming], as your father and others have done?

PUER. No, forsooth. . . . Marry, sir, there is such moiling and toiling, and taking of great pains, with hard fare, that I must needs to London to be a townsman, there to live more at ease. . . . I pray you now show unto me the order and usage of the apprentices, how they be bound, and what the scripture saith agreeable thereunto. . . .

CIVIS. You must be bound by a pair of indentures, for so many years as your master and you can agree for, always provided when you come out of your years, before you have the liberties of London, you must be of the age of four-and-twenty years. And the same master as I told you in the duty of masters, must teach you or cause you to be taught your occupation, and he to find you meat, drink, linen, woolen, hose, shoes, and all other such necessaries. And if you have served your master truly, then he will make you a freeman of London, whereby you may live and with the aid of almighty God do full well as your master before you hath done. You must be careful and mindful to carry away good exhortations when you hear them, and willing and diligent to please your master and mistress, in which doing, you shall find great commodity and profit.

PUER. When a man is bound, shall he not go into the country to see his friends during the time of his apprenticeship, nor a shooting in the fields? I love that exercise well.

CIVIS. Not without your master and mistress give you leave, and you must take heed you do not tarry long abroad then neither, for when you are absent, you know not occasion of business they shall have for you to do.

PUER. Then the servants are at a better point in the country, although they take pains on the working days, yet they may go leap, shoot, dance, dice, card, and bowl, and use what gaming they shall think good on the Sunday and holiday.

CIVIS. You cannot do so in London. I remember there was a statute made in the sixth year of the reign of King Henry the Eighth, that all constables and other head officers finding or knowing any person using or exercising any unlawful games—as tennis play, bowls, closh [a game like croquet], and all other unlawful games prohibited by many statutes—shall have full power to commit every such offender to ward, there to remain without bail or mainprize [surety] (sigs. B2r, B3v, F4r–G1r).

ROBERT DUDLEY, EARL OF LEICESTER

Letter to Dr. Jean Hotman (23 January ?1588)

❧ Robert Dudley, Elizabeth's favorite, aspired to a style of life that was associated with the Continent. This letter demonstrates both the role that servants played in his self-fashioning and the time and energy he invested in managing them: his agent in France has found him a French gardener; he would like a French cook, as well; and he dispatches a kitchen boy to be trained in a French kitchen. The business of acquiring service of sufficient quality is little different in spirit from that of acquiring fine wines and seeds for exotic fruits and vegetables—except that servants are more troublesome, requiring strict supervision.

Ottoman [Hotman]:

I am very glad to hear that you have provided me of a gardener. I doubt not but he shall be used to his contentation [contentment].

Touching the wines: you may forbear to send any, for I find the Rhenish wines very good this year.

If you can get a good young cook and a Protestant, I will thank you for him, and you shall deliver him to my servant Arden, whom I have licensed to wait upon th'earl of Derby this journey.

I have also sent a young man, an Englishman, brought up in my kitchen and prettily entered already, to spend a year or two there with some good principal cook in Paris, such as do use to serve the most of the noble men, and is most frequented and set on work. I pray you travail with some of your acquaintance to place him. And look what allowance

Hotman. I am very glad to heare
that yow have proceded in yor degree
I dowbt not but ye shalle [illegible] to his
contentacion.
Touching the wynes yow may forbeare
to send any. for I find the Rhenish wines
very good here now
Yf yow can gett a good yong cooke and
a protestant I will thank yow for him
& yow shall delyver him to my frend
Archy whome I have [illegible] to wayt
upon [illegible] of Derby here [illegible].
I have also sent a yonge man my Inglish
man brought upp in my kitchin & prettely
entred allredy to spend a yere or ij there
with some good principall cook in parris
such as doe use to serve the most of the
noble men and the most frequented
[illegible] in [illegible]. I pray yow travell with
some of yor acquaintance to place him
and looke what allowance he will aske
for his [illegible] & his bord I shalle [illegible]
[illegible] send over for him so such as yow
shall [illegible], and doe pray yow to [illegible]

Letter from Robert Dudley, Earl of Leicester, to Dr. Jean Hotman (23 January ?1588).

he will ask for his teaching, and his board shall be quarterly sent over for him to such as you shall nominate. And do pray you to give very earnest charge for his well teaching, as also to have him kept under for royeting [rioting, or carousing] abroad. And as hitherto he hath been of good honest disposition, so being young and lacking some to keep him in awe, he may stray now abroad. But let him know that you have given order that there shall be watch over his behavior and that I have written to you earnestly to advertise me how he shall behave himself. And give charge to his master to keep him under and from liberty, but to set him to work enough. And whilst you remain there, I pray you have an eye to him and, as near as you can, let none of our papists know that I have any such cook there, for I would not have him known to them. And let him come to hear preaching and service at the Amba[ssador's], but no way to charge him.

I do send you by Arden a letter to the party for a hundred crowns for you. Arden shall also deliver you money to send the gardener away to me with speed. Willing you to take care and Arden together, to have somebody come over with him to bring him to me with your letters.

I pray you let him bring with him all manner of seeds, the best you can procure there among the Italians, as well for herbs and salads as for all kind of rare flowers beside, seeds for melons, cauliflower, and such like, asparagus and all sorts of radish.

Forget not to solicit some of the prince of Conde's ministers for my 1000 [?pounds] I lent him.

Thus for this time I end and bid you farewell at court, this 23 of January.

Your loving master,
R Leicester

ANGELL DAY

The English Secretorie. Wherein is Contayned, A Perfect Method, for the Inditing of all Manner of Epistles (London, 1586)

❧ Among the guidebooks available in the Elizabethan period were some intended for servants, especially for the educated men who served as secretaries. They had to know a variety of fine "hands," or handwriting styles, but they also had to be prepared to compose letters as well as to transcribe them. Angell Day assembled a collection of epistles to serve as models for secretaries to copy or adapt. In one, he provides an example of how to commend an attendant into another man's service. He also enjoys himself with the second letter included here, a parody, written as if on behalf of an "unprofitable" servant. The Folger's copy of this volume (originally from the collection of Ham House) is one of only two known to survive, but the book was so popular that it went into eight subsequent editions.

An epistle commendatory from a noble man, in preferment of his servant

After my very hearty commendations unto you: this bearer having of long time continued in my service, and therein at all times honestly, faithfully, and carefully behaved himself, I have thought good hereby to recommend unto your patronage. And forasmuch as by reason of your office of Lord Governor of V. in her Majesty's realm of Ireland, I am informed there are many offices and places of great commodity remaining in your gift upon your followers to be bestowed, and that himself is also therewithal so greatly desirous in that kind of service to be employed, I do most heartily pray you that you will not only for my sake be contented to receive him into your service, but also in favor thereof and my great good liking towards him, you will in any place of preferment about you do him

A French Hand, from Martin Billingsley, *The Pens Excellencie* (London, 1618). This manual illustrates a number of different handwriting styles for use by a secretary. In Elizabethan England, this was an occupation generally pursued by men.

that benefit and furtherance, as to one whom you wish thoroughly well unto you would willingly have performed. Herein if my request may prevail, and that I may hereafter understand of your loving care and good endeavor towards him, I shall find myself both greatly occasioned to thank you and, in like manner, in whatsoever you shall have mean to use me, be most willing to requite you. And thus nothing doubting of your forwardness herein, I do for the present bid you heartily well to fare. At the Court this day of, et cetera.

A letter commendatory pleasantly conceited in preferring an unprofitable servant

Sir, I do send unto your view the bearer hereof (a man shaped as you see and as bold in condition as he appeareth in show) whom by all the superfluities of summer ale that hath wrought in his giddy brain, I have been requested to commend unto you. And inasmuch as in putting so unworthy a worthy in substance of so incredible allowance, it something behooveth I hide not the single gifts which by great search in many a good hostelry, tavern, and alehouse he hath by long travel and drowsy experience ere this time gained, to his insupportable credence. I shall not spare in some sort to signify unto you what in regard of all these I am led to conjecture. Truth is, sir, that he is very well studied in the mystery of malt-worms, and for his peculiar skill in discerning the nappy taste by the nut-brown color of cellar-ale in a frosty morning, he is become a sworn brother of the ragman's number, and thereby standeth enjoined never to wear furs of other lining in the coldest winter, but only the warmth of the good ale, which inwardly must hearten him. Besides, sir, if you have occasion to credit him with a small parcel of money in dispatch of a journey, do but say the word that it shall once lie in his charge, and you may stand assured that it shall be laid up so safe as any liquor in the world can safe conduct it from his belly. Take no care for your kitchen, buttery, or larder, for once a day he loves to see all clean before him. Little apparel will serve him, for his liveries ensue weekly out of the brewers' mash-fat. His lodging he recks not [cares not about]; the chimney floor and billet's ends [chopped wood] serve for a featherbed and coverings. When you have most need of him you shall always be sure to go without him: if you delight in a pig's-knee you may be receiving of him, become sure of a hogshead. Great store of small liking you happily may have to him; we know not what wonders the world may rend out, for nothing is impossible where all things may be compassed. It may please you for recreation's sake to look upon him: so you be not in case to surfeit, look what ill liking you conceive, report back again I pray you in the inner facing of his chimney casket, *Omnia sua secum portat* [he carries everything with him], he is somewhat a foolosopher, for he carries his possessions about him, for *terram dedit filiis hominum* [he gives the land to the children of mankind], he must needs then have a large dwelling. I pray, sir, give him good words how ill-favoredly soever you favor his acquaintance. For my part I request no remuneration for the preferment I have tendered towards him.

Thus much would I have done and more long since, to be rid of him. His old master being dead, it is necessary some place to be pestered with him; he makes great choice of your housekeeping, if you can like to frame with him. Much more might be delivered in the condemnation of his worthiness, but that I leave to rehearse it, but now, sir, for your own appetite, I leave to your contentment. Blame not me, but him that lead me, and so forth to an end. Commend me, but not condemn me, for I shall once do you a better turn. This is but the first, the next may be worse—better, I would say. And so fare ye well, et cetera (sigs. N4^{r-v}, N7^{v}–N8^{v}).

Pasquils Jestes, Mixed with Mother Bunches Merriments. . . . Very Prettie and Pleasant, to Drive Away the Tediousness of a Winters Evening (London, 1609)

Any hierarchical relationship had its tensions; the question is how these tensions found expression. There is evidence enough of the viewpoint of those in power, like Bess of Hardwick complaining about her "lewd" workman and Robert Dudley fretting about his kitchen boy's conduct. While it is easy to imagine how subordinates felt, it is more difficult to document their reactions. For all its merry tone, this collection of tales, first published in 1604, conveys considerable bitterness. Among other things, there is resentment of the narrowly contractual relationship J.M. objected to in *A Health to the Gentlemanly Profession of Servingmen.* The jestbook was a flourishing genre in the period, and these extracts show one reason why: vicarious revenge. The jestbook servants spoke and acted for all those who couldn't.

Of a worshipful gentleman in Lincolnshire, and his man

A certain gentleman in Lincolnshire, being also a Justice of Peace, had an old servant many years, called Adam Milford, who upon a time came unto his master and desired him, in regard he had been his servant so many years, he would now give him something to help him in his old age. Thou saist true (quoth his master), and I will tell thee what I will do: Now, shortly I am to ride up to London. If thou wilt pay my cost and charges by the way, I will give thee shortly such a thing as shall be worth to thee an hundred pound. I am content (quoth Adam), and so paid for all the reckoning by the way. So being come to London, he put his master in mind of his former promise that he had made to him. What, did I promise thee any thing? Aye (quoth Adam), that you did: for you said you would give me that that should be worth to me a hundred pound, for paying your charges to London. Let me see your writing [evidence] (quoth his Master). I have none (quoth Adam). Then thou art like to have nothing (quoth his Master). And learn this of me, that when thou makest a bargain with any man, look thou take a writing and beware how thou makest a writing to any man. This hath availed me an hundred pounds in my days. When Adam saw there was no remedy, he was content. But when they should depart, Adam stayed behind his master to reckon with his host; and on his master's scarlet cloak borrowed so much money as came to all their charges that he had laid out by the way. His master had not ridden past two miles, but it began to rain apace, wherefore he called for his cloak. His other men made answer that Adam was behind and had it with him. So they shrouded them under a tree till Adam came. When he came, his master said all angerly, thou knave, come give me my cloak: hast thou not served me well, to let me be thus wet? Truly sir (quoth Adam), I have laid it to pawn for all your charges by the way. Why knave (quoth he), didst thou not promise to bear my charges to London? Did I? (quoth Adam). Aye (quoth his master), that thou didst. Let's see, show me your writing of it (quoth Adam). Whereupon his Master perceiving he was overreached by his man, was fain to send for his cloak again, and pay the money.

Of a lawyer and his man

A worshipful gentleman, being a counselor, keeping a very good house, kept a gentleman's son to be his clerk and to wait upon his table. So one day, having store of guests, there wanted bread on the table. He beckoned to his man to fetch some. Who, not understanding him, came to him and said, Sir, what would you have? Seest not knave (quoth he) there is no bread on the table? Therefore fetch some. There was enough even now (quoth his man), if they would have let it alone, and not have eaten it up. Another time, his guests having supped, and ready to depart, he bade his man draw a cup of wine, to make them drink before they went. The fellow coming up with the gilt cup covered, his master beckoned him to take off the cover. He, not understanding, said, Master, what would you have? Why, knave, take off the cover (quoth he) of the cup. Then hold you the candle, said his man: for I cannot do two things at once (sigs. B3^{v}–B4^{r}, C4^{r}).

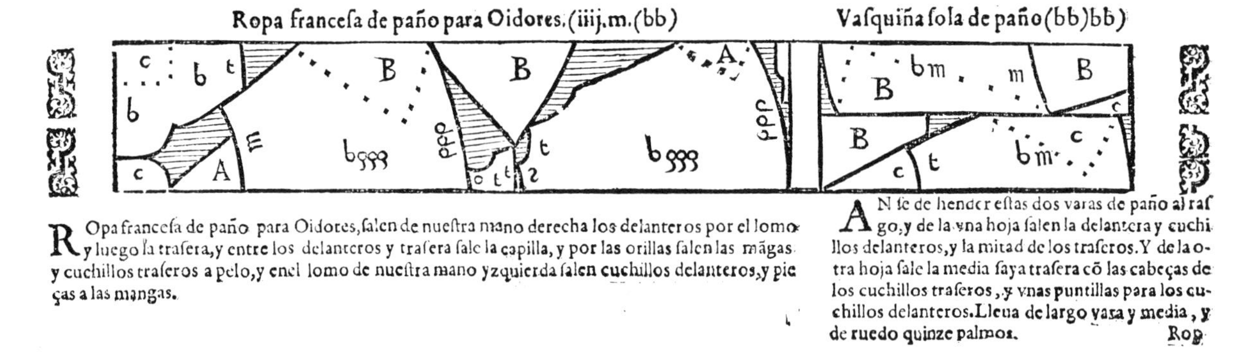

Ropa franceſa de paño para Oidores.(iiij.m.(bb)

Vaſquiña ſola de paño(bb)bb)

ROpa franceſa de paño para Oidores,ſalen de nueſtra mano derecha los delanteros por el lomo y luego la traſera,y entre los delanteros y traſera ſale la capilla, y por las orillas ſalen las mãgas y cuchillos traſeros a pelo,y enel lomo de nueſtra mano yzquierda ſalen cuchillos delanteros,y pieças a las mangas.

AN ſe de hender eſtas dos varas de paño al raſgo,y de la vna hoja ſalen la delantera y cuchillos delanteros,y la mitad de los traſeros.Y de la otra hoja ſale la media ſaya traſera cõ las cabeças de los cuchillos traſeros ,y vnas puntillas para los cuchillos delanteros.Lleua de largo vasa y media , y de ruedo quinze palmos.

Rop

Patterns for Clothing, in Diego de Freyle, *Geometria y Traça para el Oficio de los Sastres* (Seville, 1588). While some occupations were professionalized during the early modern period (like those of architects and surgeons), others became more accessible to non-specialists through printed guidebooks like this one. Tailoring, again, was a male occupation. Few households would have employed a tailor.

Maidservants ❧

SAMUEL ROWLANDS

"Like Mistress, Like Maid," from *The Night-Raven* (London, 1620)

❧ Put together the conceptual works on the place of servingmen and the practical guidebooks on their specific skills, and there is a fairly large literature for men in service. There was nothing comparable for women. In the late-medieval house, most chores had been done by servingmen, and there was still a conceptual bias against female servants in the Elizabethan years, even if practices had long since changed. Maidservants were, by definition, unattached; all women were, by common agreement, licentious. These women, in short, seemed to be a double threat to stable relationships in the household. This comic poem plays on standard fears about the sexuality of both housewives and their women.

Susan would meet with Richard and with Ned,
As soon as e'er her mistress was abed,
For a sack-posset they agree'd to eat,
And she besides would have a bit of meat,
And so be merry, that they would in sadness.
But even about the time of mirth and gladness,
When both the young men were bestow'd within,
One that had long her mistress' lover been,
Knocks at the door, whereat herself came down
(As loose of body as she was of gown)
And in the dark put Letcher in the room,
Where both the youths attend till Susan come.
Who in mean time to light a candle went,
So did her mistress for the same intent,
And meeting with her maid, "Oh strange," quoth she,
"What cause have you at this time here to be?"
"Mistress," quoth she, "unto you I'll be true,
There's two as honest youths as e'er I knew,
Came late to see me (pray you be content)."
"Wench, this may be," said she, "and no hurt meant,
For there's an honest man, to make them three,
That came in kindness for to visit me.
Good Susan, be as secret as you can,
Your master is [a] foolish jealous man,
Though thou and I do mean no hurt or ill,
Yet men take women in the worst sense still,
And fear of horns, more grief in hearts hath bred
Than wearing horns doth hurt a cuckold's head."

(sigs. C1^{r-v})

JOHN TAYLOR

"The Praise of Cleane Linnen, With the Commendable Use of the Laundres," in *All the Workes of John Taylor the Water-Poet* (London, 1630)

❧ John Taylor wrote a series of satirical pamphlets, including "The Praise of Clean Linen," first published in 1624. He derived his nickname, the "Water Poet," from a previous career as a Thames waterman. Taylor dedicated this mock-epic to Martha Legge, "the most mondifying, clarifying, purifying, and repurifying cleanser, clearer, and reformer of deformed and polluted linen." Laundry was the one household task that was always reserved for women. Following the dedicatory epistle, from which a sample follows, Taylor produced a poem in heroic couplets.

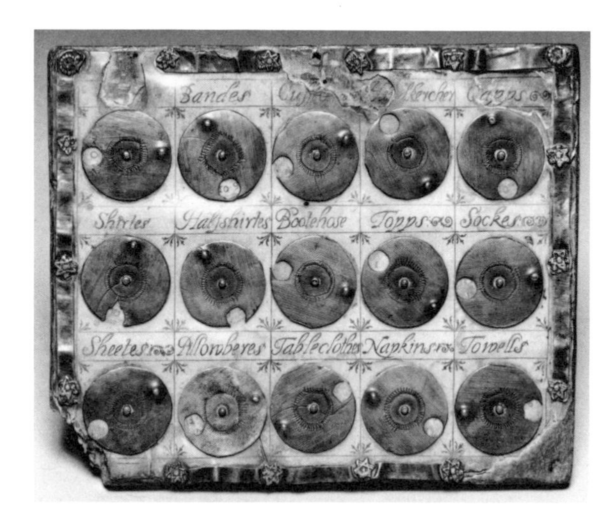

Laundry Counter (English, seventeenth century), wood covered with paper, with fifteen brass disks and brass border. By rotating each brass disk to reveal the desired number, housewives could keep track of how many sheets, pillowberes (pillowcases), and tablecloths they had sent out to laundry. Only great households had their own laundries on the premises, but even there it was important to keep track. These counters were evidently mass produced; an identical example has been found at Haddon Hall in Derbyshire. Agecroft Association.

I am struck into admiration at the undaunted valor that, champion-like, doth accompany and constantly defend your chastity. For you dare in a morning to enter a gentleman's chamber, to strip him out of his foul shirt in his bed, to have him at your bare and naked mercy, and then, like a virtuous victor, in pity and commiseration, you put a clean shirt on his back, leaving him in a clearer and far sweeter case then you found him. No doubt but such objects are provocatory temptations to frail flesh and blood, but, as I said before, your courage and constancy always brings you fairly off and on, though thousands weaker vessels of mortality would be crack'd in these unbloody bickerings. . . .

Now of the lovely laundress, whose clean trade
Is th'only cause that linen's cleanly made.
Her living is on two extremes relying:
She's ever wetting, or she's ever drying.
As all men die to live, and live to die,
So doth she dry to wash, and wash to dry.
She runs like Luna in her circled sphere;
As a perpetual motion she doth steer
Her course in compass round and endless still,
Much like a horse that labors in a mill.
To show more plain how she her work doth frame,
Our linen's foul e'er she doth wash the same.
From washing further in her course she marches:
She wrings, she folds, she pleats, she smoothes, she starches,
She stiffens, pokes [crimps], and sets, and dries again,
And folds. Thus end of pain begins her pain,
Round like a whirligig or Lenten top,
Or a most plenteous spring, that still doth drop.
The suds unto the sea I may compare,
The reek or smoke, the wind; the fishes, linen are.
The laundress fishes, foaming froth doth lighten,
The whilest her tongue doth thunder and affrighten.
The total is a tempest full of chiding,
That no man in the house hath quiet biding.
For Laundresses are testy and full of wroth
When they are lathering in their bumble broth.
Nor can I blame them, though they brawl and talk,
Men there have nought to do, they may go walk.
Yet commonly their work this profit brings:
The good-wife washeth, and her husband wrings.
But though my verse thus merrily doth stray,
Yet give the Laundress still her due I pray.
What were the painful spinner, or the weaver,
But for her labor, and her good endeavor?
What were the function of the linen drapery,
Or sempsters [seamstress's] admirable skill in napery?

(sigs. Pp1r, Pp3r)

A Laundress at Work, from Crispijn van de Passe, *Les Abus du Mariage* (N.p., 1641).

"A Booke of Account for all Manner of Layenges out Whatsoever (vizt') ffor Threshing, Hedging, Ditching, Gardening, for Buyeing of Cattell, all Manner of Necessaryes and Extreordinaryes for the Howse, and all other Layeings out Whatsoever, Belonging to my Master Sir William Pope Knight and Baronet Begineng This First Day of July 1628 and Being the Account of me Mary Petway"

❧ Female servants, like their male counterparts, represented a range of social and educational levels. This book of household accounts is fairly unusual, however, for having been kept by a woman. Mary Petway's headnote on assuming this responsibility is inscribed with pride. The entries offer a glimpse of how complicated a business it was to run and provision a great household. There are payments for goods and services, with two recipients verifying their particular transactions. In the right-hand column are the monies, given in pounds, shillings, and pence. There were twenty shillings to a pound and twelve pence to a shilling.

Cheeses	Imprimis paid by me the 2nd of July for 5. cheeses bought of Mistress Archer of Shathwell	00.05.00
Robert Binge	Item paid by me the 3rd of July to Robert Binge which he laid out for provision & other necessaries for the house from the 21st of March 1627 to the 28th of June last as by his book appears in particular	03.14.09
	per me Robert Binge	
Good: Price	Item paid the same day to Goodman Price of Swarford for his son's half year's wages due at our Lady day last	00.13.04
Goodman Baget	Item paid the same day to Goodman Baget of Swacklife for his son's half year's wages due at Michaelmas last	00.10.00
	Item paid the same day to John Sammon the groom for his half year's wages due at our Lady day last	01.10.00
	John Saman	
paid the Cooper	Item paid the 5th day of July to Thomas Walker the Cooper of Banbury for hooping & mending of all manner of hogsheads & other vessels as well pales as tubs from the 1st of May 1627 to this 5th of July 1628	01.04.00
brass nails	Item paid the same day for brass nails for the coach	00.00.04
	Item d[elivere]d to my master to give to Mistress Wickam's maid that brought 2. cheeses & 4 angelets [gold coins]	00.01.00
	Item d[elivere]d more to my master the same day to give to Goody Burden's maid that brought a couple of capons to my master	00.00.06
master Paumer	Item paid the same day to Sir Thomas Pope which he lent to my master to give to Master Paumer when he came to master Thomas Pope when he was sick of the smallpox	00.10.00
for a sieve	Item paid the same day to the sievyer [sieve-maker] of Banbury for a sieve to carry 4. cheeses in, which my master sent to the Earl of Montgomery	00.00.10
a Marlin	Item the 7th of July d[elivere]d to Thornebury by my mistress' appointment to pay to master Andrews for a marlin [small line or rope of untwisted hemp] which he bought for my master	01.10.00

193

A Booke of account for

all manner of layengs out whatsoever (viz) ffor threshing, hedging, ditching, gardening, for buying of Cattell, all manner of necessaryes and extraordinaryes for the howse, and all other layings out whatsoever, be-longing to my m[r] S[r] William Pope Knight and Baronet begining this first day of July 1628 and being the account of me Mary Petway.

Margin	Entry	li	s	d
Cheese	Imprimis paid by me the 2. of July for 5 Cheeses bought of m[ris] Arther of Shalswell	00	05	00
Robert Binge	Item paid by me the 3. of July to Robert Binge which he laied out for provision & other necessaryes for the howse from the 21th of March 1627 to the 28th of June last as by his booke appeareth in par-ticuler	03	14	09
	p me Robert Binge			
Good: Price	Item paid the same day to Goodman Price of Swarford for his sonnes half yeres wages due at o[r] Lady day last	00	13	04
Goodman Baget	Item paid the same day to Goodman Baget of Swarclift for his sonnes half yeres wages due at Michaell last	00	10	00
	Item paid the same day to John Cammon the groome for his half yeres wages due at o[r] Lady day last	01	10	00
	John Camon			
paid the Cooper	Item paid the 5th day of July to Thomas Walker the Cooper of Barbury for hooping & mending of all manner of hogsheads & other vessells aswell pales as tubbs from the [illegible] of May 1627 to this 5th of July 1628	01	04	00
Brasse nayles	Item paid the same day for brasse nailes for the Coach	00	00	04
	Item dd to my m[r] to give to m[ris] Wirkams maid that brought 2 Cheeses & 4 angelletts	00	01	00
	Item dd more to my m[r] the same day to give to Goody Budders maide that brought a couple of Capons to my m[r]	00	00	06
m[r]	Item paid the same day to S[r] Thomas Pope which he lent to my m[r] to give to m[r] [illegible]	[illegible]	[illegible]	[illegible]

Household Accounts, titled "A Booke of Account for all Manner of Layenges out Whatsoever . . . Being the Account of me Mary Petway" (1628).

for flocks	Item paid the same day to Ball the fuller for 4. tod [twenty-eight pounds] of flocks [tufts of wool] at 20 s. [shillings] the tod	02.00.00
glasses	Item paid the 8th of July for 2. drinking glasses for my master	00.01.00
	Item paid the same day for water glasses & preserving glasses	00.02.03
provision money	Item paid the same day by Anthony Lichfield to Thomas Tayler constable of Roxston for provision money for Roxston grounds	01.04.00
	Item paid more by him the same day to Richard Callcot Constable of Hookenorton for provision money for Hookenorton grounds	03.04.01
	Item paid by him the same day to Ralph Marshall of Tew for provision money for Shewell grounds	02.04.06
trenching	Item paid by him the same day to Bartholemewe Robins of Wiggenton for trenching at Showell of 144. perch [a measure of land, about 16½ feet] at i d. [denarius, or penny] the perch	00.12.00
a quarter of beef	Item paid more by him the same day for a quarter of beef to Thomas Gyles a butcher of Tiso	00.17.03
Harvey the sadler	Item paid by him the same time to Richard Harvey of Banbury for a surcingle [girth for a horse], a pair of false reins for the light horses & for mending a wanty [rope or band used to fasten the pack on a pack saddle] as by his bill appears	00.02.07

The sum is 20.17.05
(fol. 193)

PIERRE ERONDELLE

The French Garden: for English Ladyes and Gentlewomen to Walke In (London, 1605)

Pierre Erondelle, a Huguenot refugee in London, taught French and published this series of dialogues with English and French on facing pages. The dialogues are densely packed with a varied vocabulary, as suits their pedagogic purpose, but they nonetheless give us an intimate, behind-the-scenes look at life in a great house. The rapid-fire delivery of nouns and adjectives intensifies our impression that the mistress is impatient and demanding. Joly, as a waiting gentlewoman, has a fairly exalted position in the household hierarchy, but she still suffers from her lady's sharp tongue. Meanwhile, Prudence, the chambermaid, has to negotiate among all the characters: the Lady, her difficult mistress; Joly, her social superior; and the Page, whom she must supervise even though she has little authority to do so. The irony is that this book was dedicated to a lady, Elizabeth Berkeley. What did she think of this window on the life of maidservants?

LADY. Ho! Who is in the inner chamber? How now, maidens, hear you not? Are you deaf?

PRUDENCE. I am here, Madam.

LADY. Why do you suffer me to sleep so long? I am ashamed of myself, truly.

PRUDENCE. I came hither soft and fair, once or twice, to see if you were awaked, and, seeing you asleep, I durst not awake you. But it is not so late as you think.

LADY. What is it o'clock?

PRUDENCE. It is but half an hour past seven.

LADY. What, is it so far day? Oh, God! I went to bed yesternight so timely, thinking to rise this morning at the farthest at 6 o'clock: now I verify in me the grave speeches of that great philosopher the Emperor Marc[us] Aur[elius], speaking of the unsatiableness of mankind, when he said (among other things): "The more I sleep, the more I would sleep." Go to, go to, draw the window curtains. Call my page: let him bring some wood to my chamber door. Make a fire quickly, that I may rise.

PRUDENCE. Page, where are you? What, are you not ready? I think you must have a chamberlain.

THE PAGE. How now? What have you seen this morning? Hath your lover broken promise with you? How sharp you are! How well you play the mistress! My Lady could not chide better. What aileth you?

PRUDENCE. I cry you mercy, sir, have I offended you? One may not speak to you but with reverence; you have forgotten your last beating. You have great need that my Lady remember you, it is so long since she made you be whipped. Will it please you to fetch some wood? Bring some faggots [sticks bundled together] and billets [thick pieces of wood cut short for fuel]. Forget not a bavin [bundle of brushwood], and see that it be dry, for the faggots are too green. Lay them at the chamber door, and come not in the chamber until my Lady be up or that you be called. Hasten you.

LADY. O God! How long you make me tarry! Kindle the fire quickly, warm my smock, and give it me. Where is Joly? Call her. . . .

JOLY. I hear my Lady call.

LADY. Will you keep me here all the day? Where be all my things? Go fetch my clothes: bring my petticoat bodice. I mean my damask quilt bodice with whale bones. What lace do you give me here? This lace is too short, the tags are broken. I cannot lace myself with it; take it away. I will have that of green silk. When shall I have my undercoat? Give me my petticoat of wrought crimson velvet with silver fringe. Why do you not give me my nightgown? For I take cold. Where be my stockings? Give me some clean socks; I will have no worsted hose. Show me my carnation silk stockings. Where laid you last night my garters? Take away these slippers; give me my velvet pantoufles. Send for the shoemaker that he may have again these turnover shoes, for they be too high. Put on my white pumps. Set them up. I will none of them. Give me rather my Spanish leather shoes, for I will walk today. This shoeing horn hurteth me. Can you not put them on with the fur? Tie the strings with a strong double knot, for fear they untie themselves. Joly, come dress my head. Set the table further from the fire; it is too near. Put my chair in his [its] place. Why do you not set my great looking glass on the table? It is too high; set the supporter lower. Undo my night attire. Why do you not call the Page to warm the rubbers [hard brushes used for cleaning]? Let him be called: here, sirra, warm that, and take heed you burn it not. I pray you, Joly, rub well my head, for it is very full of dandruff. Are not my combs in the case? Where is my ivory comb? Comb me with the boxen comb. Give me first my combing cloth; otherwise you will fill me full of hairs; the hairs will fall upon my clothes. Comb backward. O God! You comb too hard. You scratch me. You pull out my hairs. Can you not untangle them softly with your hands before you put the comb to it? (sigs. D6v–E1v).

H. I.

An Example for All Those that Make No Conscience of Swearing and Forswearing: Shewing Gods Heavy Judgement upon a Maid-servant in London, Who Forswore Her Selfe, and Now Lies Rotting in S. Bartholomewes Hospitall in Smithfield, Where Many Resort Daily to See Her (London, c. 1625)

❦ This is the only known surviving copy of this broadside ballad, meant to be sung to a tune called "Aim not too high." Such documents are rare because they were meant to be tacked up on a wall or a post. Damage to this one shows that it was indeed displayed in such a manner at some point in its history. Roughly printed, with woodcut illustrations only some of which apply to the text, it was an ephemeral piece. The story of the larcenous maidservant, who lied about her thefts, dared God, and lost, offers a three-fold warning to its readers.

But now a story to you I will show,
Of a poor wretch that is distressed in woe.
That did the like, and did her self forswear,
Which sore example let each Christian hear.

She being in an honest service plac't,
Hath wrought her shame, and all her friends disgrac't.
Did steal and pilfer many things away,
Which now hath wrought her to this deep decay.

When things were missed, she did deny the same,
And with great impudence, devoid of shame,
Wished before God and men that she might rot,
If that such things she ever saw or got.

Yet she to prison straight way was convey'd,
And presently before she long had laid:
She did begin to rot, and stink so sore,
That they were forced to turn her out of door.

To Smithfield Hospital she then was led,
Where hundreds flock to [see her] in her bed,
Her toes and fingers do fall [off an]d rot,
With other joints; such is her heavy lot.

The surgeons strive to do their chiefest art,
And do apply their skill to every part,
But still she rots, her joints do fall away,
And God knows when shall be her dying day.

She is repentant for her wicked sin
Which in her former time she lived in,
She calls to God for mercy every day,
And to the Lord most earnestly do pray.

She doth confess that she that fact did do,
For which she now doth feel such grief and woe:
Wishing each servant might example take,
That she may be a warning for their sake. . . .

Look down, O Lord, on his distressed one,
That doth not look to thee but with a groan.
And for her wished affliction, if you please,
Comfort her soul and give her body ease.

Or if the Justice farther will proceed
To punish her for her perjurious deed,
Lord, grant her sins may thoroughly be forgiven,
Give her affliction here, her [he]aven.

Let servants that are often put in trust
Fly dealing false, and follow dealing just.
Although your ill-got goods may seem full fair,
Your seeming substance proves infectious air.

An example for all those that make no conscience of swearing and forswearing.
Shewing Gods heauy Iudgement vpon a Maid-seruant in London, who forswore her selfe, and now lies rotting in S. *Bartholomewes* Hospitall in *Smithfield*, where many resort daily to see her. *To the tune of, Aime not too high.*

Let wicked swearers all example take,
How they of God a mocking stocke do make,
Although he sits in heauen and nothing sayes,
Yet he doth see and marke our wicked wayes.

He searches in the closet of our hearts,
Where he surnayes our good and euill parts:
The soule he made to be the bodies guide,
That it should rule vs when we went aside.

But when we let the Diuill enter in,
Who still doth tempt vs vnto wicked sin,
Then grace is fled, and God on vs doth frowne,
Who with a glory vs in heauen would crowne.

Our soule must answer for our bodies deed,
As in the sacred Scriptures you may read,
And euery sinner must receiue their hyre,
Without Gods mercy in eternall fire,

The Lord hath said, that he reuenge will take,
Upon such sinners as do him forsake:
And tis most sure, for God he will not lie,
But vengeance take for our iniquity.

As late in London and in other parts,
Swearers and lyers they haue felt his smarts,
One that commited had an euill crime,
[illegible] forsweare it at the very time,

And [illegible] that she might sinke into the ground,
Or that bright heauen might her soule [illegible],
If she had done it, and did seeme to cry,
And then the ground did open presently.

Two others that the like had done in sight,
Wisht that Gods Iudgement might vpon thē light,
And so it did, for straight they fell starke dead,
The Lord aboue knowes where their souls are fled

But now a Story to you I will shew,
Of a poore wretch that is distrest in woe,
That did the like, and did her selfe forsweare,
Which sore example let each Christian heare.

She being in an honest seruice plac't,
Hath wrought her shame, & all her friends disgrac't,
Did steale and pilfer many things away,
Which now hath wrought her to this deepe decay,

When things were mist, she did deny the same,
And with great impudence, deuoyd of shame,
Wisht before God and men that she might rot,
If that such things she euer saw or got.

Yet she to prison straight way was conuey'd,
And presently before she long had laid:
She did begin to rot, and stinke so sore,
That they were forst to turne her out of dore.

To Smithfield Hospitall she then was led.
Where hundreds flocke to [illegible] in her bed,
Her toes and fingers do fal[illegible] rot,
With other ioynts, such is her heauy lot.

The Surgeons striue to do their chiefest Art,
And do apply their skill to euery part,
But still she rots, her ioynts do fall away,
And God knowes when, shall be her dying day.

She is repentant for her wicked sinne,
Which in her former time she liued in,
She cals to God for mercy euery day,
And to the Lord most earnestly do pray.

She doth confesse that she that fact did do,
For which she now doth feele such griefe and woe:
Wishing each seruant might example take,
That she may be a warning for their sake.

And all forsworen wretches in that kind.
When they do, til to beare her in their mind,
For feare the Lord doth giue to them their hyre,
As she did iustly of our great God require.

Gods mercie's great when sinners do repent,
When in their soule they truly do relent,
Christ dy'd to saue those that the truth beleeue,
And in his mercy will them sure relieue.

As I do hope that he will saue her soule,
Although her crime was very bad and foule,
For she repentant is, and craues for grace,
And hopes in heauen to haue a resting place.

Could we but thinke of Gods all-seeing eyes,
That nere were blind to our iniquities:
Our earthly minds of heauen will haue a part,
Our tongs would speake from truenesse of our heart

Though we may thinke to blind the eyes of men,
Committing sins, forswering them agen:
Yet them at last our conscience shall report,
Before a wiser [illegible] higher Court.

Let no forswearer [illegible] themsel[illegible]re,
Though with the[illegible] to[illegible]
Oh let them not presume, but let [illegible] know,
Gods hand is heauy, though [illegible] slow.

Oh may this needlesse swearing be forborne,
Oathes are the plagues for which a land doth mourn
Oh let vs mourne for oathes, and mourne our fill,
Oh may we [illegible] now, not sweare we will.

Wish not for euill falsly on thy brest,
Thinking that God will spare with thee the rest,
God pardons sins that no man might despaire,
God scourges some, that all men may beware.

Who knoweth whether himselfe the person be,
That God will punish for iniquity:
Oh with what face can men for mercy craue,
That wish themselues ill, and their wishes haue.

Gehezi did of Naaman once require,
Gold, and two shifts of raiment for a hyre:
They that will seeke for profit by a lye,
Shall lose their gaines, and gaine a leprosie.

Yet is the Lord to those that do conuert,
More kind then our desire, or our desert:
And in the midst of our iniquities,
His Iudgement doth but go, his mercie flyes.

Looke downe, O Lord, on his distressed one,
That doth not looke to thee but with a groane:
And for her wisht affliction, if you please,
Comfort her soule and giue her body ease.

Or if the Iustice farther will proceed,
To punish her for her periurious deed:
Lord grant her sins, may [illegible] be forgiuen,
[illegible] her affliction here, [illegible]auen.

Let seruants that are often [illegible]st,
Fly dealing false, and follow dealing iust:
Although your ill got goods, may seeme full faire,
Your seeming substance proues infectious ayre.

Lo[illegible]ted at for *I.W.* *FINIS.* *H.I.*

Broadside, *An Example for All Those that Make No Conscience of Swearing and Forswearing,* signed by H. I. (London, c. 1625). The woodcuts are apparently ones that the printer had readily to hand, as they have little bearing on the narrative. This was ephemeral work, in any case, meant to be tacked up on walls and quickly replaced by more recent sensations.

RICHARD COOKE

A White Sheete, Or A Warning for Whoremongers. A Sermon Preached in the Parish Church of St. Swithins by London-stone, the 19. of July, Anno Domi: 1629. The Day Appointed by Honorable Authoritie, for Penance to be Done, by an Inhabitant There, for Fornication, Continued More Then Two Yeares, with His Maide-servant (London, 1629)

☙ Needless to say, there are no statistics on sexual harrassment in the Renaissance, inasmuch as there wasn't even a concept of sexual harrassment then. It's intriguing, thus, to find this sermon, preached as a man was forced to do public penance for fornicating with a maidservant. Surprisingly enough, she doesn't come in for any of the recriminations. Nor is the main issue the murder of their bastard by the fairly familiar means of dropping the child down a privy shaft. Of course, the strictness of focus on the householder and on his crime of adultery may be due only to the facts that he is present in the parish church, that she has died, and that he apparently can't be proven to be complicit in the infanticide. Richard Cooke speaks directly to the "whoremonger."

How long you have loved and lived in this sin, your own conscience can tell you best. By your own confession, since October, 1626, near three years. And that which is worst, to keep an whore under your wife's nose—too long, and too much, if you bethink you well, [even] if it had been less and never so little. . . .

What satisfaction can you ever make to that servant of yours, who by your base and beastly fornication with her, came to a shameful and untimely death? Blessed had you both been, if you had never seen each other's faces, for had she never known your face, nor you her body, you might perhaps (I say, verily, perhaps) have proved a better husband than before, and she lived in time to have been a wife for as good a man as yourself. She lost her life and, living and dying, helped to save yours. I dispute not by what means she was wrought and brought to it: the law was satisfied, and I am contented.

What satisfaction can you make to God or the world, for the blood of that sweet newborn babe, murdered and made away by her by putting it alive, by some secret conveyance, into the house of office (an office fit for a whore and no mother). I do not say nor charge you to be privy to the putting of it into the privy. I shall leave that to God and your own conscience, who (if you were) will not go behind your back, when time shall serve to tell you of it. I judge you not; you were acquitted from the law of man. God grant you may come off as fair with God, that he may never lay this sin unto your charge.

Last of all, what satisfaction can you make, to this place and parish where you lived of late—and a little too long? What dishonor have you done us, in bringing this disgrace, and casting this aspersion on us? What favors have you had successively amongst us? How often have you been invited to our public feastings? How usually called to our counsels and meetings? How preferred to several places of offices with us? And after all this, to reward us thus, to cast this filth in our faces, to leave this stink behind you is base ingratitude. It must needs be a bad bird that thus defiles her own nest; we can count you no better, to have used us so badly. We shall be willing to pray for your well doing elsewhere, but not for your dwelling here, till you be a little sweeter. . . .

Let it now, I beseech you, be your care to return speedily unto God. Let this day's punishment beat you home to God, and like a sovereign medicine work kindly with you, to purge your soul of your sins, for the health and recovery of your soul, and when you go about this business, beware how you slight and slubber it over: it must be no easy or ordinary repentance that will serve the turn: your offence hath been great, your humiliation must not be less: *Magna peccata magna egent misericordia* [great faults need great mercy]. If you make not the plaster as large as the sore, it will do you little good (sigs. E4^{v}, F1^{v}–[F3^{r}]).

Children ❧

JOHN DOD

A Plaine and Familiar Exposition of the Ten Commandements, with a Methodicall Short Cathechisme, Containing Briefly All the Principall Grounds of Christian Religion (London, 1604)

❧ Here, the text "Honor thy father and thy mother" is held to apply not just to children's duties to their parents but also to parents' duties to their children. In this context, parents' duties include neither physical nor emotional nurture. Instead, says Dod, the first duty of parents is to instruct their children in religion; the second, detailed below, is to give them correction, including corporal punishment. Then he adds a duty that applies to mothers only: to breast-feed their babies rather than send them out to wet-nurse, as was customary among those of the upper social levels. Through his rebuttal of the imagined objections of mothers, Dod, like William Gouge above, gives us access to voices and interests otherwise obscured from us.

First, let it [correction] be seasonable, and done in time: pass it not over too long. . . . For, indeed, a small twig and a few blows, when he is yet a child, and not hardened in sin, will do more good than many rods and abundance of stripes afterwards, if this season be let slip. For if the child be not mastered when he is young, he will master his parents when he groweth elder. . . .

Secondly, it must be done in great compassion and mercy, not in bitterness to ease oneself with the pain of the child. . . . For if the child be curst and froward, is it not because he hath seen the parents brawling and contentious? If he lie, hath not his father given him a pattern of dissembling? And if he swear being young, are not oaths too rife in the family among elder folks? If he rail and speak evil, was not his parents' dealing a precedent to him? . . .

Thirdly, it must be done with prayer, that God would give them wise hearts to give most due and seasonable correction; and their children also soft hearts, to receive it with patience and to their profit. Be it that the child do well deserve it, yet to fly upon him in a passion bewrayeth more than a beast-like affection, for a sheep will not rush upon her lamb in fury, nor the cow upon her calf. And indeed this doth but harden the child's heart and embitter him, making him more stubborn and fierce. . . .

Thus much of the common duties which both the parents should jointly perform to their children in their tender years. Now followeth the special duty of the mother, which is, to nurse up her own child, if God have given her ability thereunto. . . . If the husband should use the like dealing to his wife, to thrust her out of his doors when she is weak, and place her in some poor cottage, and tell her that he could board her better cheap in another man's house, than keep her in his own: she would think this to be a bad reason against her, which she thought sufficient against her own child. And she might justly say, in this case, that her husband loved his wealth better than his wife, and so may it as truly be said of such mothers, that they respect their lucre more than their children. They allege further that, being nursed by them, it would hinder their sleep in the night. Why then should you put it to others, to break their sleep? Ought you not to love your neighbor as your self? Are you so impatient, to bear the troubles of it, that ought so tenderly to love it? And do you think that they will not grudge at it, that have no such cause to affect it? And do only entertain it, in hope of the hire, and not for love of the child? But they say further that it hindreth them from their liberty and keepeth them from many journeys, which might much delight them. . . .

Those women, therefore, that have failed in this duty, must be humbled for it, as having omitted a good work and service that God requireth at their hands. And those that have done it, must do it still (sigs. $\mathrm{S2^r}$–$\mathrm{S3^v}$).

Hornbook (London?, c. 1625). This is how English children learned their letters. The text gives the A. B. C. and the Lord's Prayer. It is covered with a protective sheet of transparent horn (accounting for the name). On the back of the wooden paddle is stamped an illustration of the patron saint of England, St. George, fighting the dragon.

JOHN LYSTER

A Rule How to Bring Up Children (London, 1588)

❧ This volume purports to model a catechism, with the father questioning his son and the son returning proper responses. In the course of this highly artificial exchange, the volume baldly lists those Biblical references to children that were most often cited in the sermons and admonitory treatises of the period. Once again, the prevailing theme is duty.

FATHER. The duty of parents would I learn, for many bring up their children wantonly. Tell me, therefore, plainly and truly: although thou be but a child in years, yet, I praise God, thou art almost a man in wisdom and knowledge.

SON. The Lord said, I know that Abraham will command his children and his household after him, that they keep the way of the Lord, and do after right and conscience. *Genesis 13*

If thy daughter be not shamefast, hold her in straitly, lest she abuse her self through too much liberty. *Ecclesiastes 26*

If thou have sons, bring them up in nurture and learning, and hold them in awe from their youth up. If you have a daughter, keep her body and show not thy face cheerful towards her. Marry thy daughter; give her to a man of understanding. *Ecclesiastes 7*

If thy daughter be wanton, keep her in straitly, lest she cause thine enemies to laugh thee to scorn. *Ecclesiastes 42*

You shall, saith God, teach all my laws and ordinances unto your children. *Deuteronomy 4*

Ye fathers, move not your children unto anger and wrath, but bring them up in the doctrine and information of the Lord. *Ephesians 6*

Ye fathers, provoke not your children to anger, lest they be of a desperate mind. *Colossians 3*

He that spareth the rod hateth his son, but who so loveth him chasteneth him betimes. *Proverbs 13*

Who so loveth his child holdeth him still under correction, that he may have joy of him afterward, and that he grope not after his neighbors' dors [mockery]. He that teacheth his son shall have joy of him and need not to be ashamed of him among his acquaintance. *Ecclesiastes 30*

Give him no liberty in his youth, and excuse not his folly. Teach thy child and be diligent therein, lest it be to thy shame. *Ecclesiastes 30*

FATHER. What saith the scripture of children to their parents?

SON. Thus saith St. Paul: children, obey your fathers and mothers in the Lord, for that is right. Honor thy father and mother that thou mayest prosper and live long on the earth. *Ephesians 6*

Ye children, obey your fathers and mothers in all things, for that is well pleasing unto the Lord. *Colossians 3*

Ye shall (saith the Lord of hosts) fear, every man, his father and mother, and keep my sabbaths. *Leviticus 19*

Give ear to the father that begat thee, and despise not thy mother when she is old. *Proverbs 23*

He that robbeth his father and his mother, and say it is no sin, he is a destroyer. *Proverbs 28*

Hold thy mother, saith Toby, as in honor all the days of the life, for thou oughtest to remember how great perils she suffered for thee in her womb. *Tobias 4*

All that the parents command them, that they ought to do diligently. Honor thy father in word and deed, in patience, that thou mayest have God's blessing, and his blessing shall abide with thee at the last. *Tobias 5*

He that defieth his father shall come to shame, and he that forsaketh his mother is cursed of God. *Ecclesiastes 3*

The blessing of the Father buildeth up the houses of the children, but the mother's curse rooteth out the foundations. *Ecclesiastes 3*

He that forsaketh his Father shall come to shame, and he that defieth his mother is accursed of God (sigs. E1ᵛ–E3ʳ).

The Office of Christian Parents: Shewing How Children Are to Be Governed Throughout All Ages and Times of Their Life (Cambridge, 1616)

❧ The fifth commandment ("honor thy father and mother") was taken to authorize political hierarchy in two analogous institutions, the household and the commonwealth. It mandated not only children's obedience to their parents but also citizens' obedience to the monarch. In both spheres questions persisted as to just how extensive was the reach of the commandment. At issue in the domestic sphere, in particular, was this: was the authority of the father so complete that he had the right to kill his own child? In abstract terms, his power was unlimited, but, in this matter, abstract political philosophy reached *its* limits. *The Office of Christian Parents* is representative of English thought in arguing against the "Roman" right of child-murder.

The first case is in regard of corruption, namely that sometime the parents, as they think, have used all means to instruct their son or daughter; they have watched over them, admonished, corrected, and exhorted them, and applied all their wisdom and diligence to keep them in good order, but it will not be: the child is malicious, willful, hardhearted, and so overcome of his natural corruption, that like a wild horse which no bridle can hold, he runneth headlong. No fear, shame, punishment, nor any thing will prevail to pull him back. . . .

And here cometh in a question: the extent of the parent his authority, whether they may (as we read of many heathen men and women) in any case put their children to death. The holy scripture commits this judgment to the magistrate, showing that in such as deserveth death, the parents ought to complain to the magistrate, and bring forth their child to be censured by him. . . . Here you see in what cases the Christian parents may seek the death of their child: namely, if he be riotous and a drunkard and stubbornly and disobediently refuse to hear the admonition of the parents. There are also two other cases wherein the child ought to die: that is, if the child smite or if the child curse father or mother. And the third is of more weight: if either son or daughter entice to idolatry, they must have no pity, they must be stoned with stones. Wherein is bewrayed the great folly and wickedness of many of our parents, who will wink at their children when they be riotous and drunkards. They will put up anything at their children's hands, and feed them and defend them with money, whereby they are strengthened in their lewd and wicked courses. Sometime it happeneth that their son hath committed murder or a rape, which by no means ought to be pardoned; yet will they labor most importunately to save their child from the gallows. And their money (which usually is strongly kept in from many good uses) is let fly to bolster out sin. But little or no pains or cost is bestowed for the child's escaping of the wrath of God and damnation. Let such parents know, that the sins of the children redound to the parents' punishment. . . .

Here is required much wisdom to guide the sick child, to look unto God, and to be patient and ruled in sickness, for foolish pity causeth parents to hurt their child. For some parents in their children's sickness are so exceeding tender and affectionate, that they can in that time use no authority over them, neither by discretion moderate their foolishness, but let them do and have what they list. This is sometime a cause of the child's death or of the continuance of the sickness, and oftentimes thereby the child proveth wayward and unfit to be governed a great while after (sigs. Q4r–R2r).

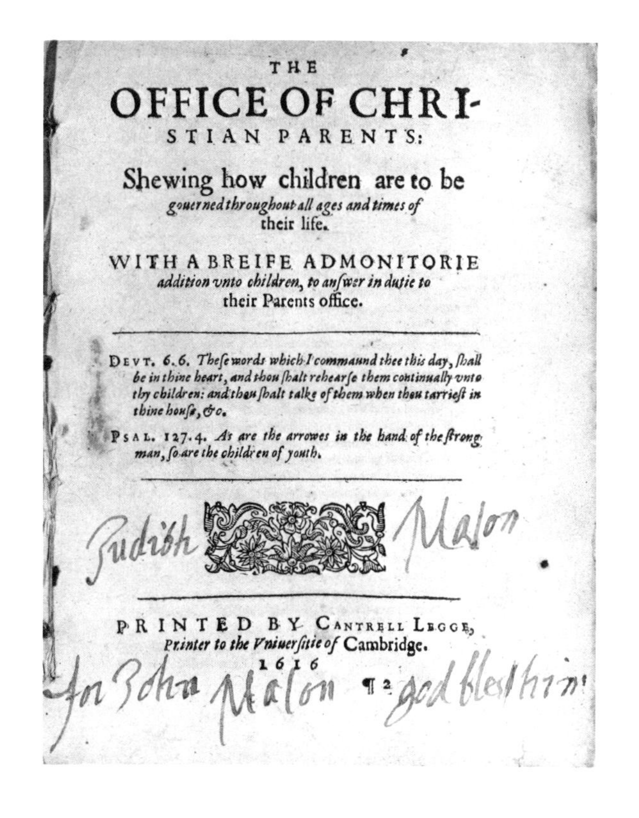

THE
OFFICE OF CHRI-
STIAN PARENTS:
Shewing how children are to be
gouerned throughout all ages and times of
their life.
WITH A BREIFE ADMONITORIE
addition vnto children, to anſwer in dutie to
their Parents office.

DEVT. 6.6. Theſe words which I commaund thee this day, ſhall be in thine heart, and thou ſhalt rehearſe them continually vnto thy children: and thou ſhalt talke of them when thou tarrieſt in thine houſe, &c.

PSAL. 127.4. As are the arrowes in the hand of the ſtrong man, ſo are the children of youth.

Judith Malon

PRINTED BY CANTRELL LEGGE,
Printer to the Vniuerſitie of Cambridge.
1616

for John Malon ¶ 2 god bless him

Title Page to *The Office of Christian Parents: Shewing How Children Are to Be Governed* (Cambridge, 1616). The Folger copy is inscribed as a gift. Judith Malon writes: "for John Malon god bless him."

HENRY GOODCOLE

Natures Cruell Step-Dames: Or, Matchlesse Monsters of the Female Sex; Elizabeth Barnes, and Anne Willis. Who were Executed the 26. Day of April, 1637. at Tyburne, for the Unnaturall Murthering of Their Owne Children . . . Further, a Relation of the Wicked Life and Impenitent Death of John Flood, who Raped His Own Childe (London, 1637)

❧ As we have seen, infanticide was not condoned in the sixteenth century, but it may not be too strong to say that it was tolerated. As the century turned, though, the law moved toward a more aggressive protection of children, until, in 1624, the concealment of the death of a newborn bastard could be produced as *prima facie* evidence of murder. This is the crime, still not all that uncommon, for which Anne Willis was prosecuted. Far more surprising are the two other crimes reported by Henry Goodcole, who ministered to condemned prisoners at Newgate and wrote a number of pamphlets on the stories he heard there. The premeditated murder of eight-year-old Susan Barnes by her mother was unnatural in the full Renaissance sense of the term: against the nature imprinted on man by God and against the nature of women to be merciful. While infanticide had a fairly high profile in the popular imagination, child sex abuse did not, making the story of the unrepentant John Flood all the more interesting.

A narration of the diabolical seduction of Elizabeth Barnes, late of Battersey in the county of Surrey, widow, mercilessly to murder Susan Barnes her own natural child

To entice the child unto its slaughter, and to go abroad with her, she provided the 24th day of March last, 1637, very early in the morning, an apple pie, a herring pie, raisins of the sun, and other fruits which she carried with her—accustomed baits used by loving parents to quiet and still their children in their unquietness, but this creature otherwise, to destroy her child by that means. . . . Thus having eaten of such things formerly provided for it, being tired with going so far a journey, it being but of the age of eight years, afterwards sweetly falleth into a fast sleep, which was very opportune for her mother's accursed design. For that same night about the hours of eleven and twelve she drew out of her sheath a knife, and with that knife barbarously did cut the throat of the child. Soon after this bloody fact being done by her, her eyes were opened, that she beheld her miserable condition, and that, that by her bloody hands had been done, that could no way be again undone. . . . She carried with her the instrument of her own death, as she did the child's, for it a knife, so a halter, wherewith to end her own life, and [she] attempted it, but had not power to lay violent hands on her self, being mercifully thereof prevented by the all-powerful hand of heaven. . . .

If this woman's house had been set on fire, doubtless she would have made such an outcry in the streets that all her neighbors must of necessity rise, and add unto her all help possible to quench the fire. Her heart was here set on fire by hell. Musing to perpetrate mischief, her tongue is silent, and mouth is shut, when it should have been wide open to cry aloud unto God for grace and mercy, and to crave the help of the effectual prayers of God's holy ministers, and congregations of his saints here on earth, to deliver her out of the snare and bondage of Satan, whom she voluntarily obeyed.

A relation [report] of John Flood, late of Saint-Giles-in-the-Field, for the committing of a rape on the body of his own natural child, being under the age of ten years

This man was most notorious, and generally reported to be of a most dissolute conversation. The fact which was laid unto his charge, fully proved by the testimony of divers grave and sober matrons, which searched the body of the child, and said she had been abused by a man without all question. The honorable judges before whom this heinous fact was tried, inquired to find out the actor of so horrid a deed. The child on whom it was done produced nor accused any other person but Flood her own father, and related very confidently the manner of their carnal knowledge of each other, to the full satisfaction of all that heard her, that none but he could be the man. Being demanded the reason why she did not immediately reveal that her father had to do with her, she answered, that she durst not speak of it again unto any body, because her father said, if she should at any time tell what he did unto her, the devil would presently tear her in pieces. This the child averred unto the court before his face, at the time of his trial.

What Flood said at the place of execution

As he impudently denied the fact at the time of his trial, he persevered to the instant of his death of the denial of the fact, with many fearful imprecations of judgments, and renunciation of God's mercies if he were any ways guilty. In great passionate hot terms he brake forth against his wife, on this wise saying: That three years she was conspiring to work his downfall, which now by her was effected (sigs. A2r–A3r, A4v, [C2v]–C3r).

Natures
Cruell Step-Dames:
OR,
Matchlesse Monsters of the Female
Sex; *Elizabeth Barnes*, and *Anne Willis*.
Who were executed the 26. day of *April*,
1637. at Tyburne, for the unnaturall murthe-
ring of their owne Children,
Also, herein is contained their severall Confessions,
and the Courts just proceedings against other notorious
Malefactors, with their severall offences
this Sessions.
Further, a Relation of the wicked Life and
impenitent Death of *John Flood*, who raped
his own Childe.

Printed at London for *Francis Coules*, dwelling in
the Old-Baily. 1637.

Title Page to Henry Goodcole, *Natures Cruell Step-Dames* (London, 1637). The woodcut shows Elizabeth Barnes cutting the throat of her sleeping child.

DOROTHY LEIGH

The Mothers Blessing: Or, The Godly Counsell of a Gentlewoman, Not Long Since Deceased, Left Behind Her for Her Children (London, 1633)

❧ It has been argued that infant mortality was so high in the Renaissance that parents did not form emotional attachments to their children. Dorothy Leigh gives the lie to that notion in the course of her apology for doing something that is not in "the usual order of women," writing a book. "Let no man blame a mother," she says, "though she something exceed in writing to her children, since every man knows that the love of a mother to her children is hardly contained within the bounds of reason." The seventh item on the agenda in this volume, first published in 1616, is the naming of her grandchildren. Particularly interesting—and, unfortunately, idiosyncratic—are her remarks about the name *Mary*. While it was a common notion that Mary redeemed Eve, Eve's sin was nonetheless cited repeatedly to justify both women's pain in childbirth and their subjection in marriage.

The seventh cause is to entreat you that, though I do not live to be a witness to the baptizing of any of your children, yet you would give me leave to give names to them all. For though I do not think any holiness to be in the name—but know that God hath his in every place and of every name—yet I see in the Bible—it was observed by God himself—to give choice names to his children, which had some good signification. I think it good, therefore, to name your children after the names of the saints of God, which may be a means to put them in mind of some virtues which those saints used, especially when they shall read of them in the Bible. And seeing many are desirous to name both their own children and others after their own names, this will be a means to increase the names of the saints in the Church. And so none shall have occasion to mislike his name, since he beareth the name of such a saint as hath left a witness to the world, that he lived and died in the true faith of Jesus Christ. The names I have chosen you are these: Philip, Elizabeth, James, Anna, John, and Susanna. . . .

It may be that some of you will marvel since I set down names for the imitation of their virtues that bore them, why I placed not Mary in the first place, a woman virtuous above all other women. My reason was this: because I presumed that there was no woman so senseless, as not to look what a blessing God hath sent to us women, through that gracious Virgin, by whom it pleased God to take away the shame which Eve our Grandmother had brought to us. For before, men might say, "The Woman beguiled me, and I did eat the poisoned fruit of disobedience, and I die." But now man may say, if he say truly: "The Woman brought me a Savior, and I feed on him by faith, and live." Here is this great and woeful shame taken from women by God, working in a woman. Man can claim no part in it; the shame is taken from us and from our posterity forever (sigs. B10^{r}–B11^{r}, C1^{v}–C2^{r}).

RICHARD MULCASTER

"Of the Top and Scourge," in *Positions Wherin Those Primitive Circumstances Be Examined, Which Are Necessarie for the Training Up of Children* (London, 1581)

❧ While books such as this one demonstrate that the Renaissance had a concept of childhood, they don't allow it to be much more than a training period for responsible adulthood. Even in discussing two favorite children's toys, the top and the whip, Richard Mulcaster pleads their health benefits, addresses the subject of right- and left-handedness, and (not excerpted here) discusses Latin and Greek analogues for these playthings. But Mulcaster, the first head of the famed Merchant Taylors' School in London, was notoriously serious of purpose and strict of discipline. It would be a mistake to think there was no room for fun in the life of the Elizabethan child.

He that will deny the top to be an exercise, indifferently capable of all distinctions in stirring, the very boys will beat him, and scourge him, too, if they light on him about Lent, when tops be in time, as every exercise hath his season, both in day and year, after the constitution of bodies and quantities in measure. . . . The harm this exercise may bring must be to the head and eyes through stooping too much forward, or to the back and shoulders by bending too much downwards. Otherwise it warmeth the body and worketh all the effects which those exercises do that, either by moving the legs or arms most, and with all the whole body in degree, enlarge and stir the natural heat either to provoke appetite or to expel superfluities. The more room the top hath to spin in, the better for the legs and feet; the bigger it is, the better for the arms and hands. The uprighter one scourgeth, the better for all parts, whom neither bending doth crush nor moisture corrupt. It were to be wished that it were whipped with both the hands, in play to train both the arms, seeing use makes the difference, and [if there is] no infirmity in nature. As both Plato, wishing the same, professeth it to be most true, and our experience teacheth us, both in left-handed people, which use but the left, and in double right-handed, which use both the hands alike, and bear the name of the right hand as the more common in use. But because the place of Plato concerning the left hand is very pithy to this purpose, though I use not to avouch much in the Greek tongue, yet methink I may not overpass it. . . . For the performance of any kind of labor there is no difference, sayeth he, in the legs and lower parts. But for our arms, through ignorant nurses and mothers, we be every one of us half lamed. For whereas naturally both the arms be almost of equal strength, through our own default we make the difference. And so he passeth on, still proving the unnatural handling of the left hand, when it is left weaker than the right hand is.

These be the exercises which I term within doors, because they may be practiced at home under covert, when we cannot abroad for the weather: though all may be used abroad, if the room and the weather do serve abroad. Wherein I take it, that I have kept Galen's rule in choosing these exercises, and that they be all both pleasant, profitable and parable [readily pursued], the perfect circumstances of all good and general exercises, not to be costly to compass, nor unpleasant to loath them, nor unprofitable to leave them. Those that require more liberty of room, to range at will or to forage in the field, be these which I noted before: walking, running, leaping, swimming, riding, hunting, shooting, and playing at the ball (sigs. K4^{r}–L1^{r}).

Chair for a Child (English, seventeenth century), with a panel back carved with a tulip and leaves. Highchairs survive from the same period. This was more likely a fireside chair.

Guests ❧

GERVASE MARKHAM

The English Husbandman (London, 1635)

❧ The term "husbandman" refers to "a tiller of soil," not to "a married man." In other words, Markham directs his advice to farmers, referring specifically to yeomen farmers, householders, and employers of servants, not to agricultural day laborers. Even though they occupied a relatively low position on the social scale, such farmers were men of substance, as is suggested also by the architectural model Markham puts forward as appropriate to their station. This was a fairly traditional floor plan even when presented in the first edition of *The English Husbandman*, in 1613. The scheme shows that planning for guests was an integral part of building, with a bedchamber (lodging) set aside for visitors and a dining parlor for entertaining.

Here you behold the model of a plain country man's house, without plaster or embosture [carved decoration], because it is to be intended that it is as well to be built of stud and plaster as of lime and stone. Or if timber be not plentiful, it may be built of coarser wood and covered with lime and hair. Yet if a man would bestow cost in this model, the four inward corners of the hall would be convenient for four turrets, and the four gavel ends being thrust out with bay windows might be formed in any curious manner. And where I place a gate and a plain pale [fence], might be either a terrace or a gatehouse of any fashion whatsoever. Besides, all those windows which I make plain, might be made bay windows, either with battlements or without. But the scope of my book tendeth only to the use of the honest husbandman, and not to instruct men of dignity, who in architecture are able wonderfully to control me. Therefore that the husbandman may know the use of this facsimile, he shall understand it by this which followeth.

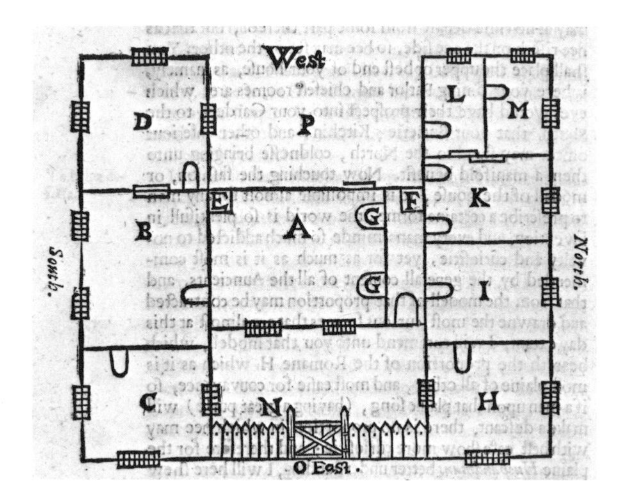

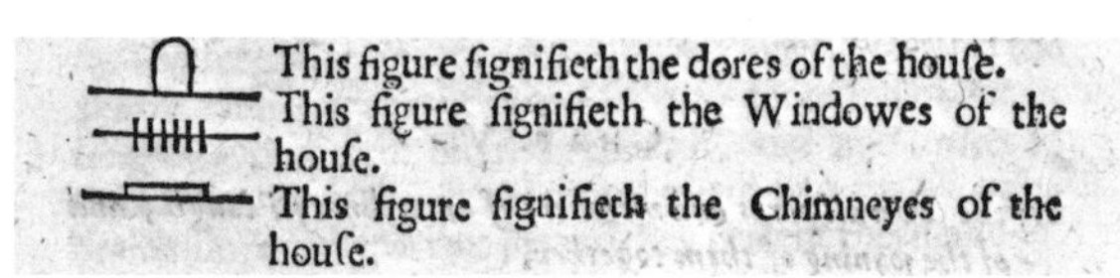

Floorplan for a Plain Countryman's House, from Gervase Markham, *The English Husbandman* (London, 1635). The plan is H-shaped, with a central great hall (A) and two cross wings. The overall design is somewhat obscured in this illustration by the fence closing in the front courtyard (N).

A. Signifieth the great hall.
B. The dining parlor for entertainment of strangers.
C. An inward closet within the parlor for the Mistress's use, for necessaries.
D. A stranger's lodging within the parlor.
E. A staircase into the rooms over the parlor.
F. A staircase into the goodman's rooms over the kitchen and buttery.
G. The screen in the hall.
H. An inward cellar within the buttery, which may serve for a larder.
I. The buttery.

K. The kitchen, in whose range may be placed a brewing lead, and convenient ovens, the brewing vessels adjoining.
L. The dairy house for necessary business.
M. The milk house.
N. A fair fawn pale [fence] before the foremost court.
O. The great gate to ride in at to the hall door.
P. A place where a pump would be placed to serve the offices of the house (sigs. D4[v]–E1[r]).

JOHN SAVILE

King James His Entertainment at Theobalds (London, 1603)

❧ While Henry VIII liked to acquire property, build, and improve, his children did not. Elizabeth notoriously encouraged her courtiers to build to her standards of magnificence and then to host her on her "progresses" around the countryside. William Cecil constructed Theobalds to this purpose, and his son Robert put the house to similar use with her successor, James. Royal visits engendered vast expense, for the monarch traveled with an enormous entourage and then, in addition, attracted crowds of followers from the local populace. The host had to hold open house, with lavish hospitality for all. Especially with supplies at a premium in the face of such demand, the tab was staggering. The price fixing undertaken here was a small countermeasure. This reporter emphasizes that the scale of activity was so large that no single witness could take it all in, and he details his stratagems for producing a credible account.

As his Highness was espied coming toward Theobalds, for very joy many ran from their carts, leaving their team of horse to their own unreasonable direction.

After his approach nigh unto Theobalds, the concourse of people was so frequent, every one more desiring a sight of him, that it were incredible to tell of. And it was wonderful to see the infinite number of horsemen and footmen that went from the city of London that day thitherwards, and likewise from the counties of Kent, Surrey, Essex, and Middlesex, besides many other countries. There were in my company two more who (after I had put it into their minds, what infinite numbers of horse and foot passed by us), after our breakfast at Edmonton, at the sign of the Bell, we took occasion to note how many would come down in the next hour. So coming up into a chamber next to the street where we might both best see and likewise take notice of all passengers, we called for an hourglass. And after we had disposed of ourselves, who should take the number of the horse and who the foot, we turned the hourglass, which, before it was half run out, we could not possibly truly number them, they came so exceedingly fast. . . .

When we were come to Theobalds, we understood his Majesty to be within the compass of three quarters of a mile of the house, at which tidings we divided ourselves into three parts, each one taking a place of special note to see what memorable accidents might happen within his compass—one standing at the upper end of the walk, the second at the upper end of the first court, the third at the second court door. And we had made choice of a gentleman of good sort to stand in the court that leads into the hall, to take notice what was done or said by his Highness to the nobility of our land, or said or done by them to his Majesty, and to let us understand of it, all which accidents as they happened in their several places, you shall hear in as few words as may be. Thus then for his Majesty's coming up the walk: there came before his Majesty some of the nobility, some barons, knights, esquires, gentlemen, and others, amongst whom was the sheriff of Essex, and the most of his men. . . . the whole nobility of our land and Scotland round about him, observing no place of superiority, all bare-headed. . . .

Supper time, at which there was such plenty of provision for all sorts of men in their due place, as struck me with admiration. And first to begin with the ragged regiment, and such as were debarred the privilege of any court, these were so sufficiently rewarded with beef, veal, mutton, bread, and beer, that they sung holiday every day and kept a continual feast. As for poor maimed and distressed soldiers which repaired thither for maintenance, the wine, money, and meat . . . they had in very bounteous sort. . . . Some of them, hearing that I was about to publish this small remembrance, made means to give me true information of such princely exhibition as they daily received during the time of his Majesty's abode at Theobalds.

But let us a little look back into the mirror of Majesty, our sovereign's own self, who, in his princely wisdom (considering the multitude of people assembled together), had that provident care over us his loving subjects, foreseeing that victuals would be dear both for horse and man, had it been permitted to have disposed of according to the insatiable desire of the town inhabitants, ratified a deposition to that effect taken before the clerk of the market, for such and such victuals, meal, bread, butter, eggs, cheese, beef, mutton, veal, and the like, with lodging, and many more such necessary matters, that they should not be out of measure dear, beyond ordinary course and custom, within the verge of his Majesty's court, so long as it continued at Theobalds (sigs. A4^{v}–B2^{r}).

A Royal Visitor Arrives at Gidde Hall, from Jean Puget de la Serre, *Histoire de l'Entree de la Reyne Mere du Roy . . . dans la Grande-Bretaigne* (London, 1639).

The Devise to Entertayne her Ma[jes]ty att Harfielde, the House of S[i]r Thomas Egerton Lo[rd] Keeper and His Wife the Countess of Darbye (July 1602)

❧ In addition to sumptuous lodgings and banquets, the host was also expected to provide entertainment and gifts for a visiting monarch. When Elizabeth arrived at Harefield in 1602, she was greeted by a lady who presented her with a rainbow-colored gown. The verse welcome, which has been attributed to Sir John Davies, refers to a superstition that if it rains on St. Swithin's Day (the 15th of July), forty more days of rain will follow. Here, through a pun on "rain" and "reign," this potential disaster to the host is turned into a tribute to the Queen.

Beauty's rose, and Virtue's book,
Angel's mind, and Angel's look,
To all Saints and Angels dear,
Clearest Majesty on earth,
Heavens did smile at your fair birth,
And since, your days have been most clear.

Only poor St. Swithin now
Doth hear you blame his cloudy brow.
But he, poor saint, devoutly swears,
It is but a tradition vain
That his much weeping causeth rain,
For saints in heaven shed no tears.

But this he saith, that to his feast
Comes Iris, an unbidden guest,
In her moist robe of colors gay.
And when she comes, she ever stays
For the full space of forty days
And more or less rains every day.

But the good saint, when once he knew
This rain was like to fall on you,
If saints could weep, had wept as much
As when he did the Lady lead
That did on burning iron tread.
To Ladies his respect is such.

He gently first bids Iris go
Unto th'Antipodes below,
But she for this more sullen grew.
When he saw that, with angry look
From her her rainy robes he took,
Which here he doth present to you.

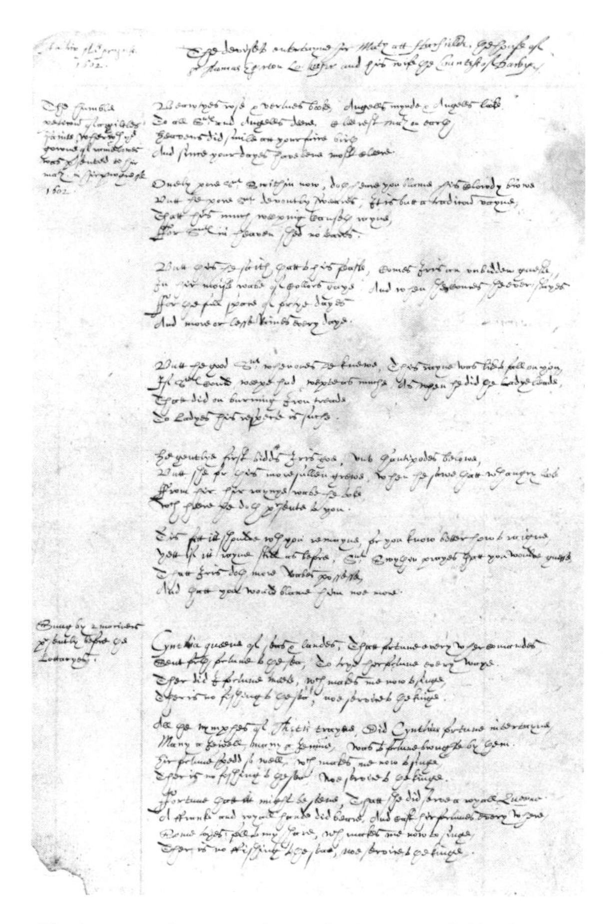

The Devise to Entertayne her Ma[jes]ty att Harfielde, the House of S[i]r Thomas Egerton (July 1602).

'Tis fit it should with you remain,
For you know better how to reign.
Yet if it rain still as before,
St. Swithin prays that you would guess
That Iris doth more robes possess,
And that you would blame him no more.

(fol. 4v)

CALEB DALECHAMP

Christian Hospitalitie: Handled Common-place-wise in the Chappel of Trinity Colledge in Cambridge (Cambridge, 1632)

❧ Throughout the sixteenth and seventeenth centuries, there were laments for the decay of hospitality. Caleb Dalechamp admits that the term "hospitality" was coming to mean "the entertainment of guests," but he and others who remembered the old days and the old ways continued to insist that it meant instead "charity towards strangers." For him, the architectural achievements of the Great Rebuilding unhappily diverted funds from the poor.

Hospitality falsely so called is the keeping of a good table at which seldom or never any other are entertained than kinsfolks, friends, and able neighbors, merry companions, parasites, jesters, and tellers of news. This is no hospitality, though it be commonly graced with that title, but it is good fellowship or some such like thing, as learned expositors aver. . . . In a large sense it [hospitality] contains all the works of charity and mercy and courteous kindness, specially the feasting of mean neighbors, the relieving of the poor, and the entertaining of honest guests and travelers of the same country. . . . And so it is hospitality to build houses for the blind and maimed, the aged and decrepit, for poor widows and young orphans, which are either past their labor or not come to it . . . . Because the feasting and entertaining of such as may entertain us again, and of such as are linked unto us by kindred or any other bond, though it be lawful in itself and sometimes commendable and expedient, yet it is no true trial nor due proof or sufficient testimony of our charity. . . .

And this again is either of magnificence, or of friendship, or of humanity, or of mercy: of magnificence, when a stranger of note and ability is entertained with pomp and state; of friendship, when a stranger or acquaintance is familiarly entertained; of humanity, when a foreigner that comes to see places and, being a stranger, is in courtesy invited; of mercy, when a poor stranger is harbored and relieved in his wants. . . .

But these [hosts] are curious and costly in decking and adorning their houses, and negligent and niggardly in harboring strangers and passengers. Their sumptuous buildings may be called *Mock-strangers* as well as *Mock-beggers*, for, like the barren figtree in the Gospel, they are seen afar off, and promise good relief to the hungry passengers. But let him come to them: he shall find (at the best) many goodly leaves of complemental, but no fruit of real hospitality. Or if haply he finds any, it is like that of the Indian figtree, no bigger than a bean, though the leaves be as broad as a target—nothing in comparison of that which was expected and justly looked for by the outward show. In the Old Testament the great ones are oft reproved for their vain and ambitious wastefulness in this kind (sigs. C3^{v}–C4^{r}, D1^{r}, D1^{v}, I3^{v}).

CHARLES GIBBON

Not so New, as True. Being a Verie Necessarie Caveat for all Christians to Consider of, Wherein is Truelie Described the Iniquitie of this Present Time, by Occasion of our Confused Living (London, 1590)

❧ This dialogue survives in a unique copy held by the Folger Library. Like Dalechamp, Gibbon's Alpheus believes that the decrease in charitable hospitality is inversely proportionate to the increase in sumptuous private building. But he also has a sense of historical cause and effect, recognizing that the dissolved monasteries had lodged transients and fed the poor, and that with the Reformation this burden of charity has fallen on the private sector. Alpheus's opposite, Nicanor, argues that the dissolution was necessary to discourage papist idolatry, but he finally cedes the argument to Alpheus.

ALPHEUS. Then I pray, tell me: what are become of these ancient monuments, stately monasteries, and huge buildings that were wont to be, where the poor might have continual access for relief and the stranger free resort for succor? Are these not defaced? But their free stones have beautified most of our fair buildings. Where are become all the revenues and lands that belonged to them, which (by report) were large? Are not the better sort enriched with their livings [income]? Yea, no doubt (superstition set apart) this season were incomparable to it. We have now sumptuous houses, but slender hospitality, for all the smoke comes out of one chimney; great substance, but small charity, for everyone is for himself. Now, hospitality is turned to prodigality, all bounty to bravery. Then was good faith amongst all folks, truth went by tallies [simple reckonings], their dealing was so simple. Now, nothing will serve, men are so subtle. Then was good neighborhood without niceness [luxury]. Now, given over for grippleness [avarice], or little used without curiousness [over-particularity]. All things then were plentiful and cheap; now, dainty [precious] and dear. . . .

NICANOR. The pulling down of those superstitious places you speak of was to a good purpose and very expedient, though you think prejudicial. You know there is an old saying not so common as true, that the bird where she leaves her old nest will lightly build again. And if the sight of images will stir up the desire of the ignorant unto idolatry, no doubt the sight of those buildings may haply procure some to their old scent. And therefore such idolatrous habitations were utterly to be deposed and destroyed, and that lawfully by authority of holy writ. . . .

ALPHEUS. We have such indeed amongst us, that will make bounteous fare for their betters, sumptuous feasts for their friends, costly cheer for their kindred, and yet will scarce afford a little bread or broth to the poor. . . . Call you this hospitality? . . . For what an horrible thing is this, that any bearing the name of Christians, should have such conditions, to prefer the goods of the world, which are but earthly, before the gifts of the mind, which are excellent. Thus, if men had as much grace as they have goods, or were as mindful of their salvation as their substance, they would neither be so gripple [greedy] in gathering, so hard in withholding, or so loath in leaving this worldly wealth; but so accompt of them, to possess them as the gift of God, to dispose them as his stewards, and to impart them as Christians. So by this means the poor should be more respected, the commonwealth more increased, and this time not so justly condemned. Is there not such amongst us as do enlarge their own livings by encroaching upon the poor, by eating up their lands, in buying houses over their heads, by abridging their liberties, and taking away their commons? (sigs. E2$^{r–v}$, E4^{r}–F1^{v}).

"How Robin Good-fellow Turned a Miserable Usurer to a Good House-keeper," in *Robin Good-fellow, His Mad Prankes and Merry Jests, Full of Honest Mirth, and Is a Fit Medicine for Melancholy* (London, 1639)

Robin Goodfellow is best remembered today as Puck in Shakespeare's *A Midsummer Night's Dream.* In fact, this prankster had a long life in country folktales, where he was a house fairy who could be a good deal more sinister than was Puck. In this story, first printed in 1628, he is on the side of the angels, because he sets out to reform a usurer. He frightens the miser into remembering his duty to be a good neighbor.

In this country of ours there was a rich man dwelled who, to get wealth together, was so sparing that he could not find in his heart to give his belly food enough. In the winter he never would make so much fire as would toast a black-pudding, for he found it more profitable to sit by other men's. His apparel it was of the fashion that none did wear, for it was such that did hang at a broker's [second-hand

A Usurer, frontispiece illustration from John Blaxton, *The English Usurer* (London, 1634). The usurer is shown in his countinghouse counting his coins. His accoutrements include two coffers, two pouches, a scale, and other devices to weigh and measure. At the usurer's back is a conventional representation of a devil.

dealer's] stall, till it was as weatherbeaten as an old sign. This man for his covetousness was so hated of all his neighbors that there was not one that gave him a good word. Robin Goodfellow grieved to see a man of such wealth do so little good, and therefore practiced to better him in this manner.

One night the usurer being in bed, Robin in the shape of a night raven came to the window and there did beat with his wings, and croaked in such manner that this old usurer thought he should have presently died for fear. This was but a preparation to what he did intend, for presently after, he appeared before him at his bed's feet in the shape of a ghost with a torch in his hand. At the sight of this, the old usurer would have risen out of his bed and have leaped out at the window, but he was stayed by Robin Goodfellow, who spake to him thus:

If thou stirren out of thy bed,
I do vow to strike thee dead.
I do come to do thee good,
Recall thy wits and startled blood.
The money which thou up dost store,
In soul and body makes thee poor.
Do good with money while you may,
Thou hast not long on earth to stay.
Do good I say, or day and night,
I hourly thus will thee afright.
Think on my words and so farewell,
For being bad, I live in hell.

Having said thus, he vanished away, and left this usurer in a great terror of mind. And for fear of being frighted again with this ghost, he turned very liberal and lived amongst his neighbors as an honest man should do (sigs. C3^{v}–C4^{v}).

The Bloudy Booke, Or, The Tragicall and Desperate End of Sir John Fites (alias Fitz) (London, 1605)

❧ In a culture so heavily invested in order and control within the household, it was inevitable that the risks of hospitality would also be recognized. Here, a guest proves to be a dangerous invader. Sir John Fites had already murdered a neighbor and was fleeing from the consequences of a dissolute life when he found his way to Twickenham. The case was notorious because of his status, and in fact this pamphlet account gives us a vivid picture of the perquisites of gentility, including Fites's privilege to claim a poor householder's own bed for the night. The goodman's charity was rewarded with his murder.

In the way between Kingston and Twickenham, after he had strayed upon the heath a long while, at last he came unto a gentleman's house which stood somewhat out of the way. And there he knocked, desiring that as they were gentlemen they would respect a gentleman and help him to some lodging, and used such words to persuade thereunto as that those of the house (the time of the night considered) thought him to have either had some other company intending to rob the house, or else to be overseen in drink, or some such matter. Insomuch that loath they were to trouble the house with such a guest, and so sent him away as he came, directing him unto the next town. Whenas, traveling up and down a long time, sometimes in the way, sometime out of the way, at last he attained about two of the clock after midnight unto a little village called Twickenham, some two miles from Kingston (the town from whence he last came) and there by chance—oh cruel chance!—happened to light upon the sign of the Anchor . . . where he caused his footman to knock and beat, and knocked himself also until such time that he had awaked the goodman of the house, who, being awakened, rose unto the window and demanded who was there? Sir John Fites answered, "Here is a Gentleman, and I want lodging; therefore I pray you open the door and let me in." The host of the house replied that he was but a poor man and kept no inn but only a victualing house, and that his lodging was very slender to entertain such a gentleman of sort as he took him to be. But the gentleman Sir John Fites answered that the worst bed that was would serve his turn at that time, and that he could be content to lie anywhere. The goodman of the house, in mere commiseration of his case pitying him and in tender compassion of his present estate regarding him, opened the door, let him into the house, set up his gelding, caused his wife to arise and lay a clean pair of sheets upon their own bed and a clean pillow, herself going to bed in another room with her maid and children. . . .

Sir John . . . at last being in bed, called and knocked for the host of the house to come unto him, who, being come into the chamber (for the goodman himself had no place to go to bed in), Sir John said unto him, "I pray thee, mine host, sit by me awhile." "I will," said the goodman, and so, fetching his cloak to wrap about him, returned and sat down by his bedside. But the gentleman's mind being troubled, he could by no means sleep or take any rest. But (oftentimes starting very suddenly as if

Title-Page Illustration to *The Bloudy Booke, Or, The Tragicall and Desperate End of Sir John Fites* (London, 1605). Fites's host lies stabbed to death in the foreground; his wife kneels behind him, wounded; and Fites runs himself through with his own sword.

he had been scared) always he would be talking of some idle matter or other, uttering much disjointed talk, as telling the goodman of the house that he had lain in a better bed than that was. Whereunto the poor man replied, in the pleasingest speeches that he could (because he noted him to look somewhat wildly), "I make no question thereof, sir, but surely I have no better at this time (the bed being sufficient for an honest man). If I had better, your worship should have it. I am sorry for your sake that it is no better." . . .

The goodman of the house remained with him until between four and five of the clock in the morning, at what time, seeing that the morning was fair and he had business to go about, he left the gentleman alone, between sleeping and waking (as it were) and softly stealing away. . . . But forth comes Sir John in his shirt, with his naked rapier in his hand, his eyes looking as if they had sparkled forth fire. . . . and therewith suddenly and violently ran at the goodman of the house with his rapier. But fear made the man nimble and swift, for before Sir John could retire, the goodman had closed the gate. And his rapier point hitting in a little hole of the gate (a fatal hole it was) thrust him quite through the body between his shoulder and his breast, so that the man fell down presently and died, only with a woeful noise and hideous shriek crying out, "I am killed."

The good wife of the house (alas, poor soul) hearing the piteous outcry and grievous groan that her dying husband made, suddenly all amazed, leaps out of her bed in her smock to see what the matter was. And not well knowing on which side of the house the cry was, out she ran on the street side. Where, as soon as she was stepped out, she meets Sir John with his naked rapier in his hand, all on gore with the blood of her husband. Wherefore, in hope of pity from his pitiless hands, she fell down upon her knees in her smock, and with hands erected, prayed, "Sweet sir, spare my life, and show mercy." But he, as eager and thirsty of blood, without all compassion, twice thrust at her naked body. Twice he missed her, but still reinforcing his stroke, thrust again the third time, and then wounded her grievously in the arm (yet not mortally). Ah, happy Fortune for her three poor infants' sake, that she was not sent by his unlucky hand after their father, and they left destitute of both. . . . Wherefore most strangely (espying a mud wall close by), he takes his rapier, and laying the hilts thereto, and the point thereof (void of all pity) unto his own breast, runs forcibly thereupon (sigs. D1^{r}–E2^{r}).

Trenchers (English, mid-sixteenth century), made of sycamore and painted on one side with stylized flowers, a strapwork design in red, and moralizing epigrams. These highly decorated little plates, only 5 inches in diameter, were evidently used for serving sweetmeats. They came in their own matching wooden case. Agecroft Association.

SECTION THREE

GOODS AND ROOMS

· GOODS AND ROOMS ·

1529 WAS A LANDMARK YEAR IN THE history of the English household. A new regulation required that an inventory of possessions be taken at the death of every man and woman. The goods were generally listed room by room, as they were found, and their value was then estimated item by item. A total worth was affixed, and the document was duly witnessed. The surviving inventories constitute a vast data base that allows us to analyze the quantity, quality, and nature of personal property across the decades, among all but the poorest and most transient classes, and in every region.

In fact, the data base is sufficiently vast that it has not yet been thoroughly processed. Even so, it is possible to reach a number of large conclusions. First, the sheer quantity of household possessions increased dramatically over the course of the hundred-and-fifty years following the compulsory institution of inventories, and this increase occurred at every social register, at roughly proportionate levels. Second, there were more kinds of goods in circulation as well as goods of a wide range in quality, including an expanding list of imported items. Third, household goods assumed pride of place among possessions. While the earliest inventories listed cattle and farm equipment first and household furnishings second, the priority was soon reversed.

Fourth, there was a widespread perception of change and improvement in the material conditions of life, as objects that had been luxuries became standard fare. And fifth, this perception was not only shared among the general populace but was also marked at the highest governmental levels. The state that realized its own self-interest in promoting a patriarchal hierarchy in the family also recognized that the systematic disposition of goods conduced to the social order. As William Segar observed in 1602, "the more a man possesseth in the state, the more careful he will be to conserve it." For this reason, an interest developed in the regulation of property through inventories.

For a case study of the growth in the amount of household goods, it is helpful to look at the region known as the Arden. There, the data base has been analyzed by Victor Skipp, who has determined that in the century from 1570 to 1674 possessions increased 289% among the wealthy, 275% among other privileged classes, 310% among what has been called the "middling sort," and 247% even among peasants.

Skipp also gives some telling examples. In 1560 a farmer named Edward Kempsale died. His post mortem inventory indicated that three-fourths of his estate consisted of farm stock. He lived in a house with two rooms and owned household goods worth under £20. These included six trenchers (or plates), three sheets, one coverlet, and two tablecloths. In 1587 another farmer named Thomas Gyll died. By comparison, he had about the same holdings in arable land, farm animals, and agricultural equipment, but these amounted to only half the value of his estate. He lived in a house of four rooms with personal possessions worth over £67. Gyll owned twenty-eight pieces of pewter, five silver spoons, thirteen-and-a-half pairs of sheets, six coverlets, four tablecloths, and also pillows, pillowcases, and table napkins.

That Kempsale had two rooms and Gyll had four is part of the story of the Great Rebuilding: Gyll had two more bedchambers, or perhaps an extra bedchamber and a parlor. In the Arden area, there was an average of 2.5 rooms in the peasant household in the mid-sixteenth century; one hundred years later, there was an average of 6.5 rooms in the same social stratum. For the Oxford region between 1600 and 1640, similarly, Derek Portman has demonstrated that at a relatively low social level, the average number of rooms per household doubled from three to six; and, on a higher economic plane, the average number of rooms quadrupled from seven to twenty-eight—all in just forty years.

As the number of rooms multiplied, it was no longer necessary for each to be a multi-purpose space. Individual rooms developed associations with activities that were peculiar to them. It is one thing to have a single area in which to live, eat, and sleep. It is something very different to have different spaces, each with an assigned activity. The clearer the identity of any space, the more the space itself functioned as a socializing device, establishing rules of behavior appropriate to it. A remarkable addition to the Elizabethan home, for example, was the parlor, a room set aside for leisure entertainment. This material construct marked a conceptual revolution, as householders formally acknowledged the pleasures of leisure and practiced the appropriate activities: feasting with friends; enjoying music; playing cards, dice, and tables (or backgammon); reading aloud.

It seems natural that this increase in the number of chambers would account for the rise in household possessions. If we're looking for a cause-and-effect sequence, however, the opposite is more likely to be the case. That is, in the sixteenth century people began first to accumulate more possessions and only afterwards discovered that they needed more space to store and display them. The growth in personal property that inspired the regulation of inventories in 1529 also fueled the Great Rebuilding of 1570 to 1640. Admittedly, large social trends of this sort cannot be charted on a very precise chronology, and undoubtedly each phenomenon fed the other, but it would be a mistake to overlook the important role that possessions played in effecting the changes in private life that accompanied the Great Rebuilding.

Linens and tableware generally occupied a large proportion of any inventory, and it was typical that they were held in a chest. The chest, which not only stored possessions but also served as a seat or table surface—and which was, to top things off, transportable—was the single most common piece of furniture in medieval times. But as a household acquired more linens and more tableware, no lone chest was adequate, and the form underwent multiple metamorphoses.

In one incarnation, the chest grew taller to store more. For practical purposes, the height had to be subdivided into segmented storage spaces. Easiest access was from the front, so that drawers appeared. Eventually the "chest" developed into a "chest of drawers." For aesthetic purposes, though, some of the levels in early pieces were designed as open shelves, where objects of which the household was most proud could be displayed. These were called cupboards (literally, boards on which to place cups) or, more precisely, court cupboards. In other incarnations, the chest evolved into livery and dole cupboards for food; into buffets, sideboards, and kitchen dressers; into linen presses, and so on.

Medieval great halls were furnished with long tables of the type we commonly call "refectory tables." These came in pieces. The base could be formed of trestles or of legs joined at the top by a frieze and at the floor by stretchers. The tabletop, called the "boards" in honor of its literal constitution, was laid across this base. The whole could easily be disassembled and pulled out of the way to clear the floor. But by mid-sixteenth century people were starting to nail the boards to the bases to form permanent and stable structures. At about the same time, joiners entered the furnishings market that had previously been dominated by carpenters; they produced tables constructed, from the first, as "joined" tables, or single units.

As the size of the cupboards increased and as the tables were joined, these furnishings became progressively less transportable. By this means, they participated in the phenomena associated with the Great Rebuilding: like shutters, floorboards, window glazing, and staircases, furnishings came to be thought of as fixtures. Some were even designed with specific household locations in mind. They contributed to the household ethic of stability in material circumstances that transformed the face of private life in the sixteenth century.

In other ways, however, the growth of personal possessions undermined old social stabilities. The flood of consumer products onto the English market inspired desires, envies, and ambitions that were unsettling. There is no question that Elizabethans were house proud and that they cherished the objects they accumulated. But at the same time, many were deeply distrustful of wealth and goods and of the way friendships and family loyalties could erode under the competitive pressure to possess. This is a recurrent theme in the literature of the time.

Elizabethans were less self-aware about the effects of the disintegration of the medieval household's communal life. With activities segregated into specific spaces, the practitioners of those activities could be associated with proper and improper locations in the household. For the householder, every area was his proper domain; for women and for servants, however, this was no longer true. It was to take some centuries for the household to break into an "upstairs" and a "downstairs," but, as has already been suggested, the roots of this social split were apparent in the Elizabethan years. Divisions such as these can seem so "natural" that we lose the ability to question or second-guess them. But one lesson we can learn from charting the changes of the Great Rebuilding is that none of these structures and habits is natural. They happened as historical processes, and history always waits to be rewritten.

Possessions and Provisions ❧

WILLIAM HARRISON

An Historicall Description of the Iland of Britaine (London, 1587)

❧ William Harrison experienced urban mercantile life (growing up in London), higher education (at both Oxford and Cambridge), a small rural parish (as a country rector), ecclesiastical law (as judge in an archdeacon's court), and great-house life (as chaplain to Sir William Brooke). In addition he had the instinct for oral history and the sensitivity to regional variation demonstrated in this extract. He was extremely well positioned, in other words, to undertake a comprehensive description of Elizabethan England. At the same time, his nationalistic pride made his reports far from dispassionate. In this passage, he celebrates the explosion of consumer culture and its impact on household life at all social levels.

The furniture of our houses also exceedeth, and is grown in manner even to passing delicacy. And herein I do not speak of the nobility and gentry only, but likewise of the lowest sort in most places of our south country that have anything at all to take to. Certes in noblemen's houses it is not rare to see abundance of arras, rich hangings of tapestry, silver vessel, and so much other plate as may furnish sundry cupboards, to the sum oftentimes of a thousand or two thousand pounds at the least—whereby the value of this and the rest of their stuff doth grow to be almost inestimable. Likewise in the houses of knights, gentlemen, merchantmen, and some other wealthy citizens, it is not geason [rare] to behold generally their great provision of tapestry, Turkey work [carpets], pewter, brass, fine linen, and thereto costly cupboards of plate, worth five or six hundred or a thousand pounds, to be deemed by estimation. But as herein all these sorts do far exceed their elders and predecessors, and in neatness and curiosity, the merchant all other; so in time past the costly furniture stayed there, whereas now it is descended yet lower, even unto the inferior artificers and many farmers, who by virtue of their old and not of their new leases have for the most part learned also to garnish their cupboards with plate, their joined beds with tapestry and silk hangings, and their tables with carpets and fine napery, whereby the wealth of our country (God be praised therefore, and give us grace to employ it well) doth infinitely appear. Neither do I speak this in reproach of any man, God is my judge, but to show that I do rejoice rather to see how God hath blessed us with his good gifts. And whilst I behold how that in a time wherein all things are grown to most excessive prices, and what commodity so ever is to be had is daily plucked from the commonalty by such as look into every trade, we do yet find the means to obtain and achieve such furniture as heretofore hath been impossible.

There are old men yet dwelling in the village where I remain, which have noted three things to be marvelously altered in England within their sound remembrance. . . . One is the multitude of chimneys lately erected, whereas in their young days there were not above two or three, if so many, in most uplandish towns of the realm (the religious houses and manor places of their lords always excepted, and peradventure some great personages), but each one made his fire against a reredos [fireback] in the hall, where he dined and dressed his meat.

The second is the great (although not general) amendment of lodging, for (said they) our fathers (yea, and we ourselves also) have lain full oft upon straw pallets, on rough mats covered only with a sheet under coverlets made of dagswain [rough, shaggy material] or hapharlots [coarse coverlets] (I use their own terms) and a good round log under their heads instead of a bolster or pillow. If it were so that our fathers or the good man of the house had within seven years after his marriage purchased a mattress or flockbed, and thereto a sack of chaff to rest his head upon, he thought himself to be as well lodged as the lord of the town, that peradventure lay seldom in a bed of down or whole feathers—so well were they contented, and with such base kind of furniture, which also is not very much amended as yet in some parts of Bedfordshire and elsewhere further off from our southern parts. Pillows (said they) were thought meet only for women in childbed. As for servants, if they had any sheet above them it was well, for seldom had they any under their bodies to keep them from the pricking straws that ran oft through the canvas of the pallet and razed their hardened hides.

The third thing they tell of is the exchange of vessel, as of treen [wooden] platters into pewter, and wooden spoons into silver or tin. For so common were all sorts of treen stuff in old time that a man should hardly find four pieces of pewter (of which one was peradventure a salt) in a good farmer's house, and yet for all this frugality (if it may so be justly called) they were scarce able to live and pay their rents at their days without selling of a cow or an horse or more, although they paid but four pounds at the uttermost by the year. . . . Whereas in my time, although peradventure four pounds of old rent be improved to forty, fifty, or an hundred pounds, yet will the farmer as another palm or date tree think his gains very small toward the end of his term if he have not six or seven years' rent lying by him, therewith to purchase a new lease, beside a fair garnish of pewter on his cupboard, with so much more in odd vessel going about the house, three or four featherbeds, so many coverlets and carpets of tapestry, a silver salt, a bowl for wine (if not an whole nest) and a dozen of spoons to furnish up the suit (vol. 1, sigs. R3v–R4r).

"Leaden Hall Market," from Hugh Alley, *A Caveatt for the Citty of London* (1598), a manuscript volume with pen and wash illustrations of London's markets. Leadenhall, a private house purchased by the city in the 1440s, provided covered storage for grains, lead, and nails as well as courtyard space for an open-air market of grain, meat, pigs' heads, sausages, poultry, fruits, and vegetables, as illustrated here. On days when the food markets were not open, wool, cloth, and leather were sold. Alley indicates that the victuals and produce come from London, Middlesex, Surrey, Kent, and Essex. The water pump to the left was set up in 1576.

The Rates of Marchandizes as They Are Set Downe in the Booke of Rates for the Custome and Subsidie of Poundage, and for the Custome and Subsidie of Clothes, the Same Being Signed by the Kings Majestie, and Sealed with the Great Seale of England (London, 1604)

❧ Soon after being crowned king of Great Britain, James issued this proclamation regarding poundage, a tax on all imports and exports, twelve pence on the pound sterling and chargeable to foreigners as well as Englishmen. The subsidy was allowed by Parliament, but James also cited precedent, emphasizing that Mary had installed the charges for the defense of the realm and that Elizabeth had followed suit. The alphabetical book of rates testifies to the quantity of goods circulating in England, as does the fact that James sought not only to redress over- and under-valuations but also to add new commodities to the list. The largest entry is for "drugs," with 228 kinds enumerated, including borax, bitter almonds, musk, pepper, tobacco cane, and tobacco leaf. The excerpts below represent most letters of the alphabet and also correspond to many items illustrated in this anthology. The abbreviation *vocat.* is for "also called"; *C.* is for one hundred or for "the hundred weight" (112 pounds); *cont.* for "containing"; *s.* for a shilling or shillings; and *d.* for denarius or denarii—that is, pence.

Arras or tapestry with gold and silver, the Flemish ell [27 inches]		xl.s.
Bears, living, the bear		xx.s.
Boards	vocat. barrel boards the C. cont. vi. score boards	v.s.
	vocat. clapboards the C. cont. vi. score boards	xv.s.
	vocat. deal-boards [of pine or fir], see Deals	
	vocat. paste boards [sheets of paper pasted together to the thickness of a board] for books, the thousand	vi.s. viii.d.
	vocat. pipe boards the C., cont. vi. score	x.s.
	vocat. white boards for shoemakers, the board	xii.d.
Bodkins, the small gross, cont. xii. dozen		iii.s. iiii.d.
Bottles	of earth, covered with wicker, the dozen	xx.d.
	of glass, covered with wicker, the dozen	vi.s. viii.d.
	of glass, with vices [screw stoppers], covered with leather, the dozen	xxx.s.
	of glass, uncovered, the dozen	xviii.d.
	of wood, vocat. sucking bottles [for infants], the gross, cont. xii. dozen	v.s.
Candle sticks	of brass or latten [a yellow mixed metal like brass], the pound	viii.d.
	of wire, the dozen	iii.s. iiii.d.
Candlesnuffers, the dozen		ii.s. viii.d.
Caps	double turfed [turned up with a facing] or cocked caps, the dozen	xxiiii.s.
	for children, the dozen	x.s.
	vocat. nightcaps of satin and velvet, the dozen	xxx.s.
	vocat. nightcaps of silk knit, the dozen	xl.s.
	vocat. nightcaps of woolen, the dozen	x.s.
	vocat. nightcaps of linen, the dozen	iiii.s.

Cases	with wooden combs, garnished, the dozen	x.s.
	with small ivory combs, garnished, the dozen	xiii.s. iiii.d.
	with middle sort ivory combs, garnished, the dozen	xx.s.
	with large ivory combs, garnished, the dozen	xl.s.
	for combs single, the gross, cont. xii. dozen	vi.s. viii.d.
	for combs double, the gross, cont. xii. dozen	xiii.s. iiii.d.
	for spectacles, gilt, the gross, cont. xii. dozen	xiii.s. iiii.d.
	for spectacles, ungilt, the gross, cont. xii. dozen	vi.s. viii.d.
	vocat. needles or pincases the gross, cont. xii. dozen	vi.s. viii.d.
Chairs of walnut-tree, the piece		iiii.s. vi.d.
Chess-boards, the dozen		x.s.
Chessmen, the gross, cont. xii dozen		vi.s.
Damask	or caffa [rich silk cloth], the yard	viii.s.
	of caffa, crimson or purple, the yard	xiii.s. iiii.d.
	tabling of Holland-making, the yard	vi.s. viii.d.
	towelling and napkining, Holland-making, the yard	ii.s. ii.d.
	tabling of Sletia-making, the yard	ii.s.
	towelling and napkining of Sletia-making, the yard	viii.d.
Ear-pickers of bone, the gross, cont. xii. dozen		v.s.
Fiddles for children, the dozen		xx.d.
Flasks	covered with leather, the dozen	iii.s. iiii.d.
	covered with velvet, the dozen	xxvi.s. viii.d.
	of horn, the dozen	v.s.
Frying and dripping pans, the C. weight, cont. 112 pound		xx.s.
Glass for	Burgundy, white, the chest	xl.s.
windows	Burgundy, colored, the chest	ii.l. x.s.
	Normandy, white, the case	xx.s.
	Normandy, colored, the case	xl.s.
	Rhenish, the way or web, cont. lx. bunches	ii.l. x.s
Glasses	vocat. burning glasses [lenses to concentrate rays of the sun], the dozen	xii.d.
Glasses,	half-penny ware, the gross, cont. xii. dozen	iiii.s.
looking	pennyware, the gross, cont. xii. dozen	viii.s.
glasses	of steel, small, the dozen	vi.s. viii.d.
	of steel, large, the dozen	xiii.s. iiii.d.
	of crystal, small, the dozen under no. 6	x.s.
	of crystal, middle sort, the dozen of no. 6	xx.s.
	of crystal, large, the dozen, no. 7., 8., and upward	xl.s.
Glasses,	of Flanders-making, coarse, the gross, cont. xii. dozen	xx.s.
vocat.	of Flanders-making, fine, the dozen	vi.s. viii.d.
Hourglasses	of Venice-making, the dozen	xx.s.
Glasses	balm glasses, the gross, cont. xii. dozen	iii.s. iiii.d.
vocat.	vials, the C., cont. v. score	viii.s. iiii.d.
	water glasses, the dozen	iiii.s.

Horns	blowing horns, the dozen	xiii.s. iiii.d.
vocat.	shoeing horns, the dozen	iii.s. iiii.d.
	for lanterns, the thousand	xx.s.
Ink for printers, the C. weight, cont. 112. pound		xx.s.
Instruments	bullet screws, the dozen	xii.d.
for Barbers	incision shears, the dozen	xii.d.
and	sets, the bundle, cont. xvi.	vi.d.
Surgeons	paices or tooth-drawers, the dozen	xx.d.
vocat.	pullicans, the dozen	xx.d.
	trepans [bone saws], the piece	ii.s. vi.d.
Ivory, the pound		v.s.
Kettles	the C. weight, cont. 112. pound	iii.l.
Lace	bone lace, the dozen yards	viii.s.
vocat.	Brittany lace, the gross, cont. xii. dozen yards	x.s.
	pomet lace, the gross, cont. xii. dozen yards	viii.s.
	pearl or antlet lace of thread, the gross, cont. xii. dozen yards	ii.s. vi.d.
	silk lace of all sorts, the pound	xxvi.s. viii.d.
Lutes	Cologne-making, with cases, the dozen	iiii.l.
	Venice-making, with cases, the dozen	xii.l.
Lute-	catlings [smallest strings], the gross, cont. xii. dozen knots	xvi.d.
strings	minikins [treble strings], the gross, cont. xii.	
vocat.	dozen knots	xiii.s. iiii.d.
Mortars and pestles of brass, the pound		viii.d.
Needles	the dozen thousand	xvi.s. viii.d.
	vocat. packneedles [large, strong needles], the thousand	vi.s. viii.d.
Needle-cases, the gross, cont. xii. dozen		vi.s. viii.d.
Olephants' teeth, the C. pound		iii.l. vi.s. viii.d.
Paper	brown, the bundle	xii.d.
	brown, the C. bundles, cont. v. score	v.l.
	vocat. cap-paper [wrapping paper], the ream	ii.s. vi.d.
	cap-paper, the C. reams	xii.l. x.s.
	vocat. demi [inferior] paper, the ream	iiii.s.
	ordinary, the ream	ii.s. vi.d.
	ordinary, the C., cont. v. score	xii.l. x.s.
	painted, the ream	vi.s. viii.d.
	vocat. printing and copy paper, the ream	ii.s. vi.d.
	vocat. royal paper [paper measuring 25 by 19 or 20 inches], the ream	vi.s. viii.d.
	vocat. pressing paper, the C. leaves	vi.s. viii.d.
Paving tiles, the thousand		xx.s.
Paving tiles, vocat. galley-tiles [glazed tiles], for foot paces, the foot		iiii.d.
Pins, the dozen thousand		iiii.s.
Pinpillows	of cloth, the dozen	xx.d.
	of velvet or silk, the dozen	vi.s. viii.d.

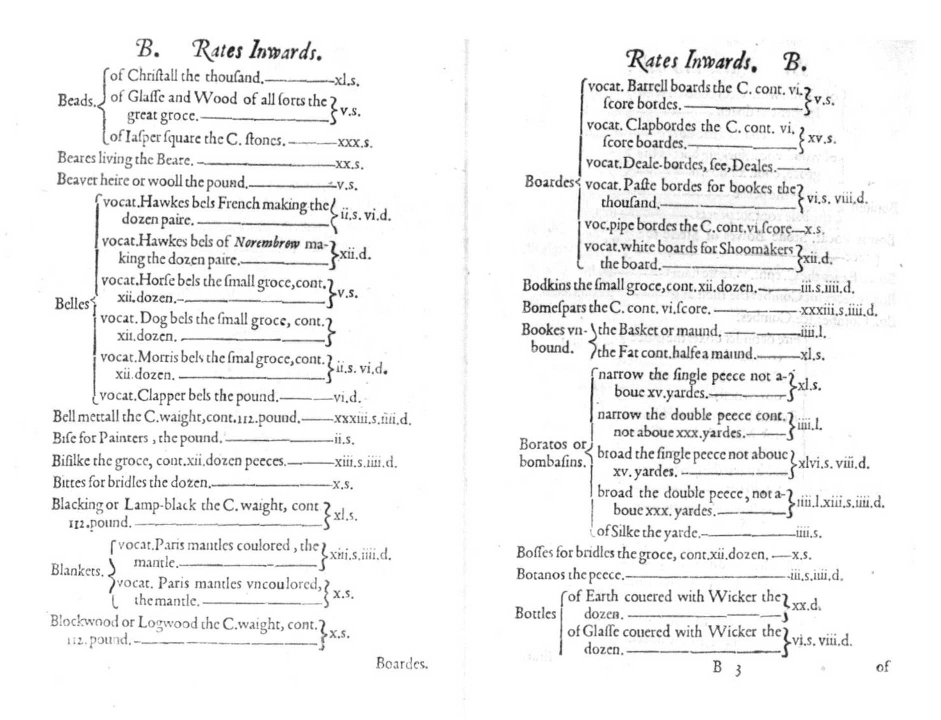

B. *Rates Inwards.*

Beads.	of Chriſtall the thouſand.	xl.s.
	of Glaſſe and Wood of all ſorts the great groce.	v.s.
	of Iaſper ſquare the C. ſtones.	xxx.s.
Beares living the Beare.		xx.s.
Beaver heire or wooll the pound.		v.s.
Belles	vocat. Hawkes bels French making the dozen paire.	ii.s. vi.d.
	vocat. Hawkes bels of *Norembrow* making the dozen paire.	xii.d.
	vocat. Horſe bels the ſmall groce, cont. xii. dozen.	v.s.
	vocat. Dog bels the ſmall groce, cont. xii. dozen.	
	vocat. Morris bels the ſmal groce, cont. xii. dozen.	ii.s. vi.d.
	vocat. Clapper bels the pound.	vi.d.
Bell mettall the C. waight, cont. 112. pound.		xxxiii.s. iiii.d.
Biſe for Painters, the pound.		ii.s.
Biſilke the groce, cont. xii. dozen peeces.		xiii.s. iiii.d.
Bittes for bridles the dozen.		x.s.
Blacking or Lamp-black the C. waight, cont 112. pound.		xl.s.
Blankets.	vocat. Paris mantles coulored, the mantle.	xiii.s. iiii.d.
	vocat. Paris mantles vncoulored, the mantle.	x.s.
Blockwood or Logwood the C. waight, cont. 112. pound.		x.s.

Boardes.

Rates Inwards. B.

Boardes	vocat. Barrell boards the C. cont. vi. ſcore bordes.	v.s.
	vocat. Clapbordes the C. cont. vi. ſcore boardes.	xv.s.
	vocat. Deale-bordes, ſee, Deales.	
	vocat. Paſte bordes for bookes the thouſand.	vi.s. viii.d.
	voc. pipe bordes the C. cont. vi. ſcore.	x.s.
	vocat. white boards for Shoomakers the board.	xii.d.
Bodkins the ſmall groce, cont. xii. dozen.		iii.s. iiii.d.
Bomeſpars the C. cont. vi. ſcore.		xxxiii.s. iiii.d.
Bookes vnbound.	the Basket or maund.	iiii.l.
	the Fat cont. halfe a maund.	xl.s.
Boratos or bombaſins.	narrow the ſingle peece not aboue xv. yardes.	xl.s.
	narrow the double peece cont. not aboue xxx. yardes.	iiii.l.
	broad the ſingle peece not aboue xv. yardes.	xlvi.s. viii.d.
	broad the double peece, not aboue xxx. yardes.	iiii.l. xiii.s. iiii.d.
	of Silke the yarde.	iii.s.
Boſſes for bridles the groce, cont. xii. dozen.		x.s.
Botanos the peece.		iii.s. iiii.d.
Bottles	of Earth couered with Wicker the dozen.	xx.d.
	of Glaſſe couered with Wicker the dozen.	vi.s. viii.d.

B 3 of

Rate Chart from *The Rates of Marchandizes as They Are Set Downe in the Booke of Rates* (London, 1604).

Pots	of earth or stone, covered, the C., cont. v. score	xiii.s. iiii.d.
	of earth or stone, uncovered, the C., cast, cont. a gallon to every cast, whether in one pot or in more	xxv.s.
	vocat. gally-pots [glazed pots], the C., cont. v. score	xx.s.
	vocat. melting-pots, for goldsmiths, the hundred	xii.d.
	of iron, French-making, the dozen	xx.s.
Puppets for children, the gross, cont. xii. dozen		vi.s. viii.d.
Quills	goose-quills, the thousand	xii.d.
Rattles for children, the gross, cont. xii. doz.		x.s.
Rings	of copper set with stones, the dozen	iii.s. iiii.d.
	for curtains, the pound	viii.d.
	for pouches, the gross, cont. xii. dozen	xv.s.
Stools	without basins, the dozen	xxx.s.
vocat. close stools	with basins, the dozen	iii.l.
Tablemen [backgammon pieces], the gross, cont. xii. dozen		viii.s.
Tables	playing tables of wainscots, & all other sorts, coarse, the pair	ii.s.
vocat.	playing tables of walnut-tree, the pair	iii.s. iiii.d.
	playing tables of brazil [wood], the pair	v.s.
	playing tables, of damask work, the pair	xiii.s. iiii.d.
Thimbles, the thousand		xx.s.
Thread	bridges [Bruge] thread, the dozen pound	xv.s.
vocat.	crossbow thread, the C. pound	xxxiii.s. iiii.d.

	Lyons or Paris thread, the bolt	ii.s.
	Lyons or Paris thread, the bale, cont. 100 bolts	x.l.
	long skein thread, the pound	viii.d.
	outnal [linen] thread, the dozen pound	xx.s.
	pack-thread [twine], in skeins, the C. pound	xvi.s. viii.d.
	pack-thread, bottom thread, the pound	iiii.d.
	piecing [mending] thread, the dozen pound	xxvi.s. viii.d.
	sisters [bleached] thread, the pound	x.s.
Toothpicks,	the gross, cont. xii. dozen	ii.s.
Trenchers	white, common sort, the gross, cont. xii. dozen	ii.s.
	red or painted, the gross, cont. xii. dozen	vi.s.
Wainscots	the C., cont. vi. score	viii.l.
Warming pans,	the dozen	xxx.s.

JOHN DOD AND ROBERT CLEAVER

A Godlie Forme of Householde Government: for the Ordering of Private Families, According to the Direction of Gods Word (London, 1598)

❧ In this passage (a familiar one in works of domestic advice), the political constitution of the household, at least as it relates to husband and wife, is given an economic rationale. The husband's responsibility to get goods and provisions is taken as a given. From it follows all the behavioral constraints on women: that their place is in the house, that they must keep silent, that they must be modest, and so on. In this respect, material goods conspired in the gender hierarchy that was so important to Elizabethan culture.

The duty of the husband is to get goods; and of the wife, to gather them together and save them. The duty of the husband is to travel abroad to seek living; and the wife's duty is to keep the house. The duty of the husband is to get money and provision; and of the wife's, not vainly to spend it. The duty of the husband is to deal with many men; and of the wife's, to talk with few. The duty of the husband is to be intermeddling; and of the wife, to be solitary and withdrawn. The duty of the man is to be skillful in talk; and of the wife, to boast of silence. The duty of the husband is to be a giver; and of the wife, to be a saver. The duty of the man is to apparel himself as he may; and of the woman, as it becometh her. The duty of the husband is to be lord of all; and of the wife, to give account of all. The duty of the husband is to dispatch all things without door; and of the wife, to oversee and give order for all things within the house. Now where the husband and wife performeth these duties in their house, we may call it a college of quietness. The house wherein these are neglected, we may terme it a hell (sigs. L5v–L6r).

THOMAS SMITH, *attributed author*

A Compendious or Briefe Examination of Certayne Ordinary Complaints of Divers of our Country Men in These our Dayes, Which although They Are in Some Parte Unjust & Frivolous, Yet Are They . . . Throughly Debated and Discussed (London, 1581)

This tract must have seemed topical when it was written in 1549, probably by Sir Thomas Smith. The reason it was still relevant when first printed in 1581 was that the rapid inflation of the first five decades of the century had only worsened. From 1500 to 1540, prices rose 50%; by 1560, another 150%; by 1580, a further 100%. In 1600, prices were 550 times their 1500 level. They affected gentlemen, merchants, artisans, and husbandmen, each of whom is given a voice of complaint in this dialogue. Meanwhile, a doctor offers a larger perspective. The runaway inflation of the decade can be attributed to population growth, urbanization, and the movement to a currency-based economy, among other factors. In this extract, the doctor recognizes also the stimulus of the national appetite for consumer goods, especially imported goods.

What number first of trifles comes hither from beyond the sea that we might either clean spare or else make them within our realm, for the which we either pay inestimable treasure every year or else exchange substantial wares and necessary for them, for the which we might receive great treasure? Of the which sort I mean as well looking glasses as drinking, and also glass windows, dials, tables, cards, balls, puppets, penners [penhorns], inkhorns, toothpicks, gloves, knives, daggers, owches [buckles], brooches, aglets [ornamental tags], buttons of silk and silver, earthen pots, pins and points, hawks' bells, paper both white and brown, and a thousand like things that might either be clean spared or else made within the realm sufficient for us. And as for some things, they make it of our own commodities and send it us again, whereby they set their people awork and do exhaust much treasure out of the realm. As of our wool they make cloths, caps, and kerseys [coarse narrow cloth]; of our fells they make Spanish skins, gloves, and girdles; of our tin, saltcellars, spoons, and dishes; of our broken linen, cloths and rags, paper both white and brown. What treasure think ye goes out of this realm for every of these things? And then for all together, it exceeds my estimation. There is no man can be contented now with any other gloves than is made in France or Spain; nor kersey, but it must be of Flanders dye; nor cloth, but French or frizado [napped woolen cloth]; nor owche, brooch, or aglet, but of Venice making or Milan; nor dagger, sword, knife, or girdle, but of Spanish making or some outward country; no not as much as a spur, but that is fetched at the milliners [vendors of fancy goods, or "Milanese" wares]. I have heard within these forty years when there were not of these haberdashers that sell French or Milan caps, glasses, knives, daggers, swords, girdles, and such things, not a dozen in all London. And now, from the town to Westminster along, every street is full of them; their shops glitters and shines of glasses, as well drinking as looking, yea, all manner vessel of the same stuff—painted cruses [pots], gay daggers, knives, swords, and girdles—that it is able to make any temperate man to gaze on them and to buy somewhat, though it serve to no purpose necessary. What need them beyond sea to travel to Peru or such far countries, or to try out the sands of the rivers of Tagus in Spain, Pactogus in Asia, and Ganges in India? . . . I think not so little as a hundred thousand pounds a year is fetched of our treasure for things of no value of themselves, but only for labors of the workers of the same, which are set awork all on our charges. What grossness of wits be we of that see it and suffer such a continual spoil to be made of our goods and treasure by such means. And specially, that will suffer our own commodities to go and set strangers awork and then to buy them again at their hands; as of our wool they make and dye kerseys, frizados, broadcloths, and caps beyond the sea and bring them hither to be sold again. Wherein, I pray you, note what they do: They make us pay at the end for our own stuff again, yea, for the strangers' custom, for their workmanship and colors, and lastly for the second custom in the return of the wares into the realm again. Whereas, by working the same within the realm, our own men should be set awork at the charges of strangers; the custom should be borne all by strangers to the Queen, and the clear gains remain within the realm (sigs. G1r–G2r).

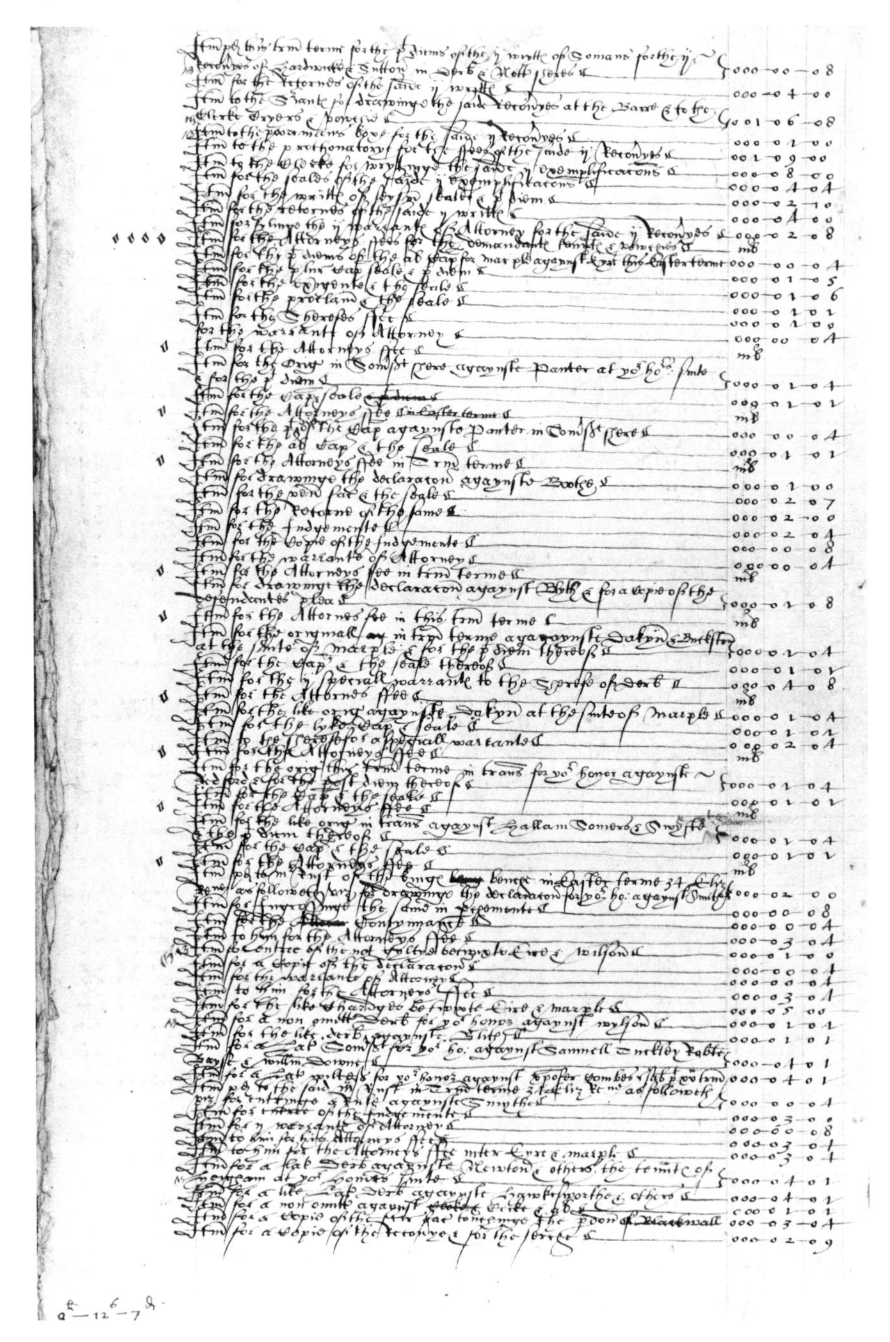

Household Accounts (1589–1592), kept for Elizabeth, Countess of Shrewsbury, by her steward Edward Whalley. Surviving account books like this one show how complicated was the process of provisioning the Elizabethan house.

HENRY PEACHAM

A Merry Discourse of Meum, and Tuum, or, Mine and Thine, Two Crosse Brothers, That Make Strife and Debate Wheresoever They Come; With their Descent, Parentage, and Late Progresse in Divers Parts of England (London, 1639)

❧ "Meum" and "Tuum"—mine and thine—represent the possessive instinct that is only intensified by possessions. This entertaining pamphlet purports to tell their life history from the time of their birth in the town of Wrangle. Along the way, we see all the arguments and conflicts they inspire, especially in courts of law.

This Harpax and his wife had only two sons [Meum and Tuum] who were twins born at one birth, who not a whit degenerating from their predecessors, for shortly after their birth they would seem to wrangle for the mother's breast. And, grown bigger, they would scratch and take hold one of another; then, after two or three years, fall out about milk, bread, and butter; and, grown great boys, at play about counters or points, insomuch as they never were without blue eyes or scratched faces. And so unhappy they were that no other children would keep them company; yea, they were charged so to do by their parents, if they meant to live in quiet and keep their estates when they were men. . . .

So calling his brother Meum from the baker's company, to set forward toward Cambridge, the clerk of [the town of] Qui desired Tuum to stay but a little, and knocking upon the table with the church-door key, called for a cap [a wooden bowl used as a drinking vessel] of Cambridge beer and drank to Tuum, craving his name; he told him.

"I am his brother," quoth Meum.

"In good time," quoth the clerk, "came you not out of the Land of Pronouns? and have you no relation to our town of Qui?"

"No," quoth Meum, "your town should rather have relation to us, for every grammar boy knows that Qui is a pronoun relative, and we are possessives."

"In good time," quoth the Suffolk man, "we have too few of you in our country" (when indeed they had too many). . . .

But to return to our new termers, Meum and Tuum: within a day or two they ordered the matter so that they gat acquaintance in all the [law] Courts of Westminster. And in no long time, by observation and practice, they grew so expert that they were still at one end of every cause that was pleaded. Not a counselor nor attorney belonging either to the King's Bench, Common Pleas, or any other Court, but grew acquainted with them. And many times in friendly manner would salute them with, "Good morrow, Master Meum"; "Save you, Master Tuum"; "I pray, let me see you at my chamber: I have been (and so have we all) much beholding unto you for your acquaintance and furtherance; we many times fare the better for you. . . ."

Being come at last down into their native country among the fens, which seemed to be in controversy between the projectors [speculators] and the country, they found all things appeased and quiet, all parties were agreed, and nothing remained for Meum and Tuum to work upon. Whereupon they resolved to go farther northward. But even at this time, they hearing of old Harpax their father's death, back they returned to Wrangle, where I hear they are now in suit, at strife, for his land and goods, Meum affirming himself to be the elder brother, Tuum saith he is as old as he, for they be twins. Which is like to prevail we shall know at this next term, when they return up to London. In the meantime I leave them wrangling at their native town of Wrangle, where I first found them (sigs. B1^{v}, C2^{v}, D2^{r}, F2^{v}).

Pasquils Jestes, Mixed with Mother Bunches Merriments. . . Very Prettie and Pleasant, to Drive Away the Tediousness of a Winters Evening (London, 1609)

❧ Like most of the humorous tales in jestbooks, this one has an angry edge. Just because the elderly father has ceded his political right to head a household, just because he has voided his economic responsibility to manage his goods, and just because he has been foolishly trusting of his only son doesn't mean he deserves what he gets. The other moral to this story, the grandson's moral, is that what goes around, comes around. Again, the story offers a sense of vicarious vindication to those who found old family and friendly relations disrupted by the new preoccupation with possessions.

Of the old man of Monmouth, that gave his son all his goods in his life time

In Monmouth dwelt an ancient man of fair possessions and great lands, having but one son to enjoy all his substance. His son being married, he gave him all that he had, and so would live free from all worldly matters in his old age with his son in his own house. After the deed of gift was made, a while the old man sat at the upper end of the table. Afterward they set him lower about the middle of the table: next, at the table's end; and then among the servants. And last of all, they made him a couch behind the door, and covered him with old sackcloth, where, with grief and sorrow, the old man died.

When the old man was buried, the young man's eldest child said unto him: "I pray you, father, give me this old sackcloth."

"What wouldst thou do with it?" said his father.

"Forsooth," said the boy, "it shall serve to cover you, as it did my old grandfather" (sig. E2v).

Court Cupboard (English, c. 1590–1600), oak, with two drawers. Such pieces were intended for the display of plate and other prized dining ware. Collection of George Way, New York City.

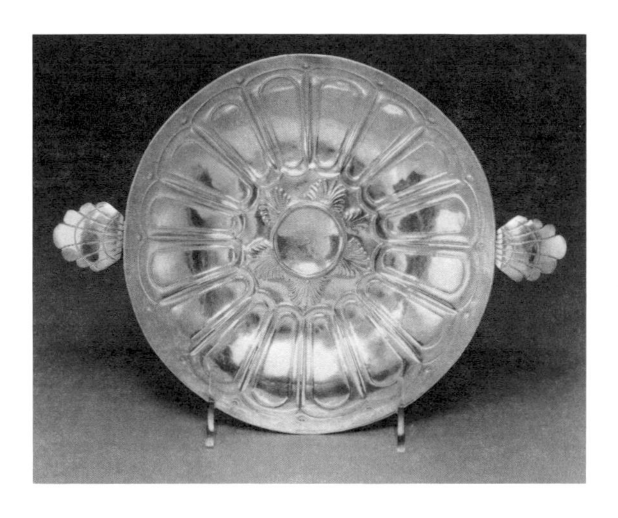

Silver Dish with Two Shell Handles (London, 1637), 10¼ inches in diameter. The maker has been identified as Thomas Maundy. Agecroft Association.

Silver Salt (possibly Dutch, c. 1600–1650). Collection of George Way, New York City.

Four-Handled Earthenware Tyg (Wrotham, 1631). The stamped initials suggest that the potter may have been John Livermore or his apprentice Nicholas Hubble. The Colonial Williamsburg Foundation.

Tigerware Malling Jug (English, 1577–1578), 9½ inches high, with silver gilt mounts. The Metropolitan Museum of Art. Gift of J. Pierpont Morgan, 1917 (17.190.308).

Cup (English, c. 1580). With trade in the Americas and the West Indies, there was a fad for cups made of coconuts, ostrich eggs, and other exotic imports. This nut has been mounted in silver gilt. The Metropolitan Museum of Art. Bequest of Irwin Untermyer, 1973 (1974.28.172).

Silver Wine Cup (English, 1618–1619). The Metropolitan Museum of Art. Gift of Irwin Untermyer, 1970 (1970.131.40).

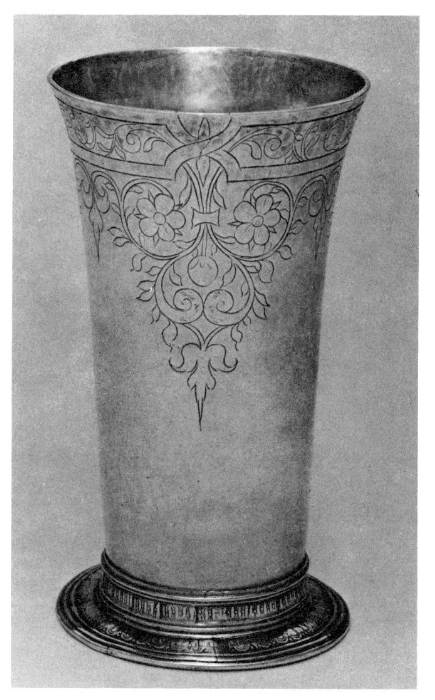

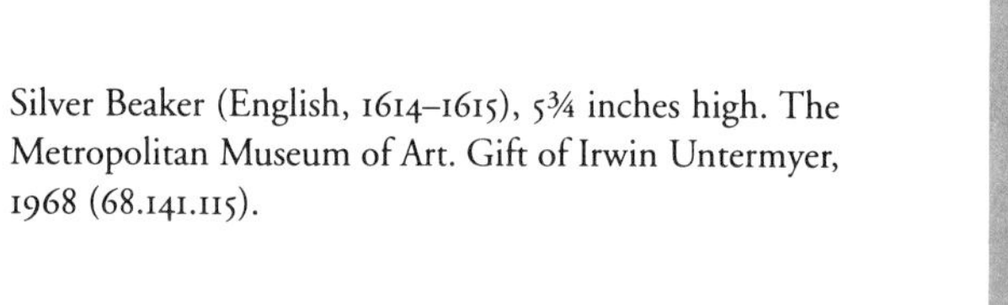

Silver Beaker (English, 1614–1615), 5¾ inches high. The Metropolitan Museum of Art. Gift of Irwin Untermyer, 1968 (68.141.115).

The Kitchen ❧

JOHN MURRELL

Murrels Two Books of Cookerie and Carving (London, 1638)

❧ The size of this modest little pocket book misrepresents its ambitious scope. John Murrell first published a cookery book in 1615 and then, over the course of several editions, enlarged it to a volume including individual recipes; a menu for a great feast with multiple courses and fifty dishes; directions for baking, boiling, and carving various meats; and the instructions for service excerpted below. He describes a complicated etiquette for table linens, bread, and salt, and along the way he also provides a glimpse of the supplies required in the various offices of a great household. The kitchen was only one of the rooms dedicated to the production of food. There were also the buttery, for storing liquids; the pantry, for bread, grains, and other dry provisions; the cellar, which could be located either above or under ground; and the ewery, for ewers of water, table linens, and towels.

The Office of the Butler and Pantler, Yeomen of the Cellar, and Ewery

Ye must have three pantry knives: one knife to square trencher-loaves [stale bread used instead of a plate], another to be a chipper [to slice or break bread into pieces], the third shall be sharp for to make smooth trenchers. Then chip your sovereign's bread hot. And all other bread let it be a day old; household bread, three days old; trencher-bread, four days old. Then look your salt be white and dry, the powder made of ivory two inches broad and three inches long. And look that your saltcellar lid touch not the salt. Then look your tablecloths, towels, and napkins be fair folded in a chest or hanged upon a perch [peg]. . . .

And when ye lay the cloth: wipe the board clean with a cloth, then lay a cloth (a couch it is called). Take your fellow the one end and hold you the other end. Then draw the cloth straight, the bought [fold] on the outer edge. Take the outer parts and hand it even. Then take the third cloth and lay the bought on the inner edge, and lay estate [make a fold opposite the head seat, in token of respect] with the upper part half a foot broad. Then cover the cupboard and thine ewery with the towel of diaper [diamond-patterned linen]. Then take thy towel about thy neck, and lay the one side of the towel upon the left arm, and thereon lay your sovereign's napkin. And lay on thine arm seven loaves of bread, with three or four trencher loaves, with the end of the towel in the left hand, as the manner is. Then take thy saltcellar in thy left hand, and take the end of the towel in your right hand to bear in spoons and knives. Then set your salt on the right side where your sovereign shall sit, and on the left side your salt. Set your trenchers, then lay your knives, and set your bread one loaf by anothers, and your spoons, and your napkin fair folded beside your bread. Then cover your bread and trenchers, spoons and knives, and at every end of the table set a saltcellar, with two trencher loaves. . . . Also see thine ewery be arrayed with basins and ewers, and water hot and cold. And see ye have napkins, cups, spoons; and see your pots for wine and ale be made clean, and to the surnap [towel for washing hands at table] make the courtesy [gesture of respect] with a cloth under a fair double napery. . . . And when your sovereign hath washed, draw the surnap even, then bear the surnap to the middest of the board. And take it up before your sovereign and bear it into the ewery again. And when your sovereign is set, look your towel be about your neck. Then make your sovereign courtesy. Then uncover your bread and lay it by the salt, and lay your napkin, knife, and spoon afore him. Then kneel on your knee till the portpain [cloth to serve bread without touching it with hands] pass eight loaves. And look ye set at the ends of the table four loaves at a mess. And see that every person have a napkin and a spoon. And wait well to the Sewer [in charge of seating and serving] how many dishes be covered, and so many cups cover ye. Then serve ye forth the table mannerly, that every man may speak of your courtesy (sigs. K7^{v}, L1^{r}–L2^{v}).

Livery Cupboard (English, 1600–1625), oak. Such a cupboard would contain a day's livery, or food rations. Collection of George Way, New York City.

The History of Frier Rush: How Hee Came to a House of Religion to Seeke Service, and Being Entertained by the Priour, Was First Made Under Cooke. Being Full of Pleasant Mirth and Delight for Young People (London, 1659)

❧ Permission to print this volume dates back to 1568–1569, though it bears the signs of being a much older story. It was evidently popular enough that it was reprinted in the 1620s (from which the earliest copies survive) and in this late issue of 1659. Although the history of Friar Rush takes place in an unnamed monastery, it obviously struck a familiar chord with those accustomed to the kitchen hierarchies of secular households, as well. Had authority in each sphere not been so clearly ranked, Englishmen would not have taken so much delight in lords of misrule like Friar Rush.

How Friar Rush threw the Master Cook into a kettle of water seething on the fire, wherein he died

It befell upon a day that Rush went forth to sport him, and it was very late before he came home again, and the Master Cook was very angry with him that he was so long absent. And as soon as Rush was entered into the kitchen, the Cook began to chide, and said unto him, "Thou whoreson knave, where hast thou been so long?" And with a great staff he laid upon Rush, and beat him sore. And when Rush saw that the Cook was angry, and so far out of reason, and that he had beaten him sore, anon he began to wax very angry with the Master Cook, and said unto him: "Thou whoreson villain, why hast thou beaten me thus? I will be revenged on thee." And suddenly he caught him in his arms, and threw him into a great kettle which was full of water seething upon the fire, and said, "Lie thou there in the Devil's name, for now thou shalt neither fight nor chide no more with me," and so Rush slew the Master Cook. Then when he had so done, he departed out of the kitchen and went to the next town to fetch the fair woman again for his master. And in his absence certain of the friars came into the kitchen to speak with Rush, but they found nobody stirring therein. And some of them went to stand by the fire's side, to tarry till Rush came in, for they thought he would not tarry long. And as they stood talking together by the fire's side they spied a man in the kettle seething upon the fire. And anon they perceived that it was the Master Cook, whereof they were greatly abashed. And with that, crying out, they went unto the Prior and showed him that the Master Cook had drowned himself in a kettle seething upon the fire in the kitchen, for which tidings the Prior was right sorry. And in the mean season Rush came home and had conveyed the woman into his master's chamber. And anon the Friars showed Rush of the great misfortune that was fallen on the Master Cook in the kitchen, and he made as he had been sorry therefore, and had known nothing therof. And he was in such great love and favor with the Prior and all the friars, that they mistrusted him nothing for that deed. And so there was no more mention of the Master Cook. Then the Prior commanded that Rush should be made Cook, and all the convent was right glad of that. And so he was himself also, for he thought his enterprises came well to pass after his mind and as he would have it. Thus Rush became Master Cook in the kitchen and dressed their meat marvelously well: for in the Lent, and in the Advent, both Fridays, and all other days, he put bacon into their pottage pot, which made the pottage to savor very well. And he dressed their meat so deliciously that the Prior and all the friars had great marvel that he did it so well. In so much that they said he did much better than their other Master Cook did, and that he was a more cunninger man in his occupation and could do much better in his office (sigs. $A4^v$–$B1^v$).

The Assise of Bread . . . Together with Sundrie Good and Needfull Ordinances for Bakers, Brewers, Inholders, Victuailers, Vintners, and Butchers (London, 1600)

❧ As bread was generally not produced in the individual household, its purchase was part of the provisioning of the house. Bread baking was a "mystery," a craft with trade secrets passed along through apprenticeship. Its production was regulated, with minimum weights established at every price level. The regulations were also protectionist, designed to ensure that foreign bakers did not realize an unfair margin of profit. The practice of publishing these ordinances dates back to at least 1532.

First, that no manner of person or persons shall keep a common bakehouse in cities and corporate towns, but such persons as have been apprenticed unto the same mystery, or brought up therein for the more space of seven years, or else otherwise skillful in the good making and true sizing of all sorts of bread, and shall put his own proper mark and seal upon all sorts of his man's bread, which he or they shall make and sell as before is mentioned.

Item, that no baker or other persons do make, bake, utter [offer on the market], and sell, any kinds or sorts of bread in the commonwealth but such which the statutes and ancient ordinances of this realm do allow them to bake and sell. That is to say, they may bake and sell simnel bread [a bread of fine flour, boiled, then baked], wastel [a bread of the finest flour], white, wheaten, household [a brown bread for ordinary household use], and horsebreads [a bread made of beans and brans for horses], and none other kinds of bread to put to sale unto her Majesty's subjects.

Item, they must make and bake farthing [quar-

Hee that giueth measure / God blesseth with tresure — It makes a poore man, / To sell flower for bran. — Looke well to thy season / With cunning and reason. — Be iust with thy waights / God plagus false sleights

The price of the quarter of wheate.	The weight of the halfpeny white Lofe drawn from the fine Cocket. An. 51. H. 3	The weight of the penye white Loafe drawne frō the fine Cocket. An. 51. H. 3.	The weight of the halfpeny white Lofe drawne frō the corse Cocket. An. 51. H. 3,
xlix.s.	iij.ʒ.q.ij.d.ob.	vi.ʒ.iij.q.	iij.ʒ.q.iiij.d
xlix.s.vj.d.	iij.ʒ.q.ij.d.	vj.ʒ.di.iiij.d.	iij.ʒ.q.iij.d.
l.s.	iij.ʒ.q.j.d.	vj.ʒ.di.ij.d.	iij.ʒ.ij.d.ob.
l.s.vj.d	iij.ʒ.q.	vj.ʒ.di.	iij.ʒ.q.ij.d.
li.s.	iij.ʒ.iiij.d.ob.	vj.ʒ.q.iiij.d.	iij.ʒ.q.j.d.
li.s.vj d	iij.ʒ.iiij.d.	vi.ʒ.q.iij.d.	iij.ʒ.q.ob.
lij.s.	iij.ʒ.iij.d.ob.	vj.ʒ.q.j.d.	iij.ʒ.q.
lij.s.vj.d.	iij.ʒ.iij.d.	vj.ʒ.q.j.d.	iij.ʒ.iiij.d.
liij.s.	iij.ʒ.ij.d.	vj.ʒ.iiij.d.	iij.ʒ.iij.d.ob
liij.s.vj.d.	iij.ʒ.j.d.ob.	vi.ʒ.iij.d	iij.ʒ.q.iij.d.
liiij.s.	iij.ʒ.i.d.	vi.ʒ.ij.d.	iij.ʒ.ij.d.ob.
liiij.s.vj.d.	iij.ʒ.ob.	vi.ʒ.i.d.	iij.ʒ.ij.d.
lv.s.	iij.ʒ.	vj.ʒ.	iij.ʒ.j.d.ob.
lv.s.vj.d.	ij.ʒ.iij.q.iiij.d.ob.	v.ʒ.iij.q.iiij.d.	iij.ʒ.ob.
lvj.s.	ij.ʒ.iij.q.iiij.d.	v.ʒ.iij.q.iij.d.	iij.ʒ.
lvi.s.vi.d.	ij.ʒ.iij.q.iij.d.ob.	v.ʒ.iij.q.ij.d.	ij.ʒ.iij.q.iiij.d.

God blesseth true labour / With plentie and fauour. — Be still quicke and kinde / Reward thou shalt finde — Pitche not at thy plesure / But in treu honest mesure — Be watchful and wise / In goodnes to rise.

The weight of the peny white Lofe according to the corse Cocket. An. 51. H. 3.	The weight of the halfe peny wheaton Lofe drawne frō the corse coket. A. 51. H. 3	The weight of the peny wheaton Lofe drawne frō the corse Cocket An. 51. H. 3.	The weight of the peny houshold Lofe drawne frō the corse Cocket. An. 51. H. 3
vj ʒ.iij.q.iij.d.	v.ʒ.iij.d.ob.	x.ʒ.q.ij.d.	xiij.ʒ.iij.q.j.d.
vj.ʒ.iij.q.j.d.	v.ʒ.j.d.	x.ʒ.ij.d.	xiij.ʒ.di.ij.d.
vj.ʒ iij.q.	v.ʒ.j.d.	x.ʒ.ij.d.	xiij.ʒ.di.
vj ʒ.di.iiij d.	v.ʒ.	x.ʒ.	xiij.ʒ.q.ij.d.
vj.ʒ.di ij.d.	iiij.ʒ.iij.q.iiij.d.	ix.ʒ.iij.q.iij.d.	xiij.ʒ.iiij.d.
vj.ʒ.di.j.d.	iiij.ʒ.iij.q.iij.d.	ix.ʒ.iij.q.j.d.	xiij.ʒ.ij.d.
vj.ʒ.di.	iiij.ʒ.iij.q..ij.d.	ix.ʒ.di.iiij.d.	xiij.ʒ.
vj.ʒ.q.iij.d.	iiij.ʒ.iij.q.j.d.	ix.ʒ.di.ij.d.	xij.ʒ.iij.q.j.d.
vj ʒ.q.ij.d.	iiij.ʒ.iij.q.	ix.ʒ.di.	xij.ʒ.di.iiij.d.
vj.ʒ.q.j.d.	iiij.ʒ.di.iiij.d.ob.	ix.ʒ.q.iiij.d.	xij.ʒ.di.ij.d.
vj.ʒ.q.	iiij.ʒ.di.iij.d.	ix.ʒ.q.i.d.	xij.ʒ.di.
vj.ʒ iiij d.	iiij.ʒ.di.ij.d.	ix.ʒ.q.j.d.	xij.ʒ.q.ij.d
vj.ʒ.iij.d.	iiij.ʒ.di.ij.d.	ix.ʒ.iiij.d.	xij.ʒ.q.i.d.
vj.ʒ.j.d.	iiij.ʒ.di.j.d.	ix.ʒ.ij.d	xij.ʒ.ij d.
vj.ʒ.	iiij.ʒ.di.	ix.ʒ.	xij.ʒ.
v.ʒ.iij.q.iij.d.	iiij.ʒ.q.iij.d.ob.	viij.ʒ.iij.q.ij.d.	xj.ʒ.iij.q.j.d.

Weight Regulations from *The Assise of Bread . . . Together with Sundrie Good and Needfull Ordinances for Bakers, Brewers, Inholders, Victuailers, and Butchers* (London, 1600).

ter-penny] white bread, half-penny white, penny white, half-penny wheaten, penny wheaten bread, penny household, and two-penny household loaves, and none of greater size, upon pain of forfeiture unto poor people all such great bread which they or any of them shall make to sell of greater size (the time of Christmas always excepted). . . .

Item, that no bakers or other person or persons shall at any time or times hereafter make, utter, or sell by retail, within or without their houses, unto any the Queen's subjects any spice cakes, buns, biscuits, or other spice breads (being bread out of size, and not by law allowed), except it be at burials or upon the Friday before Easter, or at Christmas: upon pain of forfeiture of all such spice breads to the poor.

Item, whereas there are in cities or corporate towns common bakers using the mystery of baking there, and within the same towns the foreign bakers which come into the market with their breads to be sold, [the foreign bakers] shall not only bring with them such kinds of sorts of sized breads as the law and ordinances do allow, to be made and sold as aforesaid, but also keep and observe this order in the weight of their breads, as hereafter followeth, because the said foreigners do not bear and pay, within the same cities or towns, such scot and lot [municipal tax] as the bakers of the same towns do.

First, the foreigners' half-penny white loaves shall weigh half-an-ounce more in every loaf than the bakers of the same town's half-penny white loaves do.

Item, their penny white loaves shall weigh one ounce more in every loaf than the bakers of the same town's penny white loaves do.

Item, their half-penny wheaten loaves shall weigh one ounce more in every loaf than the bakers of the same town's half-penny wheaten loaves do.

Item, their penny wheaten loaves shall weigh two ounces more in every loaf than the bakers of the same town's penny wheaten loaves do.

Item, their penny household loaves shall weigh two ounces more in every loaf than the bakers of the same town's penny household loaves do.

Item, their two-penny household loaves shall weigh four ounces more in every loaf than the bakers of the same town's two-penny household loaves do (sigs. G1r–G2r).

THOMAS MUN

A Discourse of Trade, from England unto the East-Indies, Answering to Diverse Objections which are usually Made against the Same (London, 1621)

Various anxieties were raised by the growing market in foreign goods. We get some sense of these concerns from Thomas Mun's defense of the trade of the East India Company, created by royal charter in 1600. The extract that follows is a pastiche designed to communicate the arguments as completely as possible. Mun rehearses the objections to trade throughout the text, and these objections are excerpted. He then answers them, point-for-point and at considerable length. These summaries of his defense are from an abstract at the beginning of the volume. We have only to look at recipe books represented elsewhere to see how quickly and thoroughly eastern spices were incorporated into Elizabethan and Jacobean kitchens.

THE FIRST OBJECTION:

It were a happy thing for Christendom (say many men) that the navigation to the East Indies by way of the Cape of Good Hope had never been found out. For in the fleets of ships, which are sent thither yearly out of England, Portugal, and the Low Countries, the gold, silver, and coin of Christendom, and particularly of this Kingdom, is exhausted to buy unnecessary wares.

[THE ANSWER:]

1. In the first part is showed the necessary use of drugs, spices, indigo, raw silk, and calicoes.

2. In the second part is declared the great sums of ready monies which are yearly saved to Christendom in general by fetching the wares of the East Indies directly in shipping from thence.

3. In the third part is proved that the trade from England to the East-Indies doth not consume, but rather greatly increase the general stock and treasury of this realm.

THE SECOND OBJECTION:

The timber, plank, and other materials for making of shipping is exceedingly wasted and made dearer by the building of so many great ships as are yearly sent to trade in the East Indies, and yet the state hath no use of any of them upon occasion. For

24 *A Discourse of Trade*

the Articles of agreement made with the *Dutche*, that they may not violate any of them to our hindrance or damage)all which wares in *England* will yeelde (as I doe conceaue) the prizes hereafter following, *Viz.*

In England.

	li.	s.	d.
2500000. li. of Pepper at 20. d. the pound.	208333	06	08
150000. of Cloues at 6. s. the pound.	45000	00	00
150000. of Nutmegs at 2. s. 6. d. the pound.	18750	00	00
50000. of Mace at 6. s. the pound.	15000	00	00
200000. of Indico at 5. s. the pound.	50000	00	00
107140. of China Raw-silkes at 20. s. the pound.	107140	00	00
50000. peeces of Callicoes of seuerall sorts, rated at 20. s. the peece one with another.	50000	00	00
	494223	06	08

How much the kingdomes stocke may increase yeerely by trading to the *East-Indies.*

So that here would be our owne money againe; and more, the somme of 394223. li. 06. s. 08. d. aduanced towards the generall stocke

The Import of Spices and Fabrics, from Thomas Mun, *A Discourse of Trade, from England unto the East-Indies* (London, 1621).

Spice Box (English, c. 1580), 2½ inches high. This exquisitely worked lidded box opens like a segmented orange. Each segment contains a different spice accessible from its own inner sliding panel. The beauty of the workmanship gives some sense of the value of spices. The Metropolitan Museum of Art. Gift of Irwin Untermyer, 1968 (68.141.321).

either they are not here, or else they come home very weak and unserviceable.

[THE ANSWER:]

1. In the first part is set forth the noble use of ships, and that the timber, plank, and other materials of this kingdom for the building of shipping are neither become scant nor dearer since the East India trade began.

2. In the second part is showed the great strength of shipping and warlike provisions, which the East India Company have always in readiness for the service of the kingdom.

THE THIRD OBJECTION:

The voyages to the East Indies do greatly consume our victuals and our mariners, leaving many poor widows and children unrelieved. Besides that, many ships are yearly sent forth to the East Indies, and few we see as yet returned. Also, this trade hath greatly decayed the traffic and shipping which were wont to be employed into the Straits. And yet the said trade to the East Indies is found very unprofitable to the adventurers. Neither doth the commonwealth find any benefit by the cheapness of spice and indigo, more than in times past.

[THE ANSWER:]

1. The East India Trade doth not make victuals dear, but is a means to increase our plenty.

2. It breedeth more mariners than it doth ordinarily consume, and disburdeneth the kingdom of very many lewd people.

3. It hath not destroyed any other trade or shipping of this realm, but hath increased both the one and the other, besides the great addition of itself unto the strength and traffic of this kingdom.

4. It doth not increase the number of the poor of this realm (as is erroneously supposed) but it doth maintain and relieve many hundreds of people by their employments and charity.

5. It doth save the kingdom yearly 75,000 pounds sterling or thereabouts, of that which it was accustomed to spend in spices and indigo only, when they were brought us from Turkey and Lisbon.

THE FOURTH OBJECTION:

It is generally observed that His Majesty's mint hath had but little employment ever sithence [since] the East India Trade began. Wherefore it is manifest that the only remedy for this, and so many evils besides, is to put down this trade. For what other remedy can there be for the good of the commonwealth?

[THE ANSWER:]

1. The East India Trade doth not hinder the employment of His Majesty's mint.

2. The proposition to put down the East India Trade is grounded upon idle and false reports, tending to the great hurt of the King and his people.

3. A brief narration of a kingdom's riches, with the four principal causes which may decay the general stock and treasure of this realm in particular (sigs. $A3^r$–$A4^v$, $B2^v$–$B3^r$, [$D3^r$], $E1^r$, $F3^v$).

SARAH LONGE

Mistress Sarah Longe her Receipt Booke (c. 1610)

❧ We don't think of kitchen recipes and medical treatments as inhabiting the same sphere of knowledge and household practice. In part, this is because medical procedures have moved out of the household; they have become professionalized. But in both manuscript and printed receipt [recipe] books from the Renaissance, the two kinds of instruction were intermingled, as in this example from facing pages in a book compiled by Sarah Longe. The volume is beautifully designed and carefully calligraphed. With Longe's directions for biscuits that King James reportedly liked, we find an early example of a celebrity recipe.

Another biscuit

Take 3 quarters of a pound of sugar; beat it fine; as much flour. Take a little handful of aniseeds and as much coriander seeds; beat them and search [searce, or sift] them fine. Take 7 eggs and leave out 2 of the whites. Put in 2 spoonfuls of rose water, mingle them together, and beat it an hour and half. When you put it into the oven, cast fine sugar over the top of it.

To make another biscuit, whereof King James and his Queen have eaten with much liking

Take a pound and quarter of sugar and a pound of flour very finely bolted [sifted], and, after finely searched, you must beat the sugar very fine. And then search it through a fine lawn search, and mingle the flower and sugar together. Then take 12 eggs, whereof you must take but half the whites. First beat the eggs with 3 or 4 spoonfuls of rose water.

Then put the flour and sugar that are mingled together to the eggs. Then beat them one hour together. A little before you put them into your oven, put a few caraway seeds and aniseeds into it, and cut your plates before you put on the stuff. And the oven must be not hotter than for a tart.

To stop the bleeding of a wound

Take a piece of an old hat and burn it in the fire to a coal, then grind it to powder and straw [sprinkle] it into the wound.

A remedy for such as are subject to miscarry

Take a quart or 2 of strong ale and a pound of currents, an ounce of nutmegs, and prick them full of holes. And take pith of 2 oxen, and one handful of nip, and an handful of pimpernel, one handful of clary [a pot herb], and boil them together, 'til a pint be boiled away. Brush the currents and the pith of the oxen and put them in again, and boil it again, and then drink it morning and evening warmed (fols. 20 and 21).

Receipts from Sarah Longe, *Mistress Sarah Longe her Receipt Booke* (c. 1610).

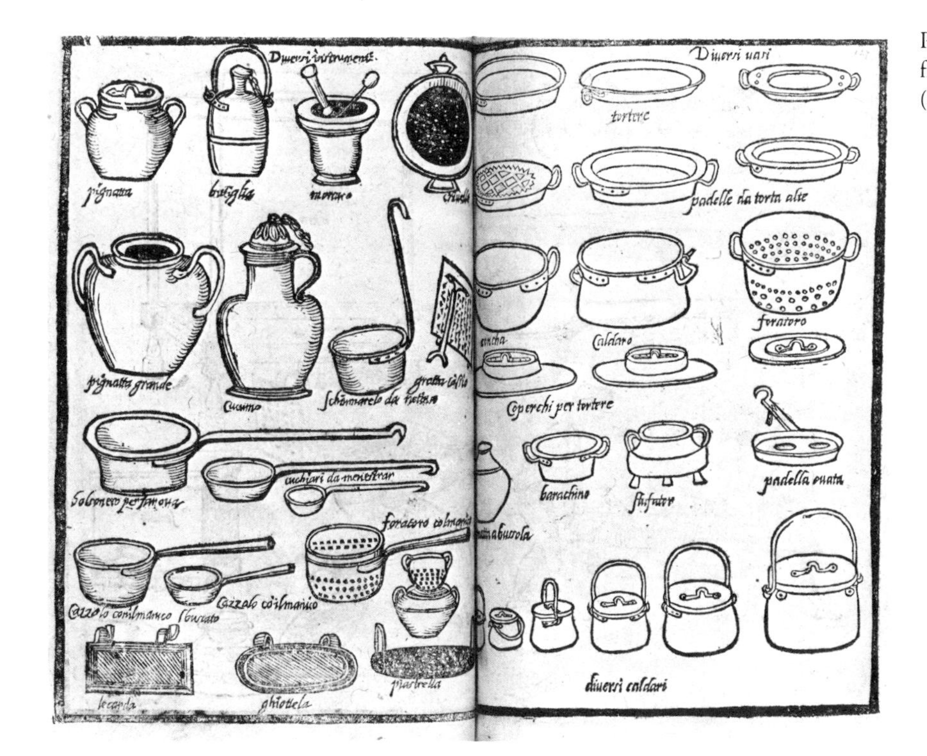

Pans and Kitchen Implements, from Bartolomeo Scappi, *Opera* (Venice, 1605).

"A True and Perfect Inventory of the Goodes & Chattles of Thomas Betts Late of the Parish of Aston in the Countie of Hartford Deceased Made and Appraised the Eleaventh Day of November in the Yeere One Thousand Six Hundred ffiftie Eight by John Hatton & John Williams as Followeth"

❧ The post mortem inventory of this householder shows how little furniture a man at the lower end of the social scale would own and how much of his worth would be represented in food stores, kitchen equipment, and bed linens. Values are in pounds (l.), shillings (s.), and pence (d.).

Inprimis, one cupboard, one table and frame, one joine[d] form [bench], three joine[d] stools, one joine[d] chair, one warming pan, two cushions, and two chairs ii.l. v.s.

In the little chamber

Item, one joined bedstead and two hutches and one box, one feather bed and one flock bed and two pillows and one bolster, two blankets and one coverlet & curtains v.l.

In the kitchen

Item, one powdering trough and one kneading trough, one small table, one chair & four kettles and one brass pot and one warming pan and other implements, and two skillets and a frying pan, one spit iii.l. vi.s. viii.d.

In the milk house

Item, one cupboard, one cheese press and milk vessels and three tubs, and one cannel [pipe, tube, or tap for a cask] and some other implements ii.l. v.s.

In the loft

Item, two boarded beds and three flockbeds with three bolsters and five pillows and five blankets and one coverlet, six coffers and one box and some other lumber v.l. iii.s. iiii.d.

In the buttery

Item, three small barrels, one lantern, and twelve pewter dishes and some other small implements ii.l. v.s.

Item, nine pair of sheets of towen [coarse flax or

hemp] and two pair of pillowbears and one dozen of napkins & two long table cloths & one pair of flaxen sheets iii.l. v.s.

In the shop

Item, six working tools and other implements l.l.

In the barn

Item, hay i.l. vi.s. iiii.d.

Item, one grindstone iii.s.

Item, wood in the yard and houses v.l.

Item, ladders in the yard v.s.

Item, one cow ii.l. x.s.

Item, his apparel and money xlv.l.

Sum total lxxviii.l. xiiii.s. iiii.d.

ROBERT PLOT

The Natural History of Staffordshire (Oxford, 1686)

❧ Local pride motivates Robert Plot to interrupt a "natural" history for this technical description of how to make a kitchen frying pan. As he explains, England has only two master manufacturers of frying pans, and one works in his county, Staffordshire.

The art of making frying pans may also be referr'd hither, the secret in great measure consisting in the regulating the heat that is given the plates whereof they are made, before they are brought to the anvil. Which together with other matters relating to the trade being found so difficult, that a novice many times is little the better though he serve a double apprenticeship to it; and so ingenious and indeed wonderful, that I thought it incredible, what I heard related of it. I shall not scruple to give the Reader the full process thereof. First, then, in order to them: there are flat round plates hammered out of bars at a forge for that purpose at the parish of Keel in this county . . . the forge little differing from those of other ironworks carrying a hammer of about 500 weight. In hammering of this flatwork they beat the plates first one by one, then two, three, or four together as they grow broader and thinner, which stick not together, having not a heat given them sufficient for that. Yet such an one they have, as will continue longer (the plates being forged many of them together) than if each plate had been forged single with a much higher heat, by which means the work is done not only with greater expedition, but profit too; the plates in this manner not only mutually preserving their heat, but keeping each other also from scaling or being beaten too much away into cinders or waste.

When the flat-work is thus finished at the forge at Keel, they are then brought to another forge at Newcastle-under-Lyme, where John Holland, who is master of both forges, works them into shape, nine frying pan-plates being commonly laid upon one another, and clasped together by turning up four labels which are ordinarily fixed to the lower plate, and so turned one within another like a nest of crucibles or boxes, the lowermost being always the biggest and the uppermost the least; the whole nine being turned nine times sooner than one single pan, for the nine together mutually preserve their heat so long that they are all turned during one heat, whereas one single pan will cool so fast that it will require at least nine heats before it can be forged, nor will it then be a good frying pan neither: for it will so scale away in the heating and forging, that it will at last be but a thin infirm pan. Now that which renders this art of making frying pans so difficult is not only the bringing them to a just heat, which shall hold a sufficient time and yet not make them liable to stick in the hammering, but the number of hammers used in this work, which are not less than twenty of several sorts, which so few know how to manage or are capable of learning, that there are but two master frying-pan makers (as I am credibly informed) in the whole kingdom: one here at Newcastle and another at Wansworth in

Surrey. They make also dripping pans at these forges, the plates being worked at the former and the pans turned at the latter: but these being forged singly and not in nests like the frying pans, there is not the same difficulty and consequently not the same ingenuity required in the fabricating of them (sigs. Tt4^{r-v}).

A Great-House Kitchen, from Bartolomeo Scappi, *Opera* (Venice, 1605).

The Housewife's Closet ❧

HENRY SMITH

A Preparative to Mariage (London, 1591)

❧ Henry Smith was the eldest son and heir of a wealthy man; his stepmother was a sister of William Cecil, Lord Burghley, Elizabeth's Lord Treasurer. At various points Smith's London preaching career was advanced through his excellent connections, and he dedicated his collection of sermons to Burghley. Ironically, Smith was unmarried when he wrote this highly popular address on marriage. The passages included below, though, do not represent original inspiration. They are so familiar in domestic literature as to seem proverbial, giving common justifications for why the housewife should be closeted at home.

We call the wife *housewife*, that is, house wife, not a street wife like Tamar, nor a field wife like Dinah, but a house wife, to show that a good wife keeps her house. And therefore Paul biddeth Titus to exhort women that they be chaste, and keeping at home. Presently after *chaste*, he saith, *keeping at home*, as though *home* were chastity's keeper. And therefore Solomon depainting the whore setteth her at the door, now sitting upon her stalls, now walking in the streets, now looking out of the windows, like curled Jezebel, as if she held forth the glass of temptation for vanity to gaze upon. But chastity careth to please but one, and therefore she keeps her closet, as though she were still at prayer. . . .

Phidias when he should paint a woman, painted her sitting under a snail's shell, signifying that she should go like a snail which carrieth his house upon his back. Solomon bade Shimei, "Go not beyond the river." So a wife should teach her feet, go not beyond the door. She must count the walls of her house like the banks of the river which Shimei might not pass, if he would please the King (sigs. F6^{r}–F7^{r}).

RICHARD BRATHWAIT

The English Gentlewoman (London, 1631)

❧ Like Smith, Brathwait believes that the housewife requires space for private contemplation—although he emphasizes how active such contemplation is or should be. While Smith coolly cites Biblical examples as if they are sufficient to argue his point, Brathwait's tactics are more emotional and intimidating. The advice to be always about some work, including needlework, is fairly standard.

You are taught to enter your chambers and be still. Still, and yet stirring still. Still from the clamors and turbulent insults of the world, still from the mutinous motions and innovations of the flesh, but never still from warring, wrestling, bickering, and embattling with the leader of those treacherous associates, tyrannous assassins. O, should you consider what troops of furious and implacable enemies are ever lying in ambuscado for you; how many soul-tempting sirens are warbling notes of ruin to delude you; what fears within you, what foes without you, what furies all about you—you would not suffer one grain of sand to drop through the cruet, without a dropping eye; not one minute pass undedicated to some good employment, to prevent the fury of such desperate assailants. Make then your chamber your private theater, wherein you may act some devout scene to God's honor. Be still from the world but stirring towards God. Meditation, let it be your companion. It is the perfume of the memory, the soul's rouser from sin's lethargy, the sweetest solace in straits of adversity. Let it be your key to open the morning, your lock to close the evening. . . . Task yourselves then privately, lest privacy become your enemy. As man's extremity is God's opportunity, so the devil's opportunity is man's security. Let not a minute be misspended, lest security become your attendant. Be it in the exercise of your needle or any other manual employment: temper that labor with some sweet meditation tending to God's honor. Choose rather with Penelope to weave and unweave than to give idleness the least leave: wanton wooers are time-wasters. They make you idolize yourselves, and consequently hazardize the state of your souls. Let not their lip-salve so anoint you as it make you forgetful of him that made you. Be you in your chambers or private closets; be you retired from the eyes of men; think how the eyes of God are on you. Do not say, the walls encompass me, darkness o'ershadows me, the curtain of night secures me: these be the words of an adultress. Therefore do nothing privately which you would not do publicly. There is no retire from the eyes of God (sigs. G4v–H1r).

GERVASE MARKHAM

The English Hus-wife, Contayning, the Inward and Outward Vertues which Ought To Be in a Compleat Woman (London, 1615)

❧ *The English Housewife* is the second part of a volume entitled *Countrey Contentments.* The first part, intended for a male audience, deals with horses, hunting, hawking, and the running of greyhounds. Following such introductions as those given below, the second part gives medical recipes and cooking instructions for a female readership.

To begin then with one of the most principal virtues which doth belong to our English housewife: you shall understand that since the preservation and care of the family, touching their health and soundness of body, consisteth most in her diligence, it is meet that she have a physical kind of knowledge, how to administer many wholesome receipts or medicines for the good of their healths, as well to prevent the first occasion of sickness as to take away the effects and evil of the same when it hath made seizure on the body. Indeed, we must confess that the depth and secrets of this most excellent art of physic is far beyond the capacity of the most skillful women, as lodging only in the breast of the learned professors. Yet that our housewife may from them receive some ordinary rules and medicines which may avail for the benefit of her family is (in our common experience) no derogation at all to that worthy science. Neither do I intend here to lead her mind with all the symptoms, accidents, and effects which go before or after every sickness, as though I would have her to assume the name of a practitioner, but only relate unto her some approved medicines and old doctrines which have been gathered together and delivered by common experience for the curing of those ordinary sicknesses which daily perturb the health of men and women. . . .

To speak then of the outward and active knowledges which belong to our English housewife: I hold the first and most principal to be a perfect skill and knowledge in cookery, together with all the secrets belonging to the same, because it is a duty really belonging to the woman. And she that is utterly ignorant therein may not by the laws of strict justice challenge the freedom of marriage, because indeed she can then but perform half her vow, for she may love and obey, but she cannot serve and keep him with that true duty which is ever expected.

To proceed then to this knowledge of cookery: you shall understand that the first step thereunto is to have knowledge of all sorts of herbs belonging to the kitchen, whether they be for the pot, for salads, for sauces, for servings, or for any other seasoning or adorning, which skill of knowledge of the herbs, she must get by her own labor and experience, and not by my relation, which would be much too tedious. And for the use of them she shall see it in the composition of dishes and meats hereafter following. She shall also know the time of the year, month and moon, in which all herbs are to be sown, and when they are in their best flourishing, that gathering all herbs in their height of goodness, she may have the prime use of the same. And because I will enable and not burden her memory, I will here give her a short epitome of all that knowledge (sigs. R2v–R3r, X2v–X3r).

MARY BAUMFYLDE

Receipt Book (1626)

❧ Manuscript compilations like this one were passed down from housewife to housewife, and this example bears some of the tokens of its long collective history. Mary Baumfylde apparently inaugurated the volume in the 1620s, but it is also signed by Katherine Foster in 1707 and Katherine Thatcher in 1712. Each of them contributed more receipts. The Baumfylde entry excerpted below, elsewhere attributed to Doctor Stevens rather than to Doctor Chambers, was extremely popular. With slight variations, it was also included in printed texts represented elsewhere in this anthology, including those assembled by Gervase Markham, John Murrell, and John Partridge.

A sovereign water of Doctor Chambers, physician, which he long time used and did many cures, and kept it secret till a little before he died. And then the Bishop of Canterbury gat it of him in writing

Rx. a gallon of Gascon wine [wine from southwestern France]. Then take ginger, galingale [an East Indian root], cinnamon, nutmegs, grains [capsules of Amonum Moleguetta, similar to cardamom], cloves, mace, aniseeds, fennel seeds, and caraway seeds, of each of these a dram. Then take sage, red mints, rose leaves, thyme, pellitory of Spain [a pungent root], rosemary, wild thyme, chamomile, lavender, of each of these a handful. Then beat the spices small, and also the herbs, and put all into the wine and let it stand xii hours, stirring it divers times. Then still it in a limbeck [used in distillation], and keep the first water by itself, for it is the best. Keep also the second, for it is very good.

The virtues of the same: It comforteth the vital spirits and helpeth inward diseases that cometh of cold, and against shaking of the palsy. It helpeth the conception of women that be barren. It killeth the worms in the body. It helpeth the stone in the bladder. It comforteth the stomach. It cureth the cold cough. It helpeth the tooth ache. It cureth the cold dropsies. It helpeth the diseases of the reins [kidneys]. It helpeth shortly a stinking breath. And whosoever useth this water sometime and not often, it preserveth him in good health and shall make him to seem young very long. It comforteth nature marvelously. With this water Doctor Chambers preserved his life till extreme age would suffer him neither to go nor stand anywhile, and he continued for five years when all the physicians judged he would not have lived. And he confessed when he was sick at any time he never used any other medicine but only this water. And if it stand in the sun all the summer it will be the better. Finis (fols. 14–16).

A Closet for Ladies and Gentlewomen, Or, The Art of Preserving, Conserving, and Candying. With the Manner How to Make Divers Kinds of Sirups, and all Kind of Banquetting Stuffes. Also Divers Soveraigne Medicines and Salves for Sundry Diseases (London, 1635)

❧ There was such a long manuscript history of recipes that, when collections such as this one appeared in print, they had a rich tradition to draw upon. It was not uncommon for these books to include more than one treatment for any single disease or condition without evaluating their comparative efficacy. This collection includes many treatments for worms, excerpted below. First published in 1608, the *Closet* went into ten editions.

For the worms

Take mare's milk and drink it as hot as you can have it from the mare, in the morning, fasting.

To know whether a child hath the worms or no

Take a piece of white leather and peck it full of holes with your knife, and rub it with wormwood, and spread honey on it, and strew the powder of Alesackatrina, and lay it on the child's navel when he goeth to bed. And if he have the worms, the plaster will stick fast; and if he have them not, it will fall off.

Two remedies very good against worms in little children

Take flour of wheat well bolted, as much as will lie upon three crowns of gold. Put it in a glass, and pour into it well-water so much as will steep the said flour, and make it look as it were milk, and no thinner. Then give the child drink of it, and you shall see with his excrements the worms come forth dead, which is a very good remedy.

The second remedy against worms

For children that be so little that the medicine cannot be ministered at the mouth, you must take very good aqua vita, wherewith you must wash or wet the stomach or breast of the child. Then pour it upon the said place with the powder of fine myrrh, and lay the child down a little while with his breast upward. And you shall see incontinently the worms, with the child's dung, come forth dead.

To heal children of the lunatic disease, which happeneth unto them by reason of a worm with two heads that breedeth in their bodies, the which worm, coming to the heart, causeth such a passion in the child that oft times it kills them

Take the tender stalks of a wilding-tree and dry them in the shadow, then stamp them well, and sift them. And take of the said powder and roots of gentian and of long peony, of each of them a quarter of an ounce, and a quarter of an ounce of myrrh. All these well beaten to powder you must put in a dish or some other vessel, and moist them with a little water. Then take of it with your two fingers and wet the lips and mouth of the child. Do this three or four times, and you shall see the worm come forth dead with the excrements (sigs. D5^{r}, G1^{v}–G2^{v}).

Ointment Pot (Antwerp?, c. 1560–1600), white tin glaze decorated in blue and manganese, 2¾ inches high. It is also possible that this pot was made at one of the newly formed delft manufactories in England. The Colonial Williamsburg Foundation.

English Woman with a Pomander, from Jost Amman, *Gynaeceum, sive, Theatrum Mulierum* (Frankfurt, 1586).

JOHN PARTRIDGE

The Treasurie of Hidden Secrets, Commonlie Called, The Good-Huswives Closet of Provision, for the Health of her Houshold. Gathered out of Sundry Experiments, Lately Practised by Men of Great Knowledge: And Now Newly Enlarged, with Divers Necessary Phisicke Helpes, and Knowledge of the Names and Naturall Disposition of Diseases, that Most Commonly Happen to Men and Women. Not Impertinent for Every Good Huswife to Use in her House, amongst her Owne Familie (London, 1600)

❧ When this collection first appeared in 1573 it bore the title *The Treasury of Commodious Conceits and Hidden Secrets, and May Be Called the Housewife's Closet of Healthful Provision.* In a verse epistle to "good houswives," the printer mentions that the book sold for four pence. The volume went through at least thirteen editions, although some have evidently been lost. Along the way, it picked up this change of title. In addition to medical and cookery recipes, Partridge included these aromatic preparations.

To make a pomander

Take benjamin [gum benzoin] one ounce, of storar calamite [a fossil plant] half an ounce, of laudanum the eight[h] part of an ounce. Beat them to powder and then put them into a brazen [brass] ladle with a little damask [water] or rose water. Set them over the fire of coals till they be dissolved and be soft like wax. Then take them out and chafe them between your hands as ye do wax. Then have these powders ready finely searched [sifted]: of cinnamon, of cloves, of sweet sanders [sandalwood], gray or white, of each of these three powders half a quarter of an ounce. Mix these powders with the other and chafe them well together. If they be too dry, moisten them with some of the rose water left in the ladle, or other. If they wax cold, warm them upon a knife's point over a chafing dish of coals. Then take of ambergris [an odiferous waxlike substance from the intestines of whales], of musk, and civet [a musk-like substance from the glands of civets], of each three grains. Dissolve the ambergris in a silver spoon over hot coals. When it is cold make it small, put to it your musk and civet. Then take your pome that you have chafed and gathered together, and by little and little (with some sweet water if need be) gather up the amber, musk, and civet, and mix them with your ball, till they be perfectly incorporated. Then make one ball or two of the lump, as ye shall think good, for the weight of the whole is about two ounces. Make a hole in your ball, and so hang it by a lace.

If you perceive that the ball is not tough enough, but too brittle, then take a courtesy [a moderate quantity] of storax liquida [balsam of the resinous styrax tree], and therewith temper your ball against the fire. But take not too much storax liquida, because it is too strong. Or the better way is to have some gum, called dragagant, ready dissolved in sweet water (it will be dissolved in two days). And with that gather your ball with the heat of the fire. This ball will be of like goodness within as without, and of great price.

Some men put in the making hereof three or four drops of oil of spike [corn oil]. Beware of too much because it is very strong.

When you will have your ball exceed in sweetness, break it and have two or three grains of musk, or civet, or ambergris, as you delight in, or altogether. Dissolve them in rose or damask water, and with the same chafe your ball over the fire, till it be drunken in. Then pierce a new hole, as before.

A fumigation for press and cloths, that no moth shall breed therein

Take of the wood of cypress, or of juniper, of rosemary dried, of storar calamite, of benjamin, of cloves, a like weight, beaten into fine powder. Then take of the powder of wormwood leaves dried, as much as all the others; mix them well together. Cast thereof upon a chafingdish of coals, and set in your press, and shut it close. And thus do oft-times, till you have well seasoned your press or coffer.

A perfume for a chamber

Take rosemary, sweet marjoram, bay leaves, of each a handful; a pennyworth of cloves; vinegar and rose water, a sufficient quantity. Boil these in your perfuming pot, which smell is sweet and wholesome.

An odiferous sweet ball against the plague

Take storar, laudanum, of each a dram; cloves, half a dram; camphor, half a scruple [half of a one-twenty-fourth ounce measure], spikenard [an aromatic Eastern plant], a scruple; nutmegs, a dram. Of all these make a paste with rose water, tempered with gum dragagant and gum arabic, stirring and bruising them well. Of this paste make your balls, and warm them (sigs. C3^{v}–D1^{r}).

Two Silver Pomanders from the Folger collection.

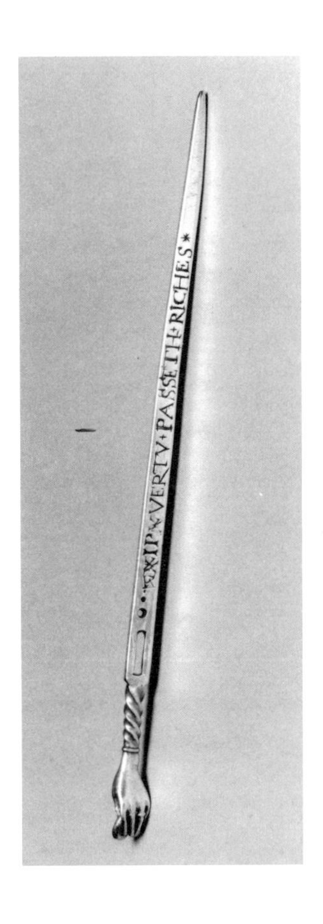

Silver Bodkin (English, c. 1620). Bodkins were used for punching holes in cloth. This one has been ornamented with the epigram "Virtue Passeth Riches" and with the initials of its owners. It ends with a spiral twist and a hand holding a heart. Agecroft Association.

Ointment Pot (London, c. 1600–1640), white tin glaze decorated in blue, 1½ inches high. The Colonial Williamsburg Foundation.

Salve pot (English, 1575–1600), of silver, 1⅝ inches high. The Metropolitan Museum of Art. Gift of Irwin Untermyer, 1970 (1970.131.3ab).

Lace Pattern, from Cesare Vecellio, *Corona delle Nobili et Virtuose Donne* (Venice, 1601).

The Bedchamber ❧

WILLIAM WHATELY

A Bride-Bush, Or A Wedding Sermon (London, 1617)

❧ In this passage, William Whately defends the sanctity of the marriage bed and reviews pollution laws that are familiar from Leviticus. Elsewhere in *A Bride-Bush,* he argues that "the sin of adultery or willful desertion dissolveth the bond and annihilateth the covenant of matrimony." Called before a high commission of the church, he was forced to retract his heretical defense of divorce. The retraction was confirmed in the second (1623) edition of this sermon and again in *A Care-Cloth.*

I come now to such as concern the marriage bed. . . . Their matrimonial meetings must have these three properties. First, it must be cheerful. They must lovingly, willingly, and familiarly communicate themselves unto themselves, which is the best means to continue and nourish their mutual natural love, and by which the true and proper ends of matrimony shall be attained in best manner: for the husband is not his own but the wife's, and the wife the husband's. Secondly, their meeting must be sanctified. Paul saith meat, drink, and marriage are good, being sanctified by prayer. Men and women must not come together as brute creatures and unreasonable beasts, through the heat of desire, but must see their Maker in that his ordinance, and crave his blessing solemnly as at meals (the Apostle speaks of both alike) that marriage may indeed be blessed unto them. To sanctify the marriage bed and use it reverently with prayer and thanksgiving, will make it moderate and keep them from growing weary each of other (as in many it falls out) and cause that lust shall be assuaged, which else shall be increased by these meetings. Propagation and chastity, the two chief ends of marriage, are best attained by prayer and thanksgiving in the use thereof, without which they will hardly come, or not with comfort. Neither is it more than needs, to see God in that which so nearly toucheth ourselves as the hope of posterity: him, as the increase of his kingdom. Let Christians therefore know the fruit of prayer even in all things. Thirdly, their nuptial meetings must be seasonable and at lawful times. There is a season when God and Nature sejoins [disjoins] man and wife in this respect. The woman is made to be fruitful, and therefore also more moist and cold of constitution. Hence it is that their natural heat serves not to turn all their sustenance into their own nourishment, but a quantity redounding is set apart in a convenient place to cherish and nourish the conception, when they shall conceive. Now this redundant humor (called their flowers or terms) [menstrual blood] hath (if no conception be) it[s] monthly issue or evacuation (and in some oftener), unless there be extraordinary stoppings and obstructions, lasting for six or seven days in the most. Sometimes also this issue, through weakness and infirmity of nature, doth continue many more days. Always after childbirth there is a larger and longer emptying because of the former retention, which continueth commonly for four, five, or six weeks, and in some longer. Now in all these three times and occasions, it is simply unlawful for a man to company with his own wife. . . . Neither let women think themselves disgraced, because I have laid this matter open in plain but modest speeches. Where God threatens death to the offender, can the Minister be faithful if he do not plainly declare the offense? (sigs. F4^{r-v}).

A Bedchamber, from *The Life and Death of Mr. Edmund Geninges, Priest* (S. Omers, 1614). This bedchamber is represented as a female space, with one wife holding a swaddled infant before the fire and another straightening the bed linens.

Lace Band (Italian, mid-sixteenth century), worked in needlepoint retecello, about 8½ inches wide and over 6 feet long. The band is fantastically detailed, with small couples, castles, and crabs. The Philadelphia Museum of Art.

EDMUND TILNEY

A Briefe and Pleasant Discourse of Duties in Mariage, Called the Flower of Friendship (London, 1587)

❧ Modeled after Castiglione's *The Courtier*, *The Flower of Friendship* (first published in 1568) purportedly records a series of conversations at the country house of one Lady Julia. In this extract, Master Pedro di Luxan tells a story that is familiar from other such works, like Marguerite de Navarre's *Heptameron*. The wife he describes is a variation on the type known as the "patient Griselda" because she accepts husbandly insults with forbearance. (The Lady Aloisa, in Pedro's audience, would not be so tolerant.) The story emphasizes the bedchamber as a symbolic site of negotiation for married couples. Pedro concludes that their bed is the "place appointed for reconcilements and renewing of love and friendship." There, the wife "may lawfully pour out into his bosom all the thoughts and secrets of her loving heart"—and may deliver "curtain" lectures.

"There was," quoth he, "a gentleman of good calling that greatly delighted in hunting, who, on a day, near to a little village, encountered with a poor widow's daughter, a simple wench but somewhat snout fair [fair-faced], whose gay eyes had so entrapped this jolly hunter that under the color thereof he oftentimes resorted unto her, and lay divers nights out of his own house. When his wife, being both fair, wise, and virtuous, understood thereof, as well by his demeanor as by other conjectures, like a wise woman she dissembled the matter and kept it secret to herself, not altering either countenance or conditions towards him, but on a time, when she was assured that he was gone another way, hied her to the house where she learned of the young woman the whole circumstance, feigning herself to be his sister. And when she had viewed the chambers and bedding wherein he lay, which was very homely, she returned home again and trussed up a good bed, well furnished, with hangings and other necessaries, which, as secretly as she could, conveyed thither, desiring both the old woman and her daughter to be good to her brother and see that he wanted nothing. The next day, came this gentleman home and, according to his custom, went a hunting to his old haunt, where he, seeing this new furniture, marveled much thereat, and inquired what the matter meant. The old mother answered that a sister of his had been there and, willing them to cherish him well, gave them besides certain money. The gentleman understanding then how the world went and knowing it to be his wife's doing, returned forthwith home and demanded of her the truth, and what she meant thereby, who denied it not. 'The cause why,' quoth she, 'I sent such furniture thither, was because I, understanding how daintily you were accustomed to lie at home, doubted you might by such hard entertainment have gotten some harm.'"

"He should," quoth the Lady Aloisa, "have had a bed of nettles or thorns, had it been for me. For sure I would not have been the cherisher of my husband in his unthriftiness."

"And so would you have made him worse," quoth master Pedro. "But it happened much better for this gentlewoman. For he, being overcome by her virtue, lived content with her ever after" (sigs. E5^{r}–E6^{r}).

ANNE TOWNSHEND

Inventory "In My Ladis Chamber," London House (1608)

As was characteristic, this bedchamber had one bedstead but many beds, or mattresses. Some would have been piled on the bed frame for the use of the lady Townshend, but others would have been placed on the floor for a servant or servants. This inventory is particularly poignant because it records the damage caused by fire. A number of items have been "all burned"; some were renewed, or repaired; some have survived, but with scorch marks.

All burned:	Item v. pieces of hangings of tapestry
	Item one field bedstead with top & valance of red cloth with green silk lace & fringe
	Item v. curtains of the same cloth lined with green taffeta sarcenet with lace & long buttons of green silk, the tester, valance, & head lined with net work, and v net work curtains
	Item a pair of inward valance of green taffeta sarcenet with a green silk fringe

---

The wool bed burned, renewed	Item one down bed & bolster & one feather bed and bolster, one white wool bed & one rose wool bed
	Item one crimson rug & a great fine blanket
all burned	Item down pillows, v.
burned	Item gilt cups & feathers, vi.
	Item a little square table with inlaid work with a drawer to it
	Item a drawing table of wainscot
	Item a court cupboard with lock and key
scorched	Item one great wicker chair lined with red cloth
	Item a chair & two stools of needlework wrought with crewel of the Irish stitch with green cotton covers
	Item one low chair of orange tawny velvet with a back with yellow silk fringe
	Item one needlework carpet
	Item iii blue carpets of broadcloth with fringe
	Item a screen of blue cloth with a frame
	Item a tawny rug
	Item frame of wainscot to set glasses in with a curtain to draw afore it
	Item a long red cushion with green silk lace
	Item a traverse of pentadous [pintado, a colored eastern cloth like chintz] with a rod
	Item a pully with a crewel stretcher
	Item a joined stool and a little stool frame
	Item a pan to burn sweet water in
	Item fire shovel a pair of andirons & tongs & a pair of bellows
	Item v. pieces of tapestry hang[ing]s containing iii Flemish ells at v s. the Flemish ell
	Item a field bedstead with top and valance of green velvet with double valance & curtains of the same lined with green taffeta sarcenet & laced with gold lace

Inventory of Furnishings "In my Ladis Chamber" (1608), from a book of inventories compiled for Anne Townshend.

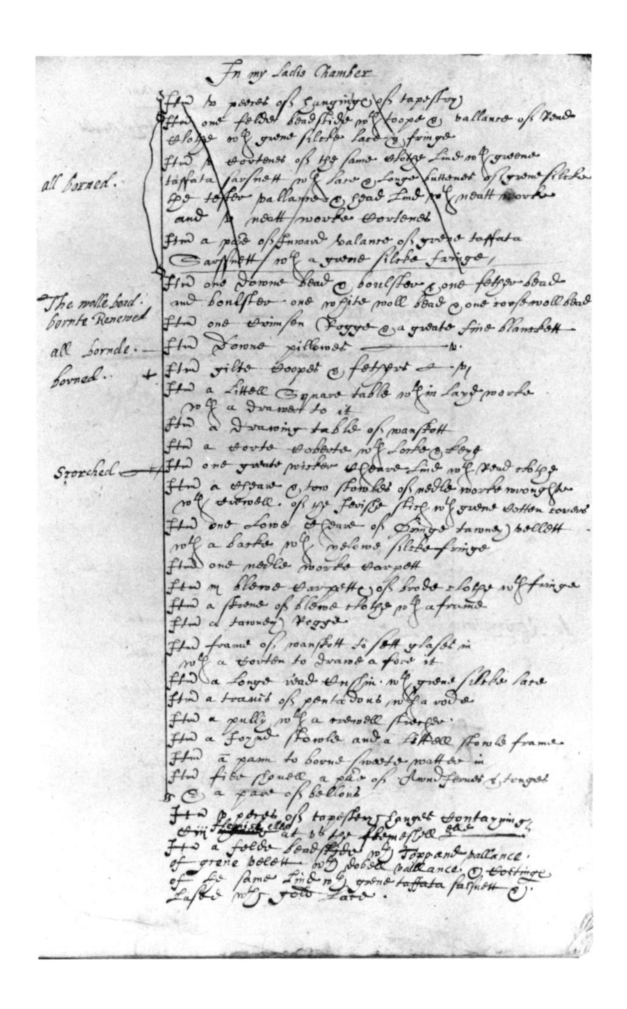
In my Ladis Chamber

all borned.

The wolle bed borne Renewed

all bornde.

borned.

Storched

ROBERT GREENE

Theeves Falling Out, True-men Come by their Goods: Or, The Bel-man Wanted a Clapper . . . Shewing, that the Villanies of Lewd Women Doe, by Many Degrees, Excell Those of Men (London, 1637)

❧ It can be difficult to comprehend how little privacy there was in the Elizabethan bedchamber, but this pamphlet, which dates back to 1592, offers a kind of parable of its collective nature. The purported author of the excerpted tale, a prostitute, is solicited by a man who pretends that he requires the strictest privacy. His point is that there is no such thing, because there is an omnipresent witness from whom there's no hiding.

I removed my lodging, and gate me into one of those houses of good hospitality, whereunto persons resort, commonly called a trugging house, or, to be plain, a whorehouse, where I gave myself to entertain all companions . . . . There resorted to our house a clothier, a proper young man, who by fortune coming first to drink, espying me, asked me if I would drink with him. There needed no great entreaty, for as then I wanted company, and so clapt me down by him and began very pleasantly to welcome him. The man being of himself modest and honest noted my personage, and judicially reasoned of my strumpet-like behavior, and inwardly (as after he reported to me) grieved that so foul properties were hidden in so good a proportion, and that such rare wit and excellent beauty was blemished with whoredom's base deformity, insomuch that he began to think well of me, and to wish that I were as honest as I was beautiful. . . .

This clothier came again to our house, whose sight cheered me up, for that, spying him out of a casement, I ran down the stairs and met him at the door and heartily welcomed him, and asked him if he would drink.

"I come for that purpose," says he, "but I will drink no more below but in a chamber."

"Marry sir," quoth I, "you shall," and so brought him into the fairest room.

In our sitting there together drinking, at last the clothier fell to kissing and other dalliance, wherein he found me not coy. At last told me that he would willingly have his pleasure of me, but the room was too lightsome, for of all things in the world he could not in such actions away with a light chamber. I consented unto him and brought him into a room more dark, but still he said it was too light. Then I carried him into a further chamber, where, drawing a curtain before the window and closing the curtains of the bed, I asked, smiling, if that were close enough?

"No, sweet love," says he, "that curtain is not broad enough for the window, some watching eye may espy us. My heart misdoubts, and my credit is my life. Love, if thou hast a closer room than this, bring me to it."

"Why then," quoth I, "follow me," and with that I brought him into a back loft where stood a little bed, only appointed to lodge suspicious persons, so dark that at noon day it was impossible for any man to see his own hands.

"How now, sir," quoth I, "is not this dark enough?"

He, sitting him down on the bed side, fetched a deep sigh, and said, indifferent, "So, so. But there is a glimpse of light in at the tiles; some body may by fortune see it."

"In faith no," quoth I, "none but God."

"God," says he, "Aye, why, can God see us here?"

"Good sir," quoth I, "why I hope you are not so simple, but you know, God's eyes are so clear and penetrating that they can pierce through walls of brass."

"And alas," quoth he, "sweet love, if God see us, shall we not be more ashamed to do such a filthy act before Him, than before men?"

At this, such a remorse of conscience, such a tearful terror of my sin strook [struck] into my mind, that I kneeled down at his feet and with tears besought him that he would help me out of that misery, for his exhortation had caused in me a loathing of my wicked life, and I would not only become a reformed woman, but hold him as dear as my father that gave me life. Whereupon he kissed me with tears. And so we went down together, where we had further communication, and presently he provided me another lodging, where I not only used myself honestly, but also was so penitent every day in tears for my former folly, that he took me to his wife (sigs. $F2^{v}$–$F4^{r}$).

JAKOB RUEFF

The Expert Midwife, Or, An Excellent and Most Necessary Treatise of the Generation and Birth of Man (London, 1637)

❧ The bedchamber was turned over exclusively to women during childbirth, with a midwife in charge of the proceedings. As indicated in this volume, originally written in Latin nearly a century earlier, many women in labor sat in special birthing stools rather than lying in bed.

Of the office of midwives, and of the apt and fit form and fashion of their stool or chair

But what the office of midwives is in the time of birth, and how the action may proceed, we will now declare. First, let the midwife know the time and observe the true pains and dolors. Also let her comfort and cheer up the laboring woman, and let her cheerfully exhort her to obey her precepts and admonitions. Likewise let her give good exhortations to other women being present, especially to pour forth devout prayers to God; afterward to do their duties at once, as well as they are able. Which done, let her bring the laboring woman to her stool, which ought to be prepared in this fashion.

Let the stool be made compass-wise, underpropped with four feet, the stay of it behind bending backward, hollow in the midst, covered with a black cloth underneath, hanging down to the ground; by that means that the laboring woman may be covered, and other women sometimes apply their hands in any place if necessity require. Let the stool be furnished and covered with many cloths and clouts [rags] at the back and other parts, that the laboring woman receive no hurt, or the infant anywhere, strongly kicking and striving because of the pains, stirrings, and motions of the mother. And after the laboring woman shall be set in her chair about to be delivered, the midwife shall place one woman behind her back which may gently hold the laboring woman, taking her by both the arms, and if need be, the pains waxing grievous, and the woman laboring, may stroke and press down the womb, and may somewhat drive and depress the infant downward. But let her place other two by her sides, which may both with good words encourage and comfort the laboring woman, and also may be ready to help and put to their hand at any time. This being done, let the midwife herself sit stooping forward before the laboring woman, and let her anoint her own hands and the womb of the laboring woman with oil of lilies, of sweet almonds, and the grease of an hen, mingled and tempered together. For to do this doth profit and help them very much which are gross and fat, and them whose secret parts are strict and narrow, and likewise them which have the mouth of the matrix dry, and such women as are in labor of their first child. It will also be profitable to commix and temper with those things the white of an egg. Lastly, all these things thus prepared, let the midwife instruct and encourage the party to her labor, to abide her pains with patience, and then gently apply her hands to the work as she ought, by feeling and searching with

Birthing Stool, from Jakob Rueff, *The Expert Midwife* (London, 1637).

her fingers how the child lieth, and by relaxing and opening the way and passage conveniently for him, while the mother is in pain, and also where there is need by enlarging and stretching out the neck of the matrix warily. And if the infant stay from proceeding forth, and be stopped anywhere, with her fingers tenderly to direct the infant to lie and proceed forth directly and naturally, when he lieth crooked and overthwart, and to futher him to an easy birth. Let her conveniently receive the infant proceeding forth to birth, and let her presently cut the navel, about the length of four fingers being left, and let her bind it hard with a double thread, as near to the belly of the child as may be. Which being done, let her have a care of the secundine [placenta] or afterbirth; let her move and stir it, the matrix as yet being stretched out and open, before being shut it be closed together again. . . . The navel being cut and the child washed, his navel, being dry, must be strewed and sprinkled with powder compounded of bole armeniac [an astringent], sanguis draconis [dragon's blood or cinnabaris, a bright red gum or resin], and myrrh, and to be pressed down with a double cloth laid upon it. For this doth remedy a flux of blood and other chances (sigs. F7v–G2r).

THOMAS HILL

The Moste Pleasaunte Arte of the Interpretacion of Dreames, Whereunto Is Annexed Sundry Problemes with Apte Aunsweares Neare Agreeing to the Matter, and Very Rare Examples, Not the Like Extant in the English Tongue (London, 1576)

❧ Thomas Hill wrote on a number of topics: physiognomy, the plague, gardening, and astronomy, as well as on the interpretation of dreams. The Elizabethan approach to the subject was schizophrenic: on the one hand, dreams were dismissed as mere fancies; on the other hand, they were understood to bring revelations from God. In this pamphlet, originally published in 1571, Hill pays tribute to their prophetic powers. At the same time, by deciphering dreams with every appearance of reason, he empties them of some of their terrors. It is interesting to note how many of the anxieties addressed in the domestic advice literature surface here in nightmare form.

What hazard of life? What loss of substance? Or what danger of limb can a dream put the dreamer unto? Even so much as when he awaketh, he wondereth how such imagination or fancy crept into his mind. Be his dream never so terrible or fearful—as falling into the hands of thieves, were wounded by them, fighting in bloody battles, or on every side beset with enemies, in such manner as it would make a stout man to quake—yet when he awaketh no skin is broken, he hath no ache in his bones, he is still in his quiet bed, as whole and as safe as when he went to rest: nothing so nor so, it was only a dream. If now he have his knowledge of divination, what a comfort will it be to him that, examining the circumstances in their due time and order, shall prognosticate what such things portend. And thereby may solace himself with good haps and labor to prevent or hinder the imminent misfortune, or at the least arm himself so strongly with patience as quietly to bear them. For a mischief known of before and diligently looked for is not so grievous as when it cometh on a sudden. It is a wonderful thing and almost incredible that dreams should have such virtue in them, were it not that God hath revealed it unto us. When he himself, as a mean, often used them, to open unto his people of Israel, his secret will and pleasure. . . .

One dreamed that he went from home into a strange country and lost the key of his house, and when he came home again, he found his daughter to have lost her maidenhead. Which dream declared to him that all things at home could not be in safety, when the key so lost was ready for another to take up. For either it signified, as it is thought, the misusage of his family; or else that his wife, daughters, or maidens were enticed to folly in his house; or else otherwise that his servants bribed and pilfered away from him. . . .

A certain woman dreamed that she thought she had her husband's privities cut from the rest of the body in her hands and that she took great care and much foresight how to keep them: who after bare her husband a son, which she brought up herself. For the husband's privities signified the son which was got by him. And that it was taken or cut away from the rest of the body signified her bringing up of her son. But her husband was after bereft of life by death. . . .

And one thought in his dream to find in his jacket or coat very many and great stinking worms and to abhor them. And that also would shake them off, but could not. Who the next day following learned or understood that his wife had her accustomed fellowship carnally with another man, and understanding the same became very pensive and perplexed of mind, insomuch that he would have departed from her, but did not because he was otherwise prohibited or stayed by a certain letter. For the jacket or coat signified the wife girt or wrapped about him; and the stinking worms, her pollution. And whereas he could not pluck and cast them away at his will signified that he could neither after his desire and purpose depart from his wife.

And one thought in his sleep that he saw his house on fire, who after received letters that his brother lay grievously sick, and whiles he prepared himself to journey, a messenger came declaring him to be dead. Who after counted the time from that hour which he saw the dream, conceived that his brother then died. But commonly this dream doth threaten death either to the dreamer or some principal of the house (sigs. A5^{v}–A6^{v}, F8^{v}, G3^{r}, I4^{r}).

WILLIAM PERKINS

Death's Knell: Or, The Sicke Mans Passing-Bell: Summoning all Sicke Consciences to Prepare Themselves for the Comming of the Great Day of Doome, Lest Mercies Gate Be Shut Against Them (London, 1628)

☙ This little pamphlet had an extensive publishing history but a low rate of survival. William Perkins died in 1602, so we know that *Death's Knell* was written before then. The first copy to survive, though, is this one, labeled the ninth edition. A fragmentary tenth edition survives in private hands, but otherwise the Folger holds the only known remaining copies: this ninth edition of 1628, the eleventh edition of 1629, and a sixteenth edition of 1637. As a *memento mori*, exhorting its readers to remember the inevitability of death, *Death's Knell* also reminds us that the bedchamber was the site of the deathbed.

Let the memory of death (good Christian) be ever the looking glass of thy life, thy continual companion, and inseparable spouse. Let thy solace be the sighs of a sorrowful soul, and those the more bitter, the better. Whilst, worm-like, thou crawlest here below, fasten all thy faculties upon the commandments of the Creator, for those, in thy small passage, must be the pilot to steer thee into the haven of heaven. Think every moment thou art in the waning, that the date of thy pilgrimage is well-nigh expired, and that the lamp of thy life lieth twinkling upon the snuff, and that now it stands thee upon to look toward thy celestial home. Thy forces are enfeebled, thy senses impaired, and, on every side, the tottering and ruinous cottage of thy faint flesh threateneth fall.

If thou wert now laid on thy departing pillow, wearied with waiting, pinched with pain, drowned in dolor, oppressed with the heavy load of thy forepast committed sins, wounded with the sting of a guilty crying conscience; if thou feltst the force of death cracking thy heart-strings asunder, ready to make the sad divorce of thy soul and body; if thou layest panting for shortness of breath, sweating a fatal sweat, and tired with struggling against deadly pangs; O, how much then wouldst thou give for a day's contrition, an hour's repentance, or a minute's amendment of life? Then worlds would be worthless in comparison of a little time, which now by whole months and years thou lavishly misspendest. How deeply would it wound thy soul, when looking back into thy life, thou shouldst espy many faults committed, but none amended; many good works omitted, but none recovered; thy duty to God promised, but not performed! How disconsolable would thy case be, thy friends being fled, thy senses affrighted, thy mind amazed, thy memory decayed, thy thoughts aghast, and every part disabled in its proper faculty, saving only the guilty conscience crying out against thee? What wouldst thou do, when stripped and turned out of thy house of clay, into the world of worms, the den of dust, and cabin of corruption; from thence to be convented [summoned] before a most severe Judge, carrying in thy own bosom thy indictment ready written, and a perfect register of all thy misdeeds (sigs. A2^{r}, A4^{v}–A5^{v}).

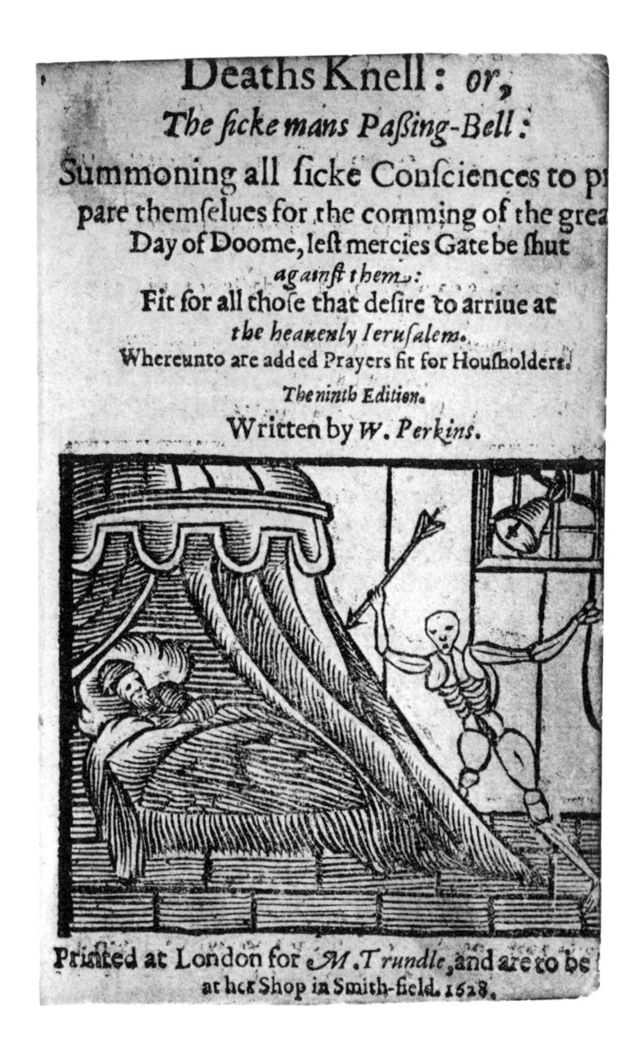
Deaths Knell: or,
The ſicke mans Paſsing-Bell:
Summoning all ſicke Conſciences to p
pare themſelues for the comming of the grea
Day of Doome, leſt mercies Gate be ſhut
againſt them:
Fit for all thoſe that deſire to arriue at
the heauenly Ieruſalem.
Whereunto are added Prayers fit for Houſholders.
The ninth Edition.
Written by *W. Perkins.*
Printed at London for *M. Trundle*, and are to be
at her Shop in Smith-field. 1628.

Title Page to William Perkins, *Death's Knell: Or, The Sicke Mans Passing-Bell* (London, 1628).

The Householder's Study ❧

THOMAS HEYWOOD, *attributed author*

The Phoenix of these Late Times: Or, The Life of M[aste]r Henry Welby, Esq.; Who Lived at his House in Grub-street Forty Foure Yeares, and in that Space, was Never Seene by Any (London, 1637)

❧ The study was an exclusive space, far more private than the bedchamber and, with certain very rare exceptions, reserved for men. The space is a suitable symbol of the self-imposed isolation of Henry Welby, who reportedly withdrew from the world in the face of his younger brother's unexplained but deadly antagonism. As he died at the age of eight-four, he evidently went into seclusion at forty. The pamphleteer, who has been identified as Thomas Heywood in part because one of a series of commendatory poems is signed by him, emphasizes that Welby did not sacrifice charity and good householding to his asceticism.

The two brothers meeting face to face, the younger drew a pistol charged with a double bullet from his side and presented upon the elder, which only gave fire, but by the miraculous providence of God no further report. At which the elder, seizing upon the younger, disarmed him of his tormentary engine and, without any further violence offered, so left him. Which bearing to his chamber, and desirous to find whether it were only a false fire, merely to fright him, or a charge, speedily to dispatch him—when he found the bullets and apprehended the danger he had escaped, he fell into many deep considerations. . . . He might be the occasion of shortening his own innocent life and hastening his brother's shameful and infamous death. . . . Since he could not enjoy his face with safety, he would ever after deny the sight of his own face to all men whatsoever.

And upon the former considerations he grounded this irrevocable resolution, which he kept to his dying day. Which that he might the better observe, he took a very fair house in the lower end of Grub Street, near unto Cripplegate. And having contracted a numerous retinue into a private and small family, having the house before prepared for his purpose, he entered the door, choosing to himself out of all the rooms three private chambers, best suiting with his intended solitude: the first for his diet, the second for his lodging, and the third for his study, one within another. And the while his diet was set on the table by one of his servants, an old maid, he retired into his lodging-chamber. And while his bed was making, into his study, still doing so, till all was clear. And there he set up his rest, and in forty-four years never, upon any occasion, how great soever, issued out of those chambers, till he was borne thence upon men's shoulders. Neither in all that time did son-in-law, daughter, or grandchild, brother, sister, or kinsman, stranger, tenant, or servant, young, or old, rich, or poor, of what degree or condition soever, look upon his face, saving the ancient maid, whose name was Elizabeth, who made his fire, prepared his bed, provided his diet, and dressed his chamber—which was very seldom, or upon an extraordinary necessity that he saw her, which maidservant died not above six days before him.

As touching his abstinence in all the time of his retirement, he never tasted flesh nor fish. He never drank either wine or strong water; his chief food was oatmeal boiled with water, which some call gruel, and in summer, now and then a salad of some choice cool herbs. For dainties, or when he would feast himself upon an high day, he would eat the

Henry Welby in His Study, from *The Phoenix of these Late Times: Or, The Life of M[aste]r Henry Welby, Esq.* (London, 1637), attributed to Thomas Heywood. Books were often kept in chests, but when they were displayed on shelves the spines were often placed facing in to the wall, as this illustration shows. The Folger owns some volumes with titles painted on the fore-edges for the purposes of identification.

yolk of an hen's egg, but no part of the white. And what bread he did eat, he cut out of the middle part of the loaf, but of the crust he never tasted. And his continual drink was four-shillings beer, and no other. And now and then, when his stomach served him, he did eat some kind of suckets [candied fruit], and now and then drank red cow's milk, which his maid Elizabeth fetched for him out of the fields, hot from the cow. And yet he kept a bountiful table for his servants, with entertainment sufficient for any stranger or tenant that had any occasion of business at his house.

In Christmas holidays, at Easter, and upon all solemn festival days, he had great cheer provided, with all dishes seasonable with the times served into his own chamber with store of wine, which his maid brought in. When he himself (after thanks given unto God for his good benefits) would pin a clean napkin before him and, putting on a pair of white holland sleeves which reached to his elbows, call for his knife and, cutting dish after dish up in order, send one to one poor neighbor, the next to another, whether it were brawn [boar], beef, capon [a castrated cock], goose, et cetera, till he had left the table quite empty. Then would he give thanks again, lay by his linen, put up his knife again, and cause the cloth to be taken away; and this would he do dinner and supper upon these days, without tasting one morsel of any thing whatsoever. And this custom he kept to his dying day, an abstinence far transcending all the Carthusian monks or Mendicant friars that I ever yet could read of. . . .

As he kept a kind of perpetual fast, so he devoted himself unto continual prayer, saving those seasons which he dedicated to his study. For you must know that he was both a scholar and a linguist; neither was there any author worth the reading, either brought over from beyond the seas or published here in the kingdom, which he refused to buy, at what dear rate soever. And these were his companions in the day and his counselors in the night. . . .

But in this gentleman, the thing most worthy our observation is that he, who was born to so fair fortunes and might have enjoyed prosperity, for his soul's sake and to enjoy the pleasures of a future world, should study adversity; to have much, and enjoy little; to be the lord of all, and a servant to all; to provide for others to eat, whilst he prepared himself to fast; and out of his great plenty to supply others, whilst himself wanted (sigs. D3^r–E3^r).

THOMAS GAINSFORD

"Oeconomick," from *The Rich Cabinet Furnished with Varietie of Excellent Discriptions, Exquisite Charracters, Witty Discourses, and Delightfull Histories* (London, 1616)

❧ The fad for gathering aphorisms and epigrams can be seen both in manuscript "commonplace" books and in printed collections like this one. A hallmark of the genre was its promiscuous inclusiveness. While advice manuals were full of internal contradictions, their logical inconsistencies were never so apparent as when they were presented in this stripped-down form and, thanks to the principal of topical organization, placed in juxtaposition. The classical term "oeconomics" refers to household management.

Oeconomic maketh marriage the first degree and foundation of a family, for as a ship cannot be governed without a rudder, so cannot a house be ordered without an overseer, which must needs be man and wife, subordinate one to the other: he to play the good husband abroad and she the good housewife at home, and both to consent in a sweet harmony of mutual help to maintain their family.

Oeconomic hath great necessity and near affinity with nurture and civility, whereby the wife must have gravity in speech and action: wisdom in governing, patience in suffering her husband, love to bring up her children, affability to conversing, diligence to lay up and save, and friendliness in entertaining and dismissing neighbors and friends when they come. . . .

Oeconomic is opposed and encumbered with many inconveniences in married folks, wherein, if fortune cannot be prevented, wisdom must mitigate the extremity. As commonly, a mild and modest maiden is a poor one; a rich one proud of her dowry; a fair one of her beauty, and is to be watched; a foul one is nasty, and is to be loathed; a wise and comely, is both willful and costly; a seamstress, a singer or dancer and no housekeeper; a housewife, irksome and imperious; and an honest one, jealous. Besides, if thou make thy wife tarry at home, she will complain; if she walk at liberty, the neighbors will talk of thee; if thou chide, she will be sullen and dumb; if thou be silent, nothing shall be heard for her chime; if she have the laying out [spending], the stock goeth to wrack; if thou dispose thy own money, she scorns to come for every penny; if thou keep thy house, thou art suspicious; if thou tarry abroad, thou art vicious; if she be trim, she must abroad to be seen; if she be but in ordinary fashion, thou art a base-minded miserable man—and so may I go infinitely on the inconveniences and crosses that are incident to housekeepers and married folks. . . .

Oeconomic giveth warning that the husbands be not rigorous, especially when they be new married to their wives. For as the wife is the honor and happiness of her husband in respect of her chastity, so the husband is the hell of his wife in regard of his cruelty.

Oeconomic giveth warning that the husband be not overjealous, for however a man may sometimes shut the doors, remove his wife from the window, bar her going abroad, and detain her from suspicious company, yet must he bring this to pass with great skill, and show that he hath always more faith in her liberty than in his own restraint or observant eye. . . .

Oeconomic instructeth the husbands that they bring no suspicious person to their houses; and the women not to be overfamiliar with any man, though a near kinsman (sigs. O5^{v}–O7^{v}).

Rental Documents and Evidences from the Book of Reckonings of Anthony Smetheley (1556–1578).

Deed Box (London, 1605), of walnut with an iron lock plate. The interior of the box is lined with block-printed paper of the sort that may also have been used on walls. The paper has Elizabeth's coat of arms, Tudor roses, and strapwork designs. The Metropolitan Museum of Art. Gift of Irwin Untermyer, 1964 (64.101.1188).

THOMAS CLAY

Briefe, Easie, and Necessary Tables of Interest and Rents Forborne: As Also, for the Valuation of Leases, Annuities, and Purchases, Either in Present, or in Reversion, Acording to the Rates Now Most in Use (London, 1624)

❧ This handy volume, first published in 1618, proclaims itself "necessary for all noblemen, gentlemen, and others who desire to understand their own estates, and to see into the managing of their own affairs; and generally for all men, in bargains and contracts of like nature." Besides this table on how to negotiate the various calendars in use, the book also shows how to figure interest. And it describes the offices of surveyors, stewards, solicitors, bailiffs, tax collectors, woodwards [officers of the woods], receivers [treasurers], and auditors.

This table serveth for the resolving of all questions concerning the dates of charters, grants, deeds, leases, or other evidences made in any king or queen's reign since the Conquest. As also, having the day of the month and year of any king's reign given, to find that year of the Lord or the number of years from the Conquest thereunto; or, contrarily, the year of the Lord or time since the Conquest being known, to find the year of the king, et cetera. Which to do, consider always whether the date of your evidence or time propounded (concerning the time of the year) do fall before or after the time of the beginning of any king or queen's reign, reckoning from the 25 of March [the first day of the new year] that present year of our Lord set at the beginning of each king's reign, and then work as followeth.

1. If the year of the king be given and the year of our Lord required, and the date fall before, add the year of the king's reign to the year of our Lord set at the beginning thereof; the product shall give the year of our Lord required. But if the date fall after, then you must subtract an unit, to show the true year of our Lord.

Example 1

A lease is dated the 24 of January in the 17 year of King Edward the First, to endure for 60 years, from Michaelmas [29 September, one of four quarter-days of the business year] next before going. I demand in what year of our Lord it began, and how long since it expired, this Michaelmas, 1623.

A Table shewing the beginning and continuance of the reignes of the Kings of England, from the Conquest to the beginning of the reigne of our Soveraigne Lord King IAMES.

Kings.	Began to reigne.	Reigned	Sin. con
Will. Conq.	1066. Oct. 14	20.y.11.m. 14.d	0
Will. Rufus	1087. Sept. 9	12.y.11.m. 17 d	20
Henry 1.	1100 August. 1	35.y. 4.m. 11.d	33
Stephen.	1135. Decem. 2	18.y. 11.m. 18 d	69
Henry 2.	1154. Octob. 27	34.y. 9.m 4.d	88
Richard 1.	1189. Iuly 6	9.y. 9.m 0.d	122
King Iohn.	1199. April 6	17.y. 7.m. 0.d	132
Henry 3.	1216. Oct. 19	56.y. 0.m. 28.d	150
Edward 1.	1272. Nou. 16	34.y. 8.m. 9.d	206
Edward 2.	1307. Iuly 7	19.y. 7.m. 16.d	240
Edward 3.	1326. Ianu. 25	50.y. 5.m. 7 d	260
Richard 2.	1377. Iune 21	22 y. 3.m. 14 d	310
Henry 4.	1399. Sept. 29	13.y. 6.m. 9.d	332
Henry 5.	1412. March 20	9.y. 5.m. 24.d	346
Henry 6.	1422. August 31	38.y. 6.m. 8 d	355
Edward 4.	1460. March 4	22.y. 1.m. 8 d	394
Edward 5.	1483. April 9	0.y. 2.m. 18.d	416
Richard 3.	1483. Iune 22	2.y. 2.m. 5.d	416
Henry 7.	1485. Aug. 22	23.y. 8.m. 2.d	418
Henry 8.	1509. April 22	37 y. 10.m. 2 d	442
Edward 6.	1546. Ianua. 28	6.y. 5.m. 19 d	480
Q. Mary.	1553. Iuly 6	5.y. 4.m. 11.d	486
Q. Elizabeth	1558. Nou. 17	44.y. 4 m. 15 d	492
King Iames.	1602. March 24 1567. Iuly 29	England, &c. Scotland.	536 *Viuat.*

A Table of Regnal Years, from Thomas Clay, *Briefe, Easie, and Necessary Tables of Interest and Rents* (London, 1624).

Here the year of the king is given, but the question must be resolved by the year of the Lord. And therefore first considering that Michaelmas before the date, being the term from which the lease is to begin, falleth before November, the beginning of the king's reign, therefore that term is in the 16 year of this king. Wherefore, to work the question to 1272, the year of our Lord set at the beginning of his reign, I add 16 and it maketh 1288, the year of our Lord in which the lease began.

Now to find when it expired, and how long since. To the year of our Lord found, I add 60, the term of the lease, and it maketh 1348, in which year it expired. Lastly, from 1623, the present year of our Lord, I take 1348, and the remain will be 275 years, and so long ago it was at Michaelmas last, since this lease expired.

Example 2

A lease beareth date the 19 day of March in the 4 year of the reign of our new sovereign Lord King James, to endure for the term of 40 years, after the expiration of a former lease bearing date the 18 day of February, in the 30 year of the late Queen Elizabeth, to endure for 21 years, beginning at the Feast of the Nativity [25 December] next before going. I demand which of these leases is yet in being, and for what term, this Nativity, 1623.

For that the later lease is in reversion, to begin at the determination of the former. To find that determination I look into the table for the year of our Lord set at the beginning of Queen Elizabeth's reign, which I find to be 1558. To this I add 30 the year of my date, and it maketh 1588. Now for so much as both my date and the beginning of my lease (as concerning the time of the year) do fall after the month in which the Queen's reign began, from the year found I subtract an unit, and there remaineth 1587, the year of our Lord which the first lease began in. To this I add 21; it maketh 1608 for the time of the determination of that lease. To that again I add 40 years, the term of the new lease; it maketh 1648, the time when it shall expire. From which I take 1623, this present year; the remain is 25 years, and so long time hath the later lease yet in being.

2. If the year of our Lord be given, and the year of the king required, and the date fall before the month and day answering to the beginning of that king's reign, which hath the year of our Lord next less to the given year set before it, then take the difference between the year given and that year set at the beginning of the king's reign, which difference is the year of the king required. But if the date fall after the said month and day, then you must add an unit to the difference found, to show the year required (sigs. A7^{r}–A8^{v}).

JOHN HARINGTON

A New Discourse of a Stale Subject, Called The Metamorphosis of Ajax (London, 1596)

❧ There were various sanitary arrangements in the Elizabethan period: privies, or internal latrines with vertical shafts to ground level; outhouses; open pits in gardens; chamber pots; and close stools, or boxes with open, padded seats over removable pots. The first two structures were notoriously malodorous, and privies, the systems of choice in great-house architecture of the early Tudor years, fell out of favor. Hardwick Hall, built in the 1590s, had only close stools. In this mock-heroic manual ("Ajax" punned on "a jakes," or privy), Sir John Harington proposed a new alternative, the water closet. Although Harington was Elizabeth's godson and was sufficiently well placed to send a water closet to Sir Robert Cecil as a gift in 1602, his invention was not to catch on until years later, in connection with other improvements in piping water into the house. For the period under consideration here, this forerunner of the modern toilet remained the concoction of a gentleman's study.

I assure you, this device of mine requires not a sea of water, but a cistern; not a whole Thames' full, but half a ton full, to keep all sweet and savory, for I will undertake from the peasant's cottage to the prince's palace. Twice so much quantity of water as is spent in drink in the house will serve the turn, which if it were at Shaftesbury, where water is dearest of any town I know, that is no great proportion. And the device is so little cumbersome, as it is rather a pleasure than a pain; a matter so slight, that it will seem at the first incredible; so sure, that you shall find it at all times infallible. For it doth avoid at once all the annoyances that can be imagined: the sight, the savor, the cold, which last, to weak bodies, is oft more hurtful than both the other, where the houses stand over brooks, or vaults daily cleansed with water. And not to hold you in too long suspense, the device is this: you shall make a false bottom to that privy that you are annoyed with, either of lead or stone, the which bottom shall have a sluice of brass to let out all the filth, which, if it be close-plastered all about it and rinsed with water as oft as occasion serves, but specially at noon and at night, you will keep your privy as sweet as your parlor, and perhaps sweeter. . . . It is nothing but to keep down the air with a stopple [plug], and let out the filth with a screw, which some will mislike, and will not endure to have such a business every time they come to that house. . . . The pains being so little as it is, I should think him a sloven that would not by himself or his man leave it as cleanly as he found it, specially considering that in Deuteronomy you are told God

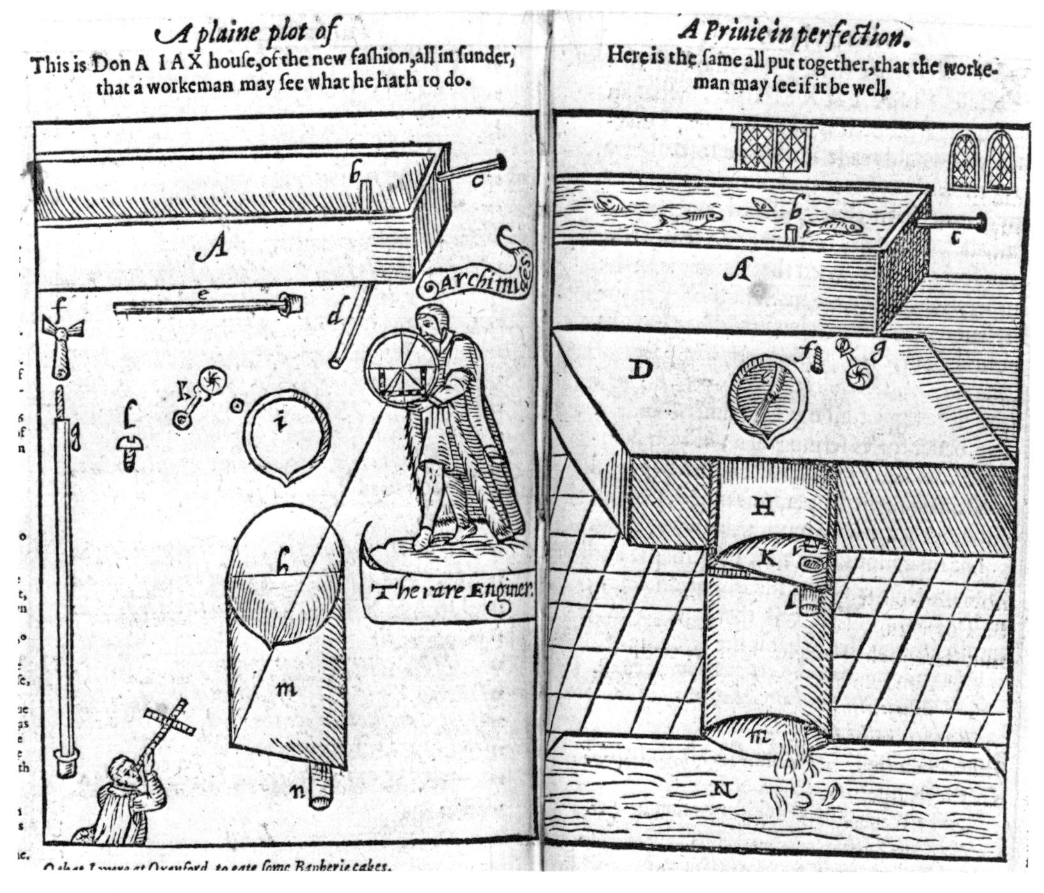

A Water Closet, from John Harington, *A New Discourse of a Stale Subject, Called The Metamorphosis of Ajax* (London, 1596). The parts are labeled: A. the cistern; B. the little asher; C. the waste pipe; D. the seat board; E. the pipe that comes from the cistern; F. the screw; G. the scallop shell to cover it when it is shut down; H. the stool pot; I. the stopple; K. the current; L. the sluice; and M. and N. the vault into which it falls. This advice is added: "always remember that at noon and at night, empty it and leave it half a foot deep in fair water. And this being well-done, and orderly kept, your worst privy may be as sweet as your best chamber."

mislikes sluttishness, and every cat gives us an example (as housewives tell us) to cover all our filthiness . . . .

In the privy that annoys you, first cause a cistern containing a barrel or upward to be placed either behind the seat or in any place either in the room or above it, from whence the water may by a small pipe of lead of an inch be conveyed under the seat in the hinder part thereof (but quite out [of] sight), to which pipe you must have a cock or a washer to yield water with some pretty strength, when you would let it in.

Next make a vessel of an oval form, as broad at the bottom as at the top, two foot deep, one foot broad, sixteen inches long. Place this very close to your feet, like the pot of a close stool; let the oval incline to the right hand.

This vessel may be brick, stone, or lead, but whatsoever it is, it should have a current of three inches; to the back part of it (where a sluice of brass must stand), the bottom and sides all smooth and dressed with pitch, rosin, and wax, which will keep it from tainting with the urine.

In the lowest part of this vessel, which will be on the right hand, you must fasten the sluice or washer of brass with solder or cement. The concavity or hollow thereof must be two inches and one-half.

To the washer's stopple must be a stem of iron as big as a curtain rod, strong and even and perpendicular, with a strong screw at the top of it, to which you must have a hollow key with a worm [spiral-cut channel] fit to that screw.

This screw must, when the sluice is down, appear through the plank not above a straw-breadth on the right hand and, being duly placed, it will stand three or four inches wide of the midst of the back of your seat.

Item, that children and busy folk disorder it not or open the sluice with putting in their hands without a key, you should have a little button or scallop shell to bind it down with a vice [screw] pin, so as without the key it will not be opened.

These things thus placed, all about your vessel and elsewhere must be passing close-plastered with good lime and hair, that no air come up from the vault but only at your sluice, which stands close-stopped. And ever it must be left, after it is voided, half-a-foot deep in clean water.

If water be plenty, the oftener it is used and opened, the sweeter; but if it be scant, once a day is enough, for a need, though twenty persons should use it.

If the water will not run to your cistern, you may with a force [pump] of twenty shillings and a pipe of eighteen pence the yard, force it from the lowest part of your house to the highest (sigs. I6^{v}–I7^{r}, K1^{r-v}, L4^{v}–L5^{r}).

HUGH PLAT

The Jewell House of Art and Nature, Conteining Divers Rare and Profitable Inventions (London, 1594)

☙ Hugh Plat's first publications were collections of Senecan sententia and indifferent poetry. Soon, however, he turned to the natural sciences, mechanics, and agriculture, in which fields he was to develop so large a reputation that King James knighted him in 1605. Plat was in contact with gardeners from around the country, and when he published a collection of garden experiments he was careful to credit his correspondents for their suggestions. This was so unusual that it may have been a form of disclaimer for methods he had not tried himself. *The Jewel House* is a potpourri of directions for husbandry, distilling, metal casting, and household inventions.

How to write a letter secretly that cannot easily be discovered or suspected

Write your mind at large on the one side of the paper with common ink, and on the other side with milk that which you would have secret. And when you would make the same legible, hold that side which is written with ink to the fire, and the milky letters will show bluish on the other side. Or else rule two papers of one bigness with lines of an equal distance; make the one full of glass windows, through which you must write your mind upon a second paper. Then fill up the spaces with some other idle words—but if all were made to hang together in good sense it would carry the less suspicion. Each friend must have one of these cut papers to read all such letters as shall be sent unto him, and this manner of writing will trouble a good decipherer to bring into perfect sense. Also you may first write an ordinary letter that may carry some good sense to your friend, but let the lines be wide asunder. Then between these lines write your secret letter with gall water only wherein the galls [excrescences from oak trees used in making ink] have been infused but a small time (for if after you have written therewith there be any sensible color left behind upon the paper, you must throw away that water and make new). This being dry and of one color with the paper will give no cause of suspicion, and the rather because the letter purporteth a sufficient sense already. Now for the discovery thereof, you must dissolve some coppers in fair water, and with a fine caliber pencil first dipped in the coppers' water, you must artly [skillfully] moist the interlining of your letter, and thereby you shall make it sufficiently legible. This is one of the most secret ways that I know. But yet the finest conceited way of all the rest, in my opinion, is the close carriage of a letter within a lawn or cambric [fine linens] ruff or handkerchief, which a man may wear for his necessary use without the defacing of any one letter contained therein. And this serveth most fitly for a love-letter, which may without all suspicion of friends be easily presented in a handkerchief to any gentlewoman that standeth well affected to her secretary. There is also a ready way without changing of the alphabet to write one's mind speedily upon paper, and yet the same not to be deciphered without the help of a rolling pin of the same scantling [measurement] with that whereon it was first written. But these two latter conceits (for some reasons best known unto myself) I may not so boldly impart as otherwise I would (sigs. D3r–D4r).

The Table.

- 56 A ready way to catch pigeons.
- 57 A worme to catch birds with.
- 58 To catch crowes, iackdawes, &c.
- 59 To kill Seapies, Seaguls, &c.
- 60 To gather Waſpes.
- 61 To keepe garments and hangings from moath eating.
- 62 To helpe beere that ſowreth or is dead.
- 63 To helpe a chimnie that is on fire preſently.
- 64 To haue Seafiſh all the yeare long.
- 65 To make beere ſtale quickly.
- 66 To ſteale bees.
- 67 To make a tallow candle laſt long.
- 68 How to tell the iuſt number of Apples, nuts, ſhillings, &c, as they ly in bulke together.
- 69 To preuent drunkenneſſe.
- 70 An excellent tent for a Diamond.
- 71 Oyle or verniſh made to dry ſpeedilie.
- 72 To fetch out any ſtaine.
- 73 To helpe wine that reboyleth.
- 74 How to make Bragget.
- 75 Clarifieng of hony in an excellent manner.
- 76 To make an artificiall Malmeſie.
- 77 To keepe Gaſcoigne wine good, a long time.
- 78 To keepe Walnuts good and moiſt, a long time.
- 79 To preſerue the gloſſe of Spaniſh leather.
- 80 To helpe ſmoking chimnies.
- 81 Tinder and matches ſweet, and of a new kind.
- 82 An excellent mixture to ſcoure pewter withal.
- 83 To defend a horſe from flies in his trauell,
- 84 To kill Rats in a garner.
- 85 To take away the offence of noiſome vaults.
- 86 Sweet and delicate dentifrices, or rubbers for the teeth.
- 87 To helpe horſe and man that is tender footed.
- 88 To keepe oyſters good ten or twelue daies.
- 89 To keepe Lobſters, Crayfiſhes, prawnes, &c. good, and ſweete, ſome reaſonable time.
- 90 To make ſmooth or gliſtering floores or wals.
- 91 To make parchment tranſparent.
- 92 A cheape morter to be vſed in buildings.
- 93 A conceited drinking glaſſe.
- 94 To diſſolue gold, and to part the ſame from gilt ſiluer.
- 95 To know when the moone is at the full by a glaſse of water.
- 96 To melt downe iron eaſilie.
- 97 To put ſeuerall wines in one glaſſe.
- 98 The Art of memorie.
- 99 To make a conceited proiection either vpon Sol or Luna.

100 To

Table of Contents, from Hugh Plat, *The Jewell House of Art and Nature* (London, 1594). A former owner has ticked off directions of particular interest.

Apostle Spoon (English, 1565–1566), of silver, 6¾ inches long. The handle of this spoon shows St. James the Greater, identified by his pilgrim staff and the pilgrim cap hanging down his back. He also bears an open book, and there is a dove on his halo. Apostle spoons were popular christening gifts, given in complete sets of twelve or in smaller numbers. They are mentioned frequently in wills of the period. The Metropolitan Museum of Art. Bequest of Mary Strong Shattuck, 1935 (35.80.89).

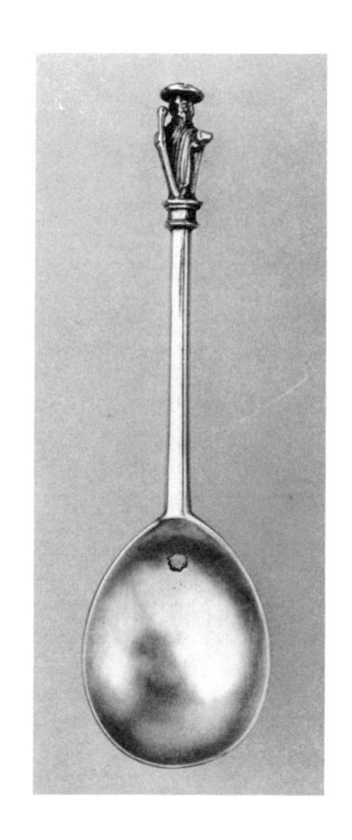

Seal Spoon (English, sixteenth century), of brass gilt, 6⅛ inches long. The handle of this spoon terminates in a small seal to imprint wax. The Metropolitan Museum of Art. Rogers Fund, 1913 (13.42.88).

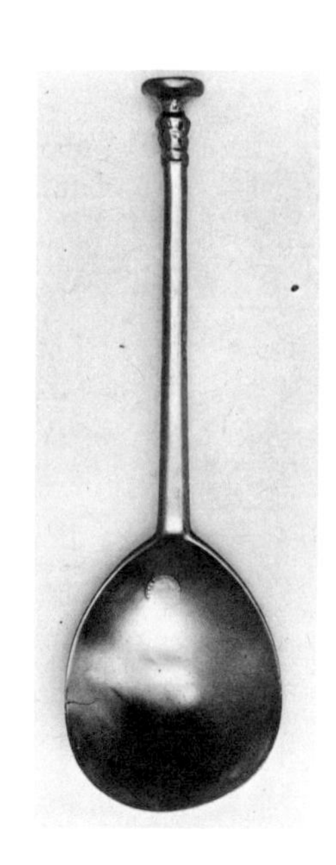

The Anatomie of mans body, and how the. xij. Signes doo gouerne in the same.

Aries. The head and face.

Taurus. Necke & throte.
Gemini Armes & shulders.
Cancer. Breast, stomack & lunges
Leo. Hart & backe.
Virgo. Guttes & belly.
Libra. Reynes & loynes
Scorpio Secrets and bladder.
Sagittarius. Thyes.
Capricornus Knees.
Aquari. Legges.

Pisces. The Feete.

The Zodiacal Man, from Walter Gray, *An Almanacke* (London, 1591). This illustration, showing perhaps the single most familiar secular image in Elizabethan England, displays the parts of the body governed by astrological signs. Pocket almanacs were extremely popular publications.

The Parlor ❧

THOMAS TUSSER

"Posies for the Parlor," in *Five Hundreth Points of Good Husbandry United to as Many of Good Huswiferie* (London, 1573)

❧ Thomas Tusser's knack for versifying practical household and agricultural advice made him very popular. In 1557 he issued a *Hundred Good Points of Husbandry* and in 1562 a *Hundred Good Points of Housewifery*; by 1573 these had grown to *Five Hundred Points.* The collection was reprinted many times over the next century and a quarter, and then in 1710 there appeared an updated review of practical advice, *Tusser Redivivus,* that retained his name as a selling point. Tusser died in debtor's prison, an irony his contemporaries were quick to note. Henry Peacham wrote, "Tusser, they tell me when thou wert alive, / Thou, teaching thrift, thyself couldst never thrive." In this poem for the parlor, Tusser pays tribute to the room as a place to entertain friends.

Parlor Scene, from a series of engravings of English customs (London, 1628). The woman on the right presents her infant: "You, sir, that have me so beguiled, / I pray receive your bastard child." She is asking for financial support. But the man returns: "O prithee, wench, let me alone / for I protest, all's spent and gone." Scattered about the chamber are the impedimenta of leisure activities—a lute, a clay pipe, a tennis racket, a wine cup—all broken and in disarray. The playing cards on the table suggest that this gentleman may have beggared himself gambling.

As hatred is the serpent's noisome rod [instrument of punishment],
So friendship is the loving gift of God.

The drunken friend is friendship very evil,
The frantic friend is friendship for the devil.

The quiet friend, all one in word and deed,
Great comfort is, like ready gold at need.

With brawling fools that wrawl [bawl] *for every wrong,*
Firm friendship never can continue long.

In time, that man shall seldom friendship miss,
That weigheth what thing touch kept in friendship is.

Ofttimes a friend is got with easy cost,
Which used evil is oft as quickly lost.

Hast thou a friend, as heart may wish, at will?
Then use him so to have his friendship still.

Wouldst have a friend, wouldst know what friend is best?
Have God thy friend, who passeth all the rest.
(sig. X4^{r})

FRANCIS BACON

"Of Frendship," from *The Essayes or Counsels, Civill and Morall* (London, 1625)

Renaissance Englishmen inherited a large classical literature in praise of friendship, and Sir Francis Bacon wrote very much in the tradition of Aristotle and Cicero. In other circles, though, there was skepticism about the possibility of reaching this classical ideal. Among puritan preachers, the rhetoric of friendship was diverted instead into the discourse of the family, where it engendered a concept that we have called "companionate" marriage. In Bacon's remark that a husband cannot talk to his wife as anything other than a wife, however, we are reminded of why the term "companionate marriage" is misleading in the hierarchical early modern period, and why the old idea of friendship continued to hold such appeal. There was no comparable tradition, by the way, for women, who had "gossips" rather than friends.

A principal fruit of friendship is the ease and discharge of the fullness and swellings of the heart, which passions of all kinds do cause and induce. We know diseases of stoppings and suffocations are the most dangerous in the body, and it is not much otherwise in the mind. You may take sarsa [sarsaparilla] to open the liver, steel to open the spleen, flowers of sulphur for the lungs, castoreum for the brain; but no receipt openeth the heart but a true friend, to whom you may impart griefs, joys, fears, hopes, suspicions, counsels, and whatsoever lieth upon the heart to oppress it in a kind of civil shrift or confession.

It is a strange thing to observe how high a rate great kings and monarchs do set upon this fruit of friendship whereof we speak: so great, as they purchase it many times at the hazard of their own safety and greatness. For princes, in regard of the distance of their fortune from that of their subjects and servants, cannot gather this fruit, except (to make themselves capable thereof) they raise some persons to be, as it were, companions and almost equals to themselves, which many times sorteth to inconvenience. . . . This hath been done not by weak and passionate princes only, but by the wisest and most politic that ever reigned, who have oftentimes joined to themselves some of their servants whom both themselves have called *friends*, and allowed others likewise to call them in the same manner, using the word which is received between private men. . . .

The second fruit of friendship is healthful and sovereign for the understanding, as the first is for the affections. For friendship maketh indeed a fair day in the affections from storm and tempests. But it maketh daylight in the understanding out of darkness and confusion of thoughts. . . . In the communicating and discoursing with another, he tosseth his thoughts more easily; he marshalleth them more orderly; he seeth how they look when they are turned into words; finally, he waxeth wiser than himself, and that more by an hour's discourse than by a day's meditation. . . .

Add now, to make this second fruit of friendship complete, that other point which lieth more open and falleth within vulgar observation, which is faithful counsel from a friend. . . . So as, there is as much difference between the counsel that a friend giveth and that a man giveth himself as there is between the counsel of a friend and of a flatterer. For there is no such flatterer as is a man's self, and there is no such remedy against flattery of a man's self as the liberty of a friend. Counsel is of two sorts, the one concerning manners, the other concerning business. For the first, the best preservative to keep a mind in health is the faithful admonition of a friend. The calling of a man's self to a strict account is a medicine sometime too piercing and corrosive. Reading good books of morality is a little flat and dead. Observing our faults in others is sometimes unproper for our case. But the best receipt—best, I say, to work, and best to take—is the admonition of a friend. It is a strange thing to behold what gross errors and extreme absurdities many (especially of the greater sort) do commit for want of a friend to tell them of them, to the great damage both of their fame and fortune. . . .

The best way to represent to life the manifold use of friendship is to cast and see how many things there are which a man cannot do himself. And then it will appear that it was a sparing speech of the ancients to say that a friend is another himself, for that a friend is far more than himself. . . . A man cannot speak to his son, but as a father; to his wife, but as a husband; to his enemy, but upon terms: whereas a friend may speak as the case requires and not as it sorteth with the person. But to enumerate these things were endless. I have given the rule where a man cannot fitly play his own part: if he have not a friend, he may quit the stage (sigs. $V3^v$–$V4^r$, $X2^v$, $X3^v$, $Y1^v$–$Y2^r$).

RICHARD BRATHWAIT

The English Gentleman (London, 1630)

❧ Reading was often a shared pursuit in the Elizabethan household, and domestic advice manuals preached the benefits of reading aloud from the scriptures to the assembled family and servants. History was also a suitably improving topic, as Richard Brathwait demonstrates. His discussion seems to tend more to private reading than communal, but it has a public end: the cultivation of informed conversation among friends.

There is no history more useful or relation more needful for any gentleman than our own modern chronicles, where he shall observe many notable passages worthy his reading. As first, how his country was first planted, how by degrees it became peopled, how to civility reduced, how by wholesome laws restrained, and how by the providence of the Almighty in so calm and peaceable manner established. Here he shall see a good king, but a bad man; there a good man, but a bad king. Again, here he shall see the state more weakened by civil broils than foreign wars, security being no less hurtful at home than hostility abroad. . . . Again, if we should but read, and reading consider, how peaceful the government, how quiet the sleeps, how cheerful the delights were of such as came by lawful and lineal succession to the crown. And the heavy nights, troubled thoughts, broken sleeps, and many tedious hours which those were owners of, who came by usurpation to enjoy (with little joy) a princely diadem. . . . For to use one example for all: who should but consider the practices which Richard the Third used to get a crown, planting his kingdom on an indirect foundation—blood—and those many strange passages and overtures which happened in his reign, with those fearful visions which appeared to him before his death, would certainly set down this for his rest: that it is not what we have without us, but what we have within us that procures us peace or disquiet. . . . Certainly, discourses of this nature cannot choose but minister much profit with delight and enable you that are gentlemen to entertain the time with much content to them that hear you. For in this treasury or storehouse of history, you shall find better means than all the helps to discourse which our weak pamphleteers can publish to enable you for discourse in all companies. For to restrain or tie yourselves to a set form of discourse, as if you were to do nothing without rules, were too pedantical. Besides, you should be sometimes so scantled [limited] for want of subjects, that unless the subject whereof you are to discourse fall happily within your own element, your ship for want of sea room would run aground. Whereas history (the sweetest recreation of the mind) will afford variety (being not curtailed by epitomes [brief abstracts], which are the moths of history) both for table-talk to delight and discourse of more serious consequence. Which in my opinion would better seem a gentleman than to entertain time in nothing but the cry of dogs or flight of hawks, which, as they are gentlemanly pleasures, and worthily approved (as I formerly noted), so are they to be used but only as pleasures and recreations—of which to speak sparingly were much better than only to discourse of them, as if our whole reading were in them (sigs. Ff1v–Ff2v).

HENRY PEACHAM

"Of Music," in *The Compleat Gentleman* (London, 1622)

❧ Henry Peacham sought royal and noble patronage by authoring a treatise on drawing and painting (in 1606) and a book of emblems (in 1612). By 1613, he had apparently succeeded. He left for two years on the Continent, reportedly as private tutor to three young gentlemen. There, he himself studied music with Horatio Vecchi in Modena, Italy. In his essay "Of Music," he praises Vecchi as "most pleasing of all other for his conceit and variety," and he also displays his familiarity with other Italian masters. At the same time, he strongly defends English musical invention. Skill in music is necessary to "the complete gentleman."

The physicians will tell you that the exercise of music is a great lengthener of the life by stirring and reviving of the spirits, holding a secret sympathy with them. Besides, the exercise of singing openeth the breast and pipes. It is an enemy to melancholy and dejection of the mind, which St. Chrysostom truly called "the devil's bath." Yea, a curer of some diseases: in Apulia, in Italy, and thereabouts, it is most certain that those who are stung with the tarantula are cured only by music. Besides the aforesaid benefit of singing, it is a most ready help for a bad pronunciation and distinct speaking, which I have heard confirmed by many great divines. Yea, I myself have known many children to have been helped of their stammering in speech only by it. . . .

I might run into an infinite sea of the praise and

use of so excellent an art, but I only show it you with the finger because I desire not that any noble or gentleman should, save his private recreation at leisurable hours, prove a master in the same or neglect his more weighty employments, though I avouch it a skill worthy the knowledge and exercise of the greatest prince. . . .

For motets and music of piety and devotion as well for the honor of our nation as the merit of the man, I prefer above all other our phoenix, Master William Byrd, whom in that kind I know not whether any may equal. I am sure none excel, even by the judgment of France and Italy, who are very sparing in the commendation of strangers in regard of that conceit they hold of themselves. . . . .

I willingly, to avoid tediousness, forbear to speak of the worth and excellency of the rest of our English composers, Master Doctor Dowland, Thomas Morley, Master Alphonso, Master Wilbye, Master Kirby, Master Weelkes, Michael East, Master Bateson, Master Deering, with sundry others inferior to none in the world, how much soever the Italian attributes to himself, for depth of skill and richness of conceit.

Infinite is the sweet variety that the theoric of music exerciseth the mind withal, as the contemplation of proportion, of concords and discords, diversity of moods and tones, infiniteness of invention, et cetera. But I dare affirm there is no one science in the world that so affecteth the free and generous spirit with a more delightful and inoffensive recreation, or better disposeth the mind to what is commendable and virtuous. . . .

How doth music amaze us, when, assure[d] of discords, she maketh the sweetest harmony! And who can show us the reason why two basins, bowls, brass pots, or the like of the same bigness, the one being full, the other empty, shall, stricken, be a just diapason in sound one to the other, or that there should be such sympathy in sounds that two lutes of equal size being laid upon a table and tuned unison, or alike in *Gamma, G sol re ut,* or any other string, the one stricken, the other untouched shall answer it?

But to conclude, if all arts hold their esteem and value according to their effects, account this goodly science not among the number of those which Lucian placeth without the gates of hell as vain and unprofitable, but of such which are . . . the fountains of our lives' good and happiness. Since it is a principal means of glorifying our merciful Creator, it heightens our devotion, it gives delight and ease to our travails, it expelleth sadness and heaviness of spirit, preserveth people in concord and amity, allayeth fierceness and anger, and, lastly, is the best physic for many melancholy diseases (sigs. O3^{r}–P2^{v}).

Lute (Italian, 1598). The maker was Michielle Harton of Padua.

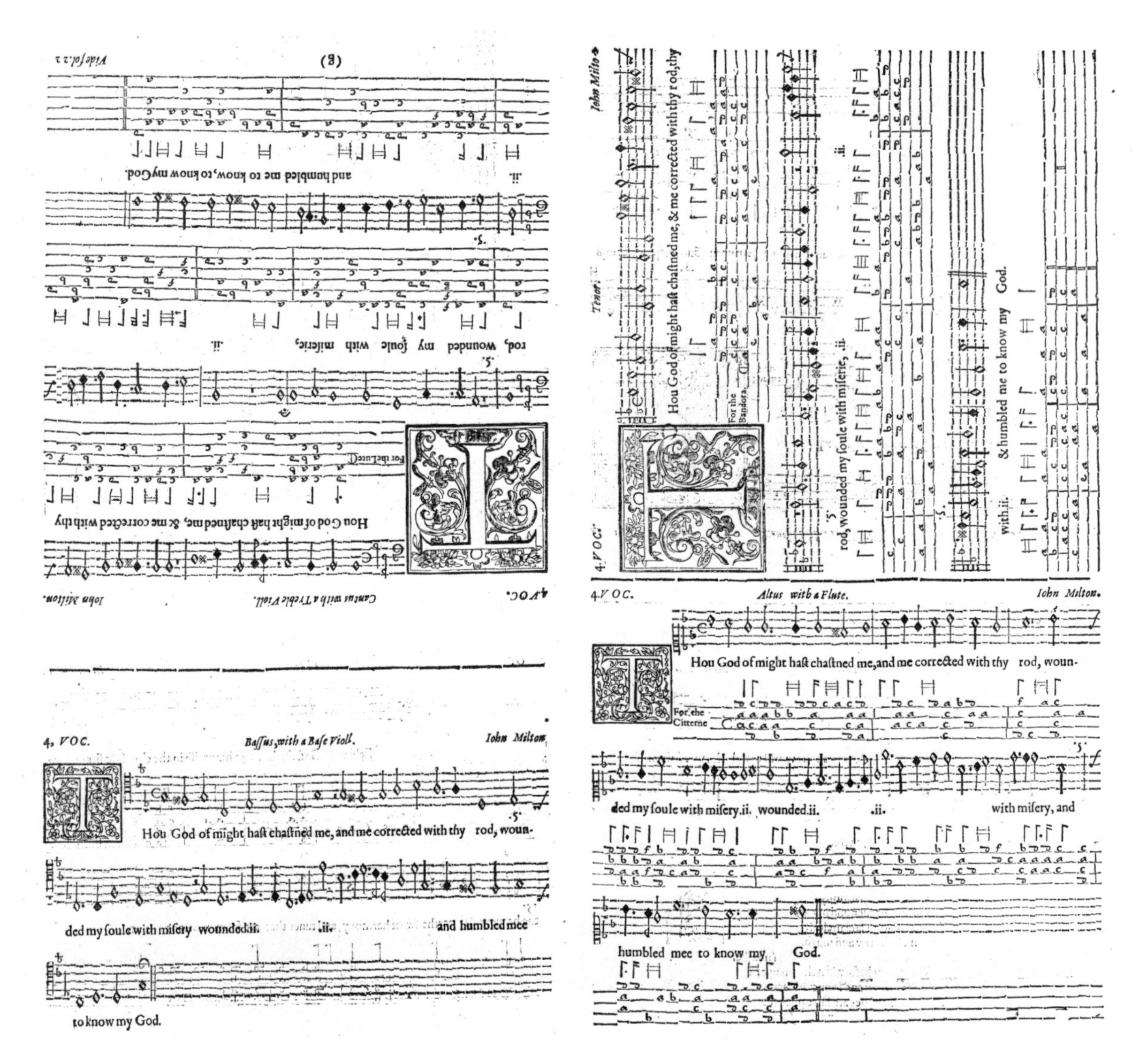

"How God of Might Hast Chastened Me," from William Leighton, *The Teares or Lamentacions of a Sorrowfull Soule* (London, 1614). Four parts are printed to be readable by four singers and instrumentalists standing around a table.

THOMAS WILCOX

A Glasse for Gamesters, and Namelie for Suche as Delight in Cards and Dise: Wherein Thei Maie See Not Onely the Vanitie, but also the Vilenesse of Those Plaies Plainly Discovered and Overthrowen by the Word of God (London, 1581)

❧ Games like tables (or backgammon), cards, and dice were very much associated with domestic entertainment, and specifically with the parlor, a room set aside for leisure pursuits. Of course, these activities had their detractors. Thomas Wilcox's treatise is interesting because he does not dismiss all games out of hand, but distinguishes among them and reserves special censure for gambling. The Puritan Wilcox lost a ministerial post in London for his reformist beliefs, and was twice imprisoned. In 1572, with John Field, he petitioned Parliament to level the ecclesiastical hierarchy and abolish the bishopric. From Newgate Prison, Field and Wilcox wrote Archbishop Parker charging him with cruelty; their wives delivered the letter.

I take play at honest and lawful games to be a thing allowable and lawful, and to be of the number of those things which are left in Christian liberty. Which liberty we must not abuse as an occasion unto the flesh, but according to such rules as God hath left for the lawful use of the same in his holy word. Wherefore I forbid not, neither do I condemn all manner of play: yea, I think it not evil that sometimes a Christian man play and refresh himself. Provided alway[s] that such recreation and delight be in things lawful and honest, and that also with moderation or measure. For it is not meet that men should spend at play (though the play itself be never so lawful) either those things or that time which God hath allotted him to other ends and purposes. For God hath given him goods for the maintenance of himself and his family and the relieving of those which want necessary succor and maintenance. . . .

I fear not to affirm that it is unlawful to play for

Chess Board (English, sixteenth century), with ivory inlays and veneers. Hunters, fleeing beasts, and flowers decorate the inset squares of this chess board, which reverses for a game of tables, or backgammon.

money, to win it, and purse it up when it is won; that is to say, either for a man to lose his own money, or to win another man's, and so to make gain of the same. . . . But some say they delight not in play, except they play for money. But I will demand of them to what use they intend to bestow that money? Peradventure they will say, upon a feast. Why not rather upon the poor? But I say, it is much better and safer not to play for any money. For although it may be that thou thyself art not touched with covetousness, the other yet with whom thou playest is peradventure touched. Let the occasions unto evil be taken away, which otherwise are very many. . . .

I take these games of dice and cards, being, as I said before, games of lot, hazard, or chance, to be flatly against the third commandment, "Thou shalt not take the name of the Lord thy God in vain." The reason that leadeth me thereunto is this: lot, or chance (as we call it), is one of the principal testimonies of the power of God, because it is ruled and governed immediately by his hand and providence, and was never ordained of God for anything but for matters of great weight, and never used amongst the godly but in causes of great importance, as in parting of goods, dividing of lands, election of magistrates, choice of ministers, and such like things, and was appointed to take away all occasion of heat in words and quarrels and corruptions in speech. Now for us to take that which God hath appointed to so great and holy uses only, and to apply it to serve our fond affections in every light trifle and case of no weight—what is it but to tread under foot the ordinance and institution of God and so, consequently, to be transgressors of that third commandment? (sigs. A6^{v}–A7^{v}, B2^{r-v}, B7^{v}–B8^{r}).

Title-Page Illustration from *The Most Ancient and Learned Playe Called The Philosophers Game* (London, 1563), attributed to Ralph Lever.

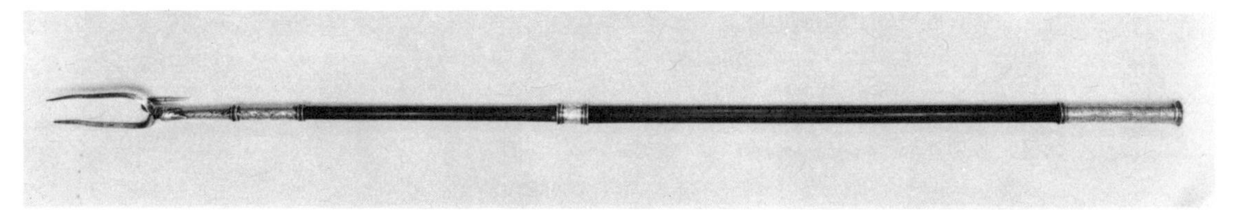

Toasting Fork (English, 1561), of exotic hardwood and silver, 34½ inches long. The Metropolitan Museum of Art. Gift of Irwin Untermyer, 1968 (68.141.297).

SECTION FOUR

SOCIAL ORDER

· SOCIAL ORDER ·

IN 1579, SIR FRANCIS AND LADY ELIZabeth Willoughby separated. Theirs had been a troubled marriage from the start. When Lady Elizabeth became publicly rebellious and disobedient to him, Sir Francis had instituted a series of measures that effectively stripped her of her accepted role in his household. She was confined to certain chambers in the house and forbidden to enter rooms containing the household stores. She was also barred from purchasing household supplies. She was prohibited from caring for her children, their supervision being entrusted instead to a nurse. And she was denied all authority over the household servants.

Lady Elizabeth would have understood each of these rights and responsibilities to have been guaranteed to her by the traditions that John Dod, Robert Cleaver, William Gouge, and William Whately represented in their sermons and advice manuals. Surviving documents record that she responded to her husband's orders with passionate outrage, threatening to kill herself. As long as she was under his roof, though, she found no allies, for the household servants recognized Sir Francis's overriding authority. When knives were accordingly removed from the Lady Elizabeth's access, she attempted to stab herself with a pair of scissors.

There was little scope for divorce in the Elizabethan years, but at her social level it was possible for Lady Elizabeth to establish independent living arrangements. Her father petitioned her husband to provide the necessary funds for her expenses, and by 1582 Sir Francis was required to do so by the Queen, in the amount of £200 per year. Lady Elizabeth also solicited support from William Cecil, Lord Burghley. Burghley's secretary, Sir Michael Hicks, wrote in response, advising the Lady Elizabeth "to submit your will to the pleasure of your head" as is "warranted by the word of God which binds all women of what birth or calling soever they be." Lady Elizabeth subsequently wrote to her husband repeatedly, asking to return to him. In 1585 she pledged that she would "perform all good duties that do become a loving and obedient wife towards her husband."

In 1587 Dorothy Willoughby, the couple's second child, married. To his shame, Sir Francis could not host her wedding feast, "because by reason of his wife's absence and the furniture of his house being much decayed, he had not designed to keep house this year." After eight years of separation, in 1588 he took Lady Elizabeth back. He had just completed his contribution to the Great Rebuilding, the impressive Wollaton Hall, and he looked forward to active hospitality there as also to the weddings of younger daughters.

As told by Alice T. Friedman, the story of the Willoughbys encapsulates the economic, political, and social meanings of the household in the Elizabethan years. First, the consequences of their separation demonstrate that, in order for the household to function effectively as an economic unit, every member of it had an integral part to play. This is easy for us to apprehend when we think of peasant farmers, poor tradesmen, and those at the lowest economic levels. But we must also understand that even in this upper register, and with a staff of forty-five or fifty servants at Wollaton Hall alone, Sir Francis Willoughby was unable to maintain his customary social obligations without the contributions of a wife. Second, the cause of their estrangement and the conditions of their reunion remind us that their roles, as also those of their servants, were given political definitions and ranks. These positions on the internal hierarchy were believed to be critical to the process of organizing individual efforts toward a shared economic purpose. Finally, the interventions of Queen Elizabeth and Sir Michael Hicks intimate the level of larger social investment in the traditional structures and functions of the household. As Gordon J. Schochet has shown, the household was a social institution.

The extracts that follow reveal how dominant this institution was, how strongly Elizabethan society relied on the household as the building block of the commonwealth, and how uneasily it dealt with exceptions to the household pattern. For one thing, the household structure, easily perceived and understood, afforded a means of conceptualizing larger social organizations. The constitution of the state, for example, was held to model itself on that of the household; the state was monarchic even as the household was patriarchal. The two were bound in a nexus of shared conventions, obligations, and expectations, and, because of their symbiotic structures, whatever affected one was believed to affect the other.

As case histories go, the Willoughbys are useful reminders of one other point. Their story starts with a marriage, just as Elizabethan households started with marriage. Each economic unit was inaugurated by a marital alliance, each accrued servants, and most were then further extended (and extended into the future) by children. In sum, the Elizabethan household *as an institution* was heterosexual and hierarchical. There were other patterns of relationship in the period, but the household is not the best point of access to them.

Alternative stories have been introduced here: the man who was killed by his wife, the maidservant who forswore herself, the householder who fornicated with his maidservant, the mother who murdered her children, and the knight who stabbed his hosts, for instance. But these disruptions occurred within conventional household frameworks. They did not break through basic ideological structures and assumptions, and their resolution reinforced prevailing beliefs and values. The power of the household as an institution was that it seemed "natural"—unideological—through its link to the most primary relationships and emotions. With the benefit of historical distance, we can ask ourselves how natural the authoritarian Elizabethan household was. And perhaps we can ask ourselves how natural our own institutions are, as well.

[ANDREW KINGSMILL]

"A Laudable and Learned Discourse, of the Worthynesse of Honorable Wedlocke, Written in the Behalfe of all . . . Maydes as Wydowes . . . for their Singuler Instruction, to Choose Them Vertuous and Honest Husbandes," in *The Schoole of Honest and Vertuous Lyfe* (London, 1579)

❧ One of three "discourses" assembled in a volume entitled *The School of Honest and Virtuous Life* and attributed to Thomas Pritchard, "The Worthiness of Honorable Wedlock" was apparently written instead by Andrew Kingsmill, a Puritan divine who died on the Continent in 1569. In 1574 his friend Francis Mills published this and other pieces by Kingsmill under the title *A View of Man's Estate.* "The Worthiness of Honorable Wedlock" was written to Kingsmill's sister, recently widowed. Kingsmill dedicated another tract to her, as well, affording a poignant glimpse of an affective relationship not otherwise explored here, that between siblings. In the early modern period, widows were always encouraged to remarry, and thus to rejoin the circle of accepted social relations. Kingsmill's perspective on the moral profits and social benefits of marriage is far from idiosyncratic, but he is unusually pithy in itemizing them.

Who will not commend honorable wedlock as a thing of great excellency? Who will not think it a state of living worthy high praise and commendation? Yea, who will not judge that it ought to be embraced with meeting and folded arms, seeing that by it, so many notable treasures do happen unto us? Virtue is maintained, vice is eschewed, houses are replenished, cities are inhabited, the ground is tilled, sciences are practiced, kingdoms flourish, amity is preserved, the public weal is defended, natural succession is continued, good arts are taught, honest order is kept, Christendom is enlarged, God's word is promoted, the conscience is quieted, lewd life is avoided, and the glory of God is highly advanced and set forth (sig. G1^{r}).

MATTHEW GRIFFITH

Bethel: Or A Forme for Families, in which all Sorts of both Sexes, are soe Squarde, and Framde by the Word, as They may best Serve in theire Severall Places, for Usefull Pieces in Gods Buildinge (London, 1633)

❧ It was not unusual for household construction to be taken as a metaphor for any ordering process. House building was accomplished in stages, from gathering materials to setting a foundation, raising the framework, placing a roof, and ornamenting the interior. These efforts resulted in a form that shaped its landscape and imprinted on the eye as a recognizably human achievement. Preacher Matthew Griffith applied this useful metaphor to the familiar genre of the domestic advice manual, finding analogies between building a house and establishing a household. Griffith was a man of passionate conviction, several times imprisoned as a royalist. Meanwhile, his daughter's derision of Oliver Cromwell's Roundheads provoked them to kill her in 1645. Griffith himself burst a blood vessel and died at the pulpit in 1665.

This building is uniform; this treatise, methodical, for I here present the whole body of the oeconomics [the subject of household management] under a continued metaphor of building an house. . . .

This building is a Bethel, for it is the Lord that builds the house. God is here the master builder, and therefore I call it God's building. We (of the ministry) are but laborers together with God, sayeth the great doctor of the Gentiles. Each master builder (as you know) hath his day-laborers to attend him, and God Himself hath been pleased to employ me (though the weakest and unworthiest) in this his work. . . .

And from those premises I infer this conclusion, that if we desire to serve God as so many members of his family, we must not only be parts of a family, as a rotten post may be part of a sound house, but we must see that we be part of God's building, who useth not to build hay, stubble, and the like trash upon a good foundation; but gold, silver, brass, stone, and other the like sound materials which will abide both wind and weather. . . .

What is God's building? A well-ordered family.

What is a well-ordered family? That which hath both an orderly head and orderly members, having mutual relation to each other. . . . But nowadays, alas, how may a man weary and wear out himself in posting from coast to coast and from the river to the world's end, before he find so well-ordered a family? For:

Some houses are now fain to hop headless, as having such governors as are either tyrants or fools. And how is it likely they should ever direct and moderate others, who are themselves so irregular? When, indeed, the head should represent that majesty of God at home which holy Job did abroad. . . . Other houses, though they have good heads, yet are their members nought and dissolute. And therefore these may be compared to a comely person who hath yet some putrified flesh, a broken leg, or a withered arm, et cetera. And such an head must know that it nearly concerns him to provide for the cure of such an epileptic member as is loose in the joints of his obedience, or else to see that it be cut off in time, for fear lest it gangrene the rest, and so the whole body perish. . . .

And as 'tis the praise of any builder that he's careful to lay a good foundation, so must we in this metaphorical building (in my text) have an eye that our foundation be sure, that so neither wind, nor weather, no, nor the gates of hell itself may ever be able to prevail against it. Now, the foundation of this our spiritual building is marriage in the Lord. . . .

The fourth thing to be mainly looked unto if we will be part of God's building is that we be of God's finishing. For as in a material building, though the foundation be never so well laid, and the body of it never so strongly erected, yet it will not hold out wind and weather unless it be finished: so it holds in this metaphorical building, which we have been so busy about all this while, both in laying the foundation and also in erecting the fabric. For we shall find little comfort and content in it unless it be finished, which now (by God's grace) we shall do. For the finishing of this our building is nothing else but the appointing of a master and his mate, to look to this structure, that there be no dilapidations, disorders, confusions, et cetera (sigs. A6^{r-v}, B2^{v}, B4^{r-v}, P8^{v}, Cc4^{r-v}).

GEFFRAY MINSHULL

Essayes and Characters of a Prison and Prisoners (London, 1618)

❧ The acquisitive pressures of early modern life had their victims. Those who fell into irredeemable debt were confined to debtors' prison. There, because they had to pay for their food and lodging, they would fall further and further behind unless rescued by kinsmen or friends. As this pamphlet reflects, there was no particular social stigma to indebtedness. But the witty tone of the text does not disguise the despair engendered by separation from home, family, friends, and the usual patterns of household life.

The Character of a Prison

A prison is a grave to bury men alive and a place wherein a man, for half a year's experience, may learn more law than he can at Westminster for an hundred pound.

It is a *microcosmus*, a little world of woe; it is a map of misery; it is a place that will learn a young man more villainy, if he be apt to take it, in one half year, than he can learn at twenty dicing houses, bowling alleys, brothel houses, or ordinaries; and an old man more policy than if he had been pupil to Machiavel.

It is a place that hath more diseases predominant in it than the pest-house in the plague-time, and it stinks more than the Lord Mayor's doghouse or Paris-garden in August.

It is a little commonwealth, although little wealth be common there; it is a desert where dessert lies hoodwinked; it is a famous city wherein are all trades, for here lies the alchemist that can rather make *ex auro non aurum* [out of gold, something not gold], than *ex non auro aurum* [out of something not gold, gold].

It is as intricate a place as Rosamond's labyrinth and is as full of blind meanders and crooked turnings that it is unpossible to find the way out, except he be directed by a silver clew [ball of thread], and can never overcome the Minotaur without a golden ball to work his own safety.

It is as Inns of Court, for herein lawyers inhabit, that have crotchets [fanciful devices] to free other men, yet all their quirks and quiddities cannot enfranchize themselves. . . .

It is an exile which doth banish a man from all contentments, wherein his actions do so terrify him, that it makes a man grow desperate.

To conclude, what is it not? In a word, it is the very idea of all misery and torments. It converts joy into sorrow, riches into poverty, and ease into discontentments (sigs. B2r–B3r).

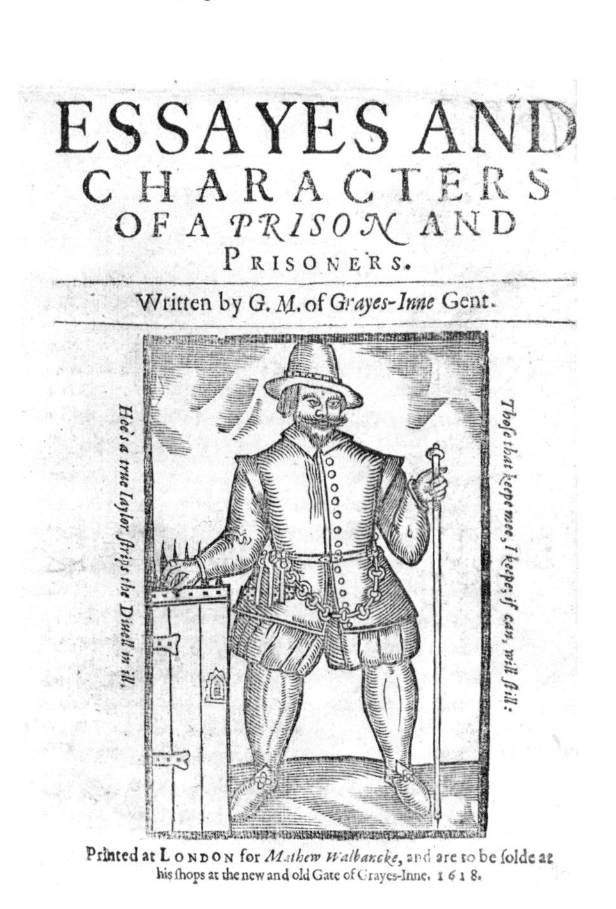

Jailer, from Geffray Minshull, *Essayes and Characters of a Prison* (London, 1618). A jailer was known by his ominous set of keys.

BY THE QUEEN

A Proclamation Concerning New Buildings and Inmates, in or about the Citie of London (1602)

❧ The rapid growth of the London population put pressure on any number of city services and institutions, only one of which was housing. It was primarily through housing, however, that remedies of containment were attempted. In this proclamation, the state acknowledged that similar efforts four and five years earlier had failed, "partly by the covetous and insatiable dispositions of some persons that without any respect of the common good and public profit of the realm do only regard their own particular lucre and gain, and partly by the negligence and corruption of others."

Whereas the Queen's most excellent Majesty, heretofore in her Princely wisdom and providence forseeing the great and manifold inconveniences and mischiefs which did then grow and were like more and more to increase unto the state of the city of London and the suburbs and confines thereof, by the access and confluence of people to inhabit the same; not only by reason that such multitudes could hardly be governed by ordinary justice to serve God and obey her Majesty without constituting and addition of more officers and enlarging of authorities and jurisdictions for that purpose, but also could hardly be provided of sustentation of victual, food, and other like necessaries for man's relief upon reasonable prices; and finally for that such great multitudes of people, being brought to inhabit in small rooms, whereof a great part being very poor, and such as must live by begging or by worse means, and being heaped up together and in a sort smothered with many families of children and servants in one house or small tenement, it must needs follow, if any plague or other universal sickness should by God's permission enter among those multitudes, that the same would not only spread itself and invade the whole city and confines, but would be also dispersed through all other parts of the realm, whereby great mortality should ensue, to the manifest danger of the whole body thereof, out of which neither her Majesty's own person (but by God's special ordinance) nor any other whatsoever could be exempted: For remedy whereof, her Majesty by her proclamation bearing date the seventh day of July, in the two and twentieth year of her reign, did charge and command all manner of persons of what quality so ever they were, to desist and forbear from any new buildings of any house or tenement within three miles from any of the gates of the said city of London, to serve for any habitation or lodging for any person, where no former house had been known to have been, in the memory of such as were then living; and also to forbear from letting or setting or suffering any more families than one only to be placed or to inhabit from thenceforth in any house that before that time had been inhabited, as by the said Proclamation, amongst other provisions, charges, and commandments therein contained, more fully and at large appeareth. . . .

(1) First, that no new buildings of any new house or tenement be from henceforth erected or attempted to be erected within the City of London, or the suburbs thereof, or within three miles of the City of London or Westminster, except the same be upon the foundation of a former dwelling house. And if any such happen to be begun, that the same be forthwith by the view of the Justices of the Peace within that limit pulled down, and the timber thereof begun to be set up to be sold to the relief of the poor of the parish, where the same shall happen to be.

(2) That from henceforth there be no dividing of any house or tenement within the precincts aforesaid into several dwellings, but to be kept as one house, nor any more dwelling houses to be built upon any former foundation of a dwelling house, than before was upon the same house.

(3) And for such tenements as have been divided within these ten years within London, Westminster, or within three miles' compass thereof, the inmates to be avoided presently, if they have no estate [tenure] for life, lives, or years yet enduring. And for such as have such estate or term, then as the same shall end and determine, so the tenement to be reduced to the former estate, and no tenant to be admitted in place of the other.

(4) All sheds and shops to be plucked down that have been builded within the places and precincts aforesaid, within seven years last past.

(5) All houses, tenements, or buildings erected within these seven years last past, and not let out, or being void of a tenant, order to be taken that the same shall not be inhabited nor let to any unless the owner shall be content that the Churchwardens and the Minister, by allowance of two or more of the Justices of the Peace of that division, shall dispose of them for some of the poor, or for the good and behalf of the poor of the parish that are destitute of houses, and at and under such rents as they shall allow.

(6) All other tenements or buildings not built upon an old foundation of a dwelling house that are not at this present finished, to be plucked down,

By the Queene.

A Proclamation concerning new buildings and Inmates, in or about the Citie of London.

Hereas the Queenes most excellent Maiestie, heretofore in her Princely wisedome and prouidence foreseeing the great and manifolde inconueniences and mischiefes, which did then grow, and were like more and more to increase vnto the State of the citie of London, and the Suburbes and confines thereof, by the accesse and confluence of people to inhabite in the same, Not onely by reason that such multitudes could hardly bee gouerned by ordinarie Justice to serue God and obey her Maiestie, without constituting and addition of more Officers, and enlarging of authorities and Jurisdictions for that purpose, but also could hardly bee prouided of sustentation of victuall, foode, and other like necessaries for mans reliefe vpon reasonable prices, And finally for that such great multitudes of people, being brought to inhabite in small roomes, whereof a great part being verie poore, and such as must liue by begging or by worse meanes, and being heaped vp together, and in a sort smothered with many families of children and seruants in one house or smal Tenement, it must needs follow, if any plague, or other vniuersal sicknes should by Gods permission enter among those multitudes, that the same would not onely spread it selfe, and inuade the whole Citie and confines, but would bee also dispersed through all other parts of the Realme, whereby great mortalitie should ensue, to the manifest danger of the whole bodie thereof, out of which neither her Maiesties owne person (but by Gods speciall ordinance) nor any other whatsoeuer could be exempted: For remedie whereof, her Maiestie by her Proclamation bearing date the seuenth day of July, in the two and twentieth yere of her Raigne, did charge and command all maner of persons of what qualitie so euer they were, to desist and forbeare from any new buildings of any house or Tenement within three miles from any of the gates of the said Citie of London, to serue for any habitation or lodging for any person, where no former house had beene knowen to haue beene, in the memorie of such as were then liuing; And also to forbeare from letting or setting, or suffering any more families then one onely, to bee placed or to inhabite from thenceforth in any house that before that time had beene inhabited, as by the said Proclamation, amongst other prouisions, charges and commandements therein contained, more fully and at large appeareth. And whereas afterwards, in the nine and thirtieth and fourtieth yeeres of her Highnesse raigne, vpon seuerall Bils of complaint exhibited by her Maiesties Atturney generall into the high Court of Starrechamber before her Highnesse Councell there, against diuers persons for diuers offences by them committed and done contrarie to the tenour of the said Proclamation, The said Councell grauely waighing and considering the manifolde mischiefes that did then happen, and were like dayly to encrease, for want of due execution of the said Proclamation, did make and set downe verie profitable and necessarie Orders and Decrees in that behalfe, as by the said Orders and Decrees remaining of Record in her said Court of Starchamber more fully and at large appeareth. And whereas the Lords and others of her Highnes Honorable Priuie Councel, perceiuing great delay, negligence, and parcialitie vsed in the execution of the said Proclamation, Orders, and Decrees, haue also at sundrie times written their letters vnto such of her Highnesse Officers to whome it did apperteine, for the putting in due execution of the saide Proclamation, Orders and Decrees: Her Maiestie perceiuing, that notwithstanding her gracious and Princely Commandement signified by her said Proclamation, and the Honourable care of her priuie Councell touching the same, yet it falleth out, partly by the couetous & insatiable dispositions of some persons, that without any respect of the Common good and publike profite of the Realme, doe onely regard their owne particular lucre and gaine, and partly by the negligence and corruption of others, who by reason of their offices & places ought to see the said Proclamation, Orders, and Decrees duely perfourmed, and yet doe vndutifully neglect the same, that the said mischiefes and inconueniences do daily encrease and multiplie, to the great contempt of her Maiesties royall commandement, the manifest danger of the whole Realme, and especially of the saide Citie of London and the confines thereof, and to the great offence of many of her faithfull and louing subiects: Doth by the aduice of her said Councell, straightly charge and command the Lorde Maior of the Citie of London, and all other Officers hauing authoritie within the same, and also all Justices of peace, Lords and Bailiffes of Liberties, not being within the Jurisdiction of the said Lorde Maior of London, faithfully and diligently to execute and perfourme, and cause to be executed and perfourmed within the Citie of London, and within all places being within three miles of the Cities of London or Westminster, these Articles following.

A Proclamation Concerning New Buildings and Inmates, in or about the Citie of London (London, 1602).

and the builders or leasers that bind or tie the tenants to build upon their ground to be bound to appear in the Star Chamber, and to commit the workmen to prison that shall persist after warning given by any Justice of the Peace or Constable.

(7) Those houses and tenements that are already demised or letten, diligently to enquire what term they have, and if they have them from year to year, then the tenant to be commanded to avoid and to provide himself elsewhere without the precincts aforesaid before the end of three months. And order to be also taken that the house be not let again, but in such sort as is before expressed.

(8) When and as often as any tenant shall avoid, decease, or leave any of the said new erected tenements, or that their terms do expire, then, and so often, strict order to be taken, that the same be not afterwards let or set, but in manner before set down and allowed. And if any person shall demise or take any the tenements aforesaid or any part of any of them, contrary to the true meaning and intent of this proclamation, every such person to be committed to prison, until advertisement shall thereof be given to the Lords of her Majesty's Privy Council, and not to be delivered before he be bound to answer the same in the Star Chamber, as contemners of this her Majesty's proclamation.

(9) And if any shall henceforth offend in new building or in dividing of any tenement contrary to the true intent and meaning of this proclamation, and all workmen continuing the same work after they shall be forbidden thereof by any Justice of Peace or Constable of the place or limit where the same shall happen to be, shall be committed to prison until they shall find sufficient sureties for their appearance in the Star Chamber, to answer their contempts there, and for their good behavior in the mean season.

To our Wel-Beloved Friends, to Whom this Present Writing Shall Come. Wee the Mayor, Justices, Minister, Aldermen, and Burgesses of the Borough of Banbury in the County of Oxon. Wish all Welfare and Happinesse (London, 1628)

❧ The disaster that inspired this announcement is described in the title of William Whately's pamphlet on the subject: *Sin No More, Or A Sermon Preached in the Parish Church of Banbury on Tuesday the Fourth of March Last Past* [i.e., 1628], *upon Occasion of a Most Terrible Fire that Happened There on the Sabbath Day Immediately Precedent, and within the Space of Four Hours was Carried from the One End of the Town to the Other with that Fury as, Continuing to Burn all the Night, and Much of the Next Day, It Consumed 103 Dwelling Houses, 20 Kiln-Houses, and Other Outhouses* [outbuildings], *to the Number of 660 Bays* [an architectural unit, generally fifteen or twenty feet wide] *and Upwards, Together with So Much Malt and Other Grain and Commodities, as Amounted at the Least to the Value of Twenty Thousand Pounds.* Whately is one of the twenty leading citizens of Banbury, Oxfordshire, who signed the letter transcribed below, which survives in a unique copy in the Folger collection. Among a group of "neighbor bordering ministers" also testifying to the "lamentable ruins" and mass homelessness of Banbury are John Dod and Robert Cleaver. All events such as these—including monstrous births, floods, and earthquakes—were taken as warnings against the sins of the larger populace, not just those immediately affected. Charity was solicited in the same communal spirit.

Our grievous loss, we presume, hath sufficiently been witnessed by too true report, which emboldeneth us to seek to you, as feeling members, for relief. The King's mercy in granting letters patents [royal authorization of the appeal] hath been so many ways abused, that in the general (we know) it hath much dulled the edge of men's liberality, especially to places remote. Might we have been permitted therefore, our letters only should have made relation of our lamentable condition and petitioned your supplies. But seeing the road way is the safest and most usual in these evil events, we make bold to send both together. A fearful fire of late furiously raging amongst us hath consumed so much that, unless [except] to spectators [eyewitnesses], it may seem incredible. But if our honest credits may be a sufficient testimony, we assure you all the particulars in his Highness' letters patents mentioned, and in the briefs thereof, are true. And the losses (though therein rated at twenty thousand pounds) are rather far under, than one whit overvalued. The number of poor was great before but is now increased, and the substance of those that did relieve them by this accident is much diminished. We doubt not, therefore, but in this extremity you will extend your charity, promising our prayers, to entreat him that can give and take at his pleasure to bless you with such continual safety and prosperity, that you may be always so happy as to give rather than receive. And thus presenting the sighs, groans, and tears of all these miserable afflicted Christians (now left harborless and succorless) to your charitable considerations, we humbly take leave, with such respects as every of your places and qualities require. Resting, from our distressed town of Banbury, July 1628, your loving friends and well wishers.

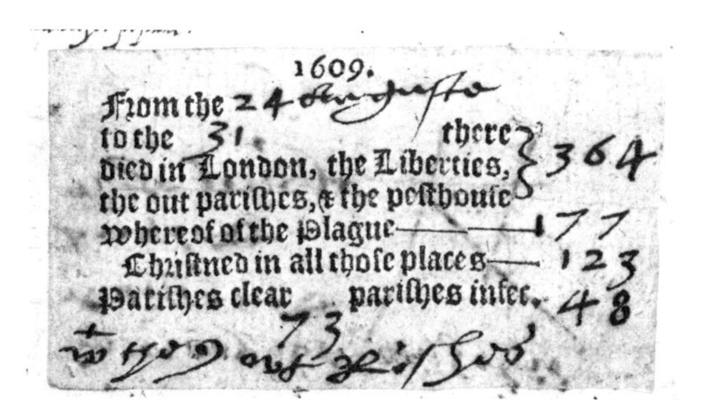
1609.
From the 24 Augusto
to the 31 there
died in London, the Liberties, 364
the out parishes, & the pesthouse
whereof of the Plague 177
Christned in all those places 123
Parishes clear 73 parishes infec. 48

Plague Bill (London, 1609). During seasons of great pestilence, the number of deaths from plague was published each week on preprinted forms. This count for the week of 24–31 August 1609 survives only because the Baron von Offenbach's traveling companion bound it into his diary; no other copy is known to exist. Plague was another threat of which Englishmen and women were uncomfortably aware.

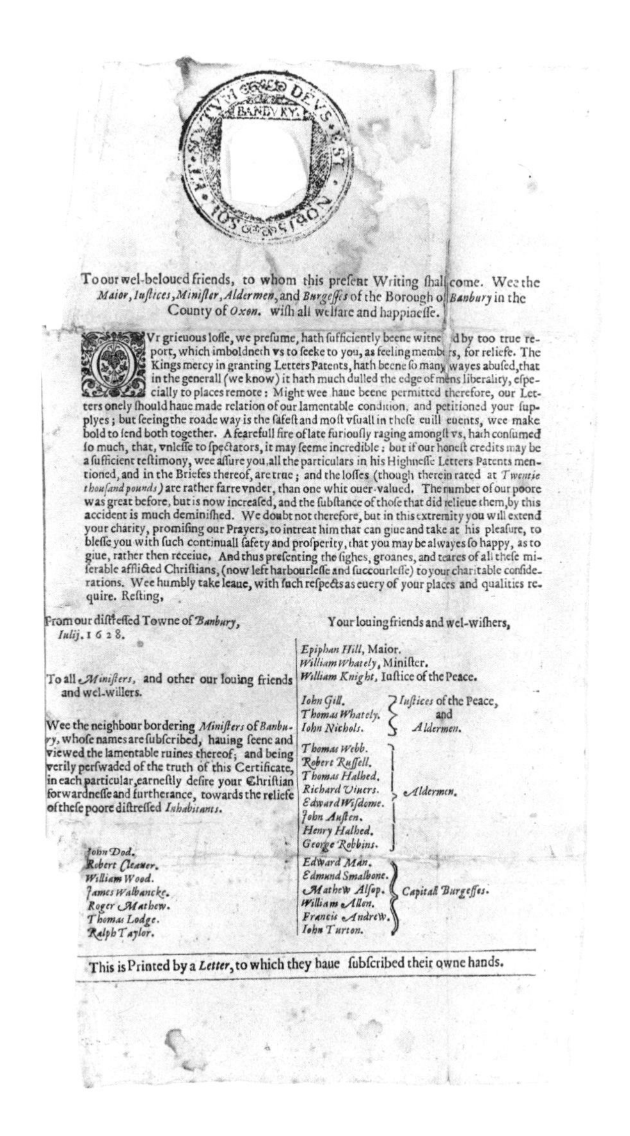
To our wel-beloued friends, to whom this preſent Writing ſhall come. Wee the *Maior, Iuſtices, Miniſter, Aldermen*, and *Burgeſſes* of the Borough of *Banbury* in the County of *Oxon.* wiſh all welfare and happineſſe.

OVr grieuous loſſe, we preſume, hath ſufficiently beene witne[ss]ed by too true report, which imboldneth vs to ſeeke to you, as feeling memb[e]rs, for reliefe. The Kings mercy in granting Letters Patents, hath beene ſo many wayes abuſed, that in the generall (we know) it hath much dulled the edge of mens liberality, eſpecially to places remote: Might wee haue beene permitted therefore, our Letters onely ſhould haue made relation of our lamentable condition, and petitioned your ſupplyes; but ſeeing the roade way is the ſafeſt and moſt vſuall in theſe euill euents, wee make bold to ſend both together. A fearefull fire of late furiouſly raging amongſt vs, hath conſumed ſo much, that, vnleſſe to ſpectators, it may ſeeme incredible: but if our honeſt credits may be a ſufficient teſtimony, wee aſſure you, all the particulars in his Highneſſe Letters Patents mentioned, and in the Briefes thereof, are true; and the loſſes (though therein rated at *Twentie thouſand pounds*) are rather farre vnder, than one whit ouer-valued. The number of our poore was great before, but is now increaſed, and the ſubſtance of thoſe that did relieue them, by this accident is much deminiſhed. We doubt not therefore, but in this extremity you will extend your charity, promiſing our Prayers, to intreat him that can giue and take at his pleaſure, to bleſſe you with ſuch continuall ſafety and proſperity, that you may be alwayes ſo happy, as to giue, rather then receiue. And thus preſenting the ſighes, groanes, and teares of all theſe miſerable afflicted Chriſtians, (now left harbourleſſe and ſuccourleſſe) to your charitable conſiderations. Wee humbly take leaue, with ſuch reſpects as euery of your places and qualities require. Reſting,

From our diſtreſſed Towne of *Banbury*, *Iulij*. 1628.

Your louing friends and wel-wiſhers,

Epiphan Hill, Maior.
William Whately, Miniſter.
William Knight, Iuſtice of the Peace.

Iohn Gill.
Thomas Whately.
Iohn Nichols.
} *Iuſtices* of the Peace, and *Aldermen.*

Thomas Webb.
Robert Ruſſell.
Thomas Halhed.
Richard Viners.
Edward Wiſdome.
Iohn Auſten.
Henry Halhed.
George Robbins.
} *Aldermen.*

Edward Man.
Edmund Smalbone.
Mathew Alſop.
William Allen.
Francis Andrew.
Iohn Turton.
} *Capitall Burgeſſes.*

To all *Miniſters*, and other our louing friends and wel-willers.

Wee the neighbour bordering *Miniſters* of *Banbury*, whoſe names are ſubſcribed, hauing ſeene and viewed the lamentable ruines thereof; and being verily perſwaded of the truth of this Certificate, in each particular, earneſtly deſire your Chriſtian forwardneſſe and furtherance, towards the reliefe of theſe poore diſtreſſed *Inhabitants*.

Iohn Dod.
Robert Cleauer.
William Wood.
Iames Walbancke.
Roger Mathew.
Thomas Lodge.
Ralph Taylor.

This is Printed by a *Letter*, to which they haue ſubſcribed their owne hands.

An Appeal for Aid (Banbury, 1628).

M. S.

The Poore Orphans Court, Or, Orphans Cry. Being a Wel-Wisher for a Speedy Helpe of their Misery, and an Eye-Witnesse of their Present Calamitie (London, 1636)

❧ The author of this slender pamphlet, who has been identified as Michael Spark, paints a picture of epidemic homelessness for the orphaned young, particularly in London. His first request is that there be a daily accounting of the number of orphans at an appointed location. Like John Kendrick, he would have these orphans put to trade or apprenticeship. He also suggests sending them to work in America.

Those that be able to help themselves, I speak not for. But for these poor orphans whose court is kept in a cage, or under a stall, or in St. Paul's amongst the forms [benches], the more is the pity. . . . These few lines it may be will be laughed at; I care not though they be. I give myself content and wish but that may be done here as is at this present in Dorchester, Norwich: not one seen to beg. Let us learn of them or of the Dutch, as in the University of Leiden, where 800 orphans are daily fed and set at work, and well provided for. How do the Dutch or French parishioners in London—can they do so, and not we? It is nothing but our hard hearts. . . . These orphans with good looking-to would keep themselves. Witness the willingness of some who you shall have of the bigger sort in Fleet Street in the evenings, with links ready to earn a penny to light men. Nay, in Smithfield, standing by day to sweep clean the ways, how ready are many of them? But the weakest go to the wall, as we see by woeful experience, many whose toes and legs are ready to rot off, and worser miseries, which make many a man blush to see that they are no better provided for. It may be I am deceived; would I were. I am verily persuaded that many spend more in the tavern idly than they give the poor willingly. Will not many a lady spend ordinarily day-by-day five shillings to see an idle play, or five pounds at a rare banquet, rather than give five shillings—I believe five tokens—to help these poor miserable children? If they hear of a new play, on goes all the best clothes; the coach-horses must be fetched; and that they may hurry from the poor, the coach man shall have his charge to drive away when he cometh amongst them. And what's the word? "Away with these stinking beggars." But when they come home, they will call to the servants to see the dog have his dinner, but the poor shall go supperless to bed under a stall, or in a porch, dying with misery, or starving with cold and hunger. These are reasons able to draw a man into a serious consideration for a speedy remedy, and I leave them to those in authority, and rest ever wishing, but not obtaining my desire, that there were a court for the poor orphans as well as the rich.

I desire you in office and in whose power it lies, to look with their eyes and pity with their hearts these poor wretched miserable wretches, those who have neither father nor mother, no, nor any friends; those that want wit, reason, and are not come to understanding; those whose years speak not discretion, nor have wit to help themselves. And those be they that make blood drop from my heart, whilst my pen cannot express their misery (sigs. A3v–A4v, B1v).

Frontispiece to M. S., *The Poore Orphans Court* (London, 1636).

The Last Will and Testament of M[aste]r John Kendricke late Citizen and Draper of London: Who Departed this Life the 30. Day of December, Anno. 1624. Full of Notable Workes of Charity, Worthy of Lasting Memory and Imitation (London, 1625)

❧ This will found its way into print for the reason stated in the title: it was "worthy of lasting memory and imitation." As W. K. Jordan has pointed out, charity was remade in the sixteenth century into a civic virtue—necessarily so, given the dissolution of the monasteries. John Kendrick's testament is particularly interesting in the present context because of his concern to support the social structures and hierarchies of householding, domestic labor, marriage, and service. He honored these ideas with legacies to kinsmen and women, by establishing workhouses and funding hospitals, through wedding gifts to young women and apprenticeships for young boys, by returning debtors to their homes, and in his touching remembrance of his former master.

The said Mayor and Burgesses [of Reading] shall buy and purchase unto them and their successors for ever a fair plot of ground within the said town of Reading, or the liberties [suburbs] thereof, and thereupon shall erect and build a strong house of brick fit and commodious for setting of the poor on work therein. . . . Then the whole residue and remainder of the same seven thousand and five hundred pounds shall make and be a common stock to be employed and bestowed in trade of clothing, either in making of colored cloths or whites, as the time shall require, and also in working of wool, hemp, flax, iron, grinding of Brazil woods, and other stuffs for dying—or otherwise, as to the said Mayor and Burgesses aforesaid and their successors for ever shall seem convenient for the employment of poor people and for the preservation and increase of the said common stock. . . .

Item, I give and bequeath to the Mayor, Aldermen, and Burgesses of the town of Newbury in the county of Berks[hire] (I mean the body corporate of the same town) the sum of four thousand pounds to buy and purchase therewith a commodious house and garden, within the same town, or the liberties thereof, to set the poor on work: and with the residue of the same sum to make a common stock for the employment of the poor in the said house. . . .

The sum of twenty-four pounds thereof yearly for ever, to be bestowed in the month of December for the releasing of six poor prisoners out of these prisons in London: to wit, the two Compters, Ludgate, Newgate, and the Fleet, by four pounds for each prisoner. . . .

More, to the poor prisoners in London ten pounds yearly for ever: namely, to the prisoners of the Compters in the Poultry and in Woodstreet, and in Newgate. To each of these prisons forty shillings yearly for ever.

To the poor Prisoners in Ludgate and in the Fleet, to each house thirty shillings yearly for ever.

And to the poor prisoners in Bedlam twenty shillings yearly for ever. . . .

More, five-and-twenty pounds yearly for ever to be distributed by the said Wardens among poor religious men and women in the City of London, to some more and to some less, as the said Wardens shall find their necessity and dessert to be. Wherein my desire is that poor clothworkers and their widows shall be first preferred, and next, the poor of the Drapers Company. The residue of the said sum of one hundred pounds a year, being four pounds yearly for ever, I entreat the four Wardens of the said Company to accept for their pains, to be equally divided between them by twenty shillings to each of them for the time being yearly for ever. . . .

Item, I give and bequeath to be given at the marriages of poor maids within the City of London two hundred pounds to be distributed by forty shillings apiece upon the days of their marriage, to such as have served one master or mistress by the space of five years together.

Item, I give and bequeath to be given and distributed to poor maids in the town of Reading in the county of Berks[hire] at their several marriages, by forty shillings apiece, at the discretion of the Mayor and Burgesses of that town, the sum of one hundred pounds. Provided none enjoy the benefit thereof, but such as have served one master, or mistress, or dame, by the space of seven years together. . . .

Item, I give and bequeath to the Mayor, Aldermen, and Burgesses of the Town of Newbury in Berkshire the sum of fifty pounds, to be by them bestowed and distributed to twenty-five maids of the same town at the several days of their marriages, none to enjoy this gift but such as have well and honestly served with one master, mistress, or dame by the space of seven years at least. And this fifty pounds to be paid to the said Mayor, Aldermen, and Burgesses within one year next after my decease.

Item, I give and bequeath towards the setting on work of forty idle vagrant boys, such as go up and down the streets in the City of London begging and pilfering, the sum of two hundred pounds, to be . . . placed and bound apprentice with a master for the term of seven years at the least, with artmasters, as glovers, pinners, shoemakers, or any other occupation or art which they shall be thought most fit for, to learn in the said house, whereby in time they may prove good members and live like honest men in the Commonwealth. . . .

Item, I give and bequeath to M[aster] John Quarles who was my master the sum of five hundred pounds, to be paid him within a year next after my decease. And my earnest desire and request unto M[aster] Lawrence Halstead is, that unto the end of our contract of partnership, which will be the five and twenty day of October, A.D. 1626, the same M[aster] Quarles may have his diet, lodging, and washing, in his the said M[aster] Halstead's house free and without paying anything therefore, as he now hath it with me. . . . And I do hereby freely and absolutely forgive the said M[aster] John Quarles the sum of three hundred pounds, which he oweth me payable at pleasure, being lent him the last of March, anno 1615, and being all that he oweth me at the date of this my will.

Item, I give and bequeath to M[aster] George Lowe, merchant, heretofore my partner, the sum of three hundred pounds, to be paid him within one year next after my decease. And I do hereby also absolutely forgive him all that is due unto me for his lodging, diet, firing, and washing, which he hath had of me now six years together (sigs. $A4^{v}$–$B1^{v}$, $B2^{v}$, $B3^{v}$–$B4^{v}$, $C2^{r-v}$, $D3^{r}$).

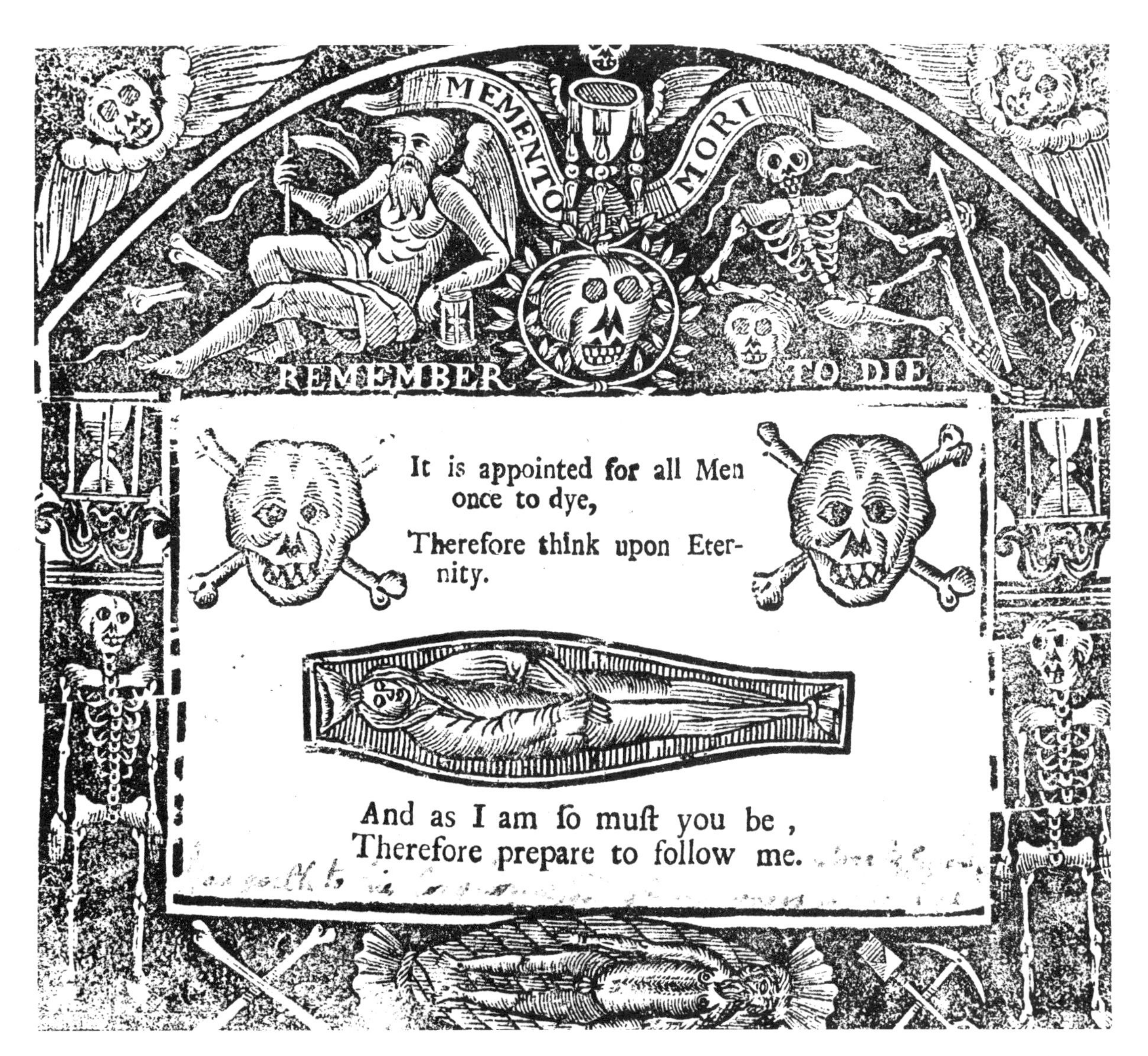

Memento Mori: Remember to Die (London? c. 1640). This little panel is the sort of thing Nehemiah Wallington would have brooded over in his period of depression. Englishmen and women kept reminders of death about them to inspire godly behavior while alive.

SUGGESTED READING

A note from the author: Much of the background research for this anthology was conducted in connection with two other publications, which should be consulted for more complete documentation than the anthology format permits. These include *Private Matters and Public Culture in Post-Reformation England* (Ithaca: Cornell University Press, 1994), and "'The Causes and Reasons of all Artificial Things' in the Elizabethan Domestic Environment" (in *Medieval and Renaissance Drama in England*, 7 [1995], 19–75). Research for these publications was conducted with the aid of sabbaticals from the Folger Shakespeare Library and with grants from the National Endowment for the Humanities, from the Huntington Library, and from the Center for Advanced Study in the Visual Arts at the National Gallery of Art.

Amussen, Susan D. *An Ordered Society: Gender and Class in Early Modern England.* Oxford: Basil Blackwell, 1988.

Barley, Maurice W. *Houses and History.* London: Faber and Faber, 1986.

Chartier, Roger, ed. *Passions of the Renaissance*, Vol. 3 of *A History of Private Life*, ed. Philippe Ariès et al. Trans. Arthur Goldhammer. Cambridge: Belknap Press of Harvard University Press, 1989.

Cressy, David. *Literacy and the Social Order: Reading and Writing in Tudor and Stuart England.* Cambridge: Cambridge University Press, 1980.

Friedman, Alice T. *House and Household in Elizabethan England: Wollaton Hall and the Willoughby Family.* Chicago: University of Chicago Press, 1989.

Gillis, John R. *For Better, For Worse: British Marriages, 1600 to the Present.* Oxford: Oxford University Press, 1985.

Girouard, Mark. *Robert Smythson and the Elizabethan Country House.* New Haven: Yale University Press, 1983.

Hoskins, W. G. *Provincial England: Essays in Social and Economic History.* London: Macmillan, 1963.

Houlbrooke, Ralph A. *The English Family, 1450–1700.* Themes in British Social History. London: Longman, 1976.

Howard, Maurice. *The Early Tudor Country House: Architecture and Politics, 1490–1550.* London: George Philip, 1987.

Ingram, Martin. *Church Courts, Sex, and Marriage in England, 1570–1640.* Past and Present Publications. Cambridge: Cambridge University Press, 1987.

Jordan, W. K. *Philanthropy in England, 1480–1660: A Study of the Changing Pattern of English Social Aspirations.* London: George Allen and Unwin, 1959.

Laslett, Peter. *The World We Have Lost—Further Explored.* 3d ed. London: Methuen, 1983.

Macfarlane, Alan. *The Family Life of Ralph Josselin: A Seventeenth-Century Clergyman.* Cambridge: Cambridge University Press, 1970.

Mercer, Eric. *Furniture, 700–1700.* London: Weidenfeld and Nicolson, 1969.

Palliser, D. M. *The Age of Elizabeth: England under the Later Tudors, 1547–1603.* Social and Economic History of England. London: Longman, 1983.

Portman, Derek. "Vernacular Building in the Oxford Region in the Sixteenth and Seventeenth Centuries." In *Rural Change and Urban Growth, 1500–1800*, ed. C. W. Chalklin and M. A. Havinden, pp. 135–68. London: Longman, 1974.

Schochet, Gordon J. *Patriarchalism in Political Thought: The Authoritarian Family and Political Speculation and Attitudes Especially in Seventeenth-Century England.* New York: Basic Books, 1975.

Seaver, Paul S. *Wallington's World: A Puritan Artisan in Seventeenth-Century London.* Stanford: Stanford University Press, 1985.

Sharpe, J. A. *Crime in Early Modern England, 1550–1750.* Themes in British Social History. London: Longman, 1984.

Skipp, Victor. *Crisis and Development: An Ecological Case Study of the Forest of Arden, 1570–1674.* Cambridge: Cambridge University Press, 1978.

Slack, Paul. *Poverty and Policy in Tudor and Stuart England.* Themes in British Social History. London: Longman, 1988.

Stone, Lawrence. *The Family, Sex, and Marriage in England, 1500–1800.* New York: Harper and Row, 1977.

Thirsk, Joan. *Economic Policy and Projects: The Development of a Consumer Society in Early Modern England.* Oxford: Clarendon Press, 1978.

Thomas, Keith. *Religion and the Decline of Magic: Studies in Popular Beliefs in Sixteenth- and Seventeenth-Century England.* London: Weidenfeld and Nicolson, 1971.

West, Trudy. *The Timber-Frame House in England.* Newton Abbot: David and Charles, 1971.

Wrightson, Keith. *English Society, 1580–1680.* London: Hutchinson, 1982.

INDEX
of Books and Manuscripts

INDEX
of Objects

Elizabethan Households
was designed and printed at
The Stinehour Press.
The text was set in Adobe Garamond,
a recutting of the 16th-century font
drawn by Robert Slimbach.
The paper stocks used are Mohawk Opaque
for the text, and Mohawk Tomohawk
for the endleaves and cover.
Catalogue design by
Dean Bornstein.

CW00763705

Facebook

The Top 100 Best Ways To Use Facebook For Business And Marketing

By Ace McCloud

Disclaimer

Table of Contents

DEDICATED TO THOSE WHO ARE PLAYING THE GAME OF LIFE TO

KEEP ON PUSHING AND NEVER GIVE UP!

Ace McCloud

Be sure to check out my website for all my Books and Audio books.

www.AcesEbooks.com

Introduction

I want to thank you and congratulate you for buying the book, "Facebook: The Top 100 Best Ways To Use Facebook For Business, Marketing And Making Money ."

Facebook is a very powerful social media platform that has been around since the early 2000's. What started out as just a social network for college students has quickly expanded over the years into a worldwide network of people that can be joined for free. With its 1.9 billion users, Facebook is a great way to reach people who share the same goals and interests that you do. Although Facebook is best known for its personal profile pages, there is also a function called Facebook Pages, which can be used by businesses around the world. This great feature has helped many businesses step into the 21st century as well as gain more clients, drive more sales and boost traffic to their websites and physical locations.

It is important for any business, whether big or small, to establish a presence on Facebook. Not only is the potential client reach almost limitless, but it serves as a two-way interactive tool that you can use to get to know your audience and give your business a personal feel. By adding a little creativity, there are many ways that you can uniquely communicate with your audience through Facebook. Next, having a Facebook page for your business can save you hundreds to thousands of dollars on marketing costs, as Facebook is essentially free. While you may have to invest some time and money, Facebook can ultimately help you lower your costs and boost profits at the same time.

One of the best features about Facebook is that you can use some its features, such as the paid ads application, to customize your marketing strategy and reach specific members of your target audience. The insights and analysis tools built into the Facebook page can help you track your professional progress and serve as your guide for tweaking your marketing strategy. Finally, having a Facebook business page can help you drive more traffic to your actual website and boost brand loyalty.

This book contains proven steps and strategies on how to master all the features built into your Facebook pages so that you can build your business for success. In the following pages, you will discover all of the best ways to use Facebook for business, marketing, making money and so much more. You will also learn how to combine it with other social media marketing platforms to make the biggest dent in your brand awareness and sales for the amount of time and money you spend. There are many tips and tricks provided throughout this book that are aimed at helping you become a master at Facebook for business. At the end, you will find a step by step guide that puts it all together for you. Simply follow that formula at the end of the book and you are bound to be a successful business owner with an awesome, appealing Facebook page.

Chapter 1: Discover How To Optimize Your Facebook Page For Maximum Results

Facebook is useful to have both as an individual and as a business. As a business owner, your personal Facebook page can serve as your identity while your business Facebook page can serve as your brand. Facebook is free and relatively easy to use. This chapter will bring you through all the steps you need to take in order to optimize your business Facebook page for the best results.

Optimizing Your Facebook Page

Step 1: Create the actual Facebook page. It's really easy—all you do is click on Pages, which is located on the left side of the screen under you name and avatar. When you come to that page, you will see a button that says Create a Page in the top right-hand corner. Click that button to create a page. There, you can upload a picture and fill out the basics like your business name, address, phone number, website, etc.

Step 2: Think about your cover photo, because this area is one of the first things your audience will see and it's bigger than your profile picture, so you want it to be significant. It really depends on your business and what you do, but some of the more popular ways to take advantage of this space is to display your slogan, more contact information, or an image that is directly related to your business. Sometimes it can be more specific. For example, if you're trying to start a music career, you can choose to put the cover of your latest album up there. Be creative and make the most you can of this space. For inexpensive options, be sure to check out Fiverr.com, which can give you a great Facebook header for just five dollars. Perfect dimensions for the header are 851 wide by 315 high.

Step 3: Think about your profile picture. This part should be a no-brainer. If you have a company logo, it would be best to use that. If you're a small business or independent contractor, a good idea would be to use a high-resolution professional picture of yourself. Your audience will see this image in their timeline so make sure it is memorable and inviting. The best kinds of photos to use are ones that are square-shaped. It is a good idea to get a professional photo for this. Not only should the photo look great, but ten years from now you will be glad to have it!

Step 4: Fill out your description and about me areas. These spaces are important because this is where your audience will go to learn more about you and your business. Be sure to use lots of SEO terms and keywords to make sure that your page comes up first in search results. Be engaging and inviting—make your audience want to know more. Take your time with this and do a good job. If you’re not a good writer, find or hire someone who is to make this section really good!

Step 5: Once you have completed every inch of your profile, the next step is to start posting status updates. These are short blurbs that you can share with anyone who likes your page to keep them engaged and informed. It's just the same as if you were posting with your personal profile except it comes up on your business page. POSTING STATUS UPDATES IS IMPORTANT! If you are not consistently active on your Facebook page, you will likely not engage anybody at all and there won't be much activity. **Make it a goal to post a certain number of status updates each week.** Doing it here and there won't work—you need to be consistent. One strategy that works well is to use automation software to post statuses that you put together on your behalf. Buffer has a really good service, it's free for up to 10 or so statuses and you can link them to your other social media accounts if you have them.

Make sure that your status updates are the type that will engage your audience. The more your audience interacts with your page, the more likely it is to spread and grow. Facebook is currently set up so that if a friend on your personal profile likes or comments on something posted by a page, you may see that activity and chose to jump in on the conversation or like the page yourself. To stir up some audience engagement, you can ask questions, ask for opinions, take polls or surveys, or participate in a like and share campaign that will encourage your audience to help spread the word about you and your products to their friends.

Always think about "quality versus quantity" when it comes to your status updates. You can post a hundred posts in a week, but if they're dull or boring, you likely will not get much audience engagement. Try and build a good reputation by posting quality material that people will be interested in. Also, try to break up business posts with the occasional interesting article, blog post, or YouTube video (It is ideal if you have any of those channels and you then link them to your posts—a strategy known as 'back-linking'). Sometimes you can slyly break up your posts with a nice inspirational quote or two—I've noticed that the best kind are any that can relate to your industry, be inspirational, or just bring some happiness and joy into the lives of others. Always try to keep your content different and unique; otherwise your audience may grow bored easily.

One awesome thing about Facebook pages is that Facebook will analyze your posts for you. This allows you to see which posts your audience is engaging with the most, whether its likes, comments, or shares. This tool lets you measure each post and see if you can find a trend among the posts with the most engagement. Keep an eye on this weekly if not daily and see what you're doing right on your best posts. If Facebook notices that more people are engaging with one post more than usual, it will send you an additional notification about it, prompting you to check out the analysis. This will be critical information if you truly want to be a pro and get results from Facebook.

Another good strategy for analyzing your posts is to go under your Insights page and use the Pages to Watch tool. This tool allows you to add up to 5 other pages that are similar to yours. You can then track the performance of that page and compare it to the performance of yours. You can choose your own pages or Facebook will suggest some for you. The Insights tab also breaks down and analyzes your page likes, reach, and visits, where you can compare your performance to yourself between different periods of time. The People tab under Insights is especially useful for fine-tuning your target audience. It breaks your fans and people reached down by gender, age, and location.

Finally, don't forget that audience engagement is a two-way street. If a person interacts with your page, be sure to write something back or acknowledge it in some way. This is easier for small businesses and not so easy for medium to large-sized businesses, but with the right strategies, which you will discover in a bit, it is totally possible.

The last cool thing about Facebook pages is that you can time your status updates to go out even if you're not using an app like Buffer. All you have to do is click on the little clock icon in the bottom left-hand corner of your status update. If you can manage to figure out when your audience is online most, this tool can be invaluable for reaching the most people at the best times. You can also use this tool to get your posts on a schedule. Posting at the times that will get you maximum results is another technique you should really take seriously if you want to get peak performance results.

Step 6: Last but not least, you'll also want to stay consistent in your endeavors at building your audience. The bigger your audience is, the more people you are likely to reach. There are several ways to build your audience. The key is to build upon each "like" that you get—so for each Facebook user who likes your page, you have the potential to reach however many friends they all have on their pages. There will be more about strategies on how to naturally do this later, but for now, you will discover the two easiest ways to build your base audience.

The first common way to build your audience base is to invite all your friends, which you can do under the Build Audience tab. Although it can be tempting to invite all 705 of your friends at once, I would suggest only sending out 15-25 requests at a time. I've noticed that the first couple of people you invite are more likely to like the page and by the time you get to the end, you're not bound to hear from anyone. The first couple of people you invite will get a notification on their personal page with an invitation but I feel like after that, your invitation goes to limbo with everyone else. I don't know if this is a glitch or what and it's not a fact, just my hunch, but it does seem to have a small effect.

The second strategy build for building your audience base is to experiment with paid ads. These are the ads that pop up on the sidebar of your Facebook page when you're browsing. You can target these paid ads to your audience by selecting a location, age range, gender and some interest keywords. You can then choose whether to run the ad continuously or only run it only for a select period of time. Lastly, the paid ads feature allows you to choose a budget for yourself. The higher your budget, the more likely your estimated reach will be. For example, a $10 budget may only get you 32 likes a day for the duration of your ad but a $100 budget may get you two hundred or more likes per day.

More Optimization Tips and Tricks

Under the Settings tab along the top, you can further optimize your page. You can activate/deactivate profanity filters and you can manage what countries are able to view your page. Here, you can also change your name (but beware—Facebook only lets you change it one time before you have to make a brand new page) and manage your notifications. You can also choose to have notifications from your page be sent to your email or personal Facebook page. And if you really love interacting with Facebook, you can set things up so you get updates on your smartphone from your email. You can also moderate how often you get these updates.

Another nice feature about Facebook is there is a tab under Settings called Page Roles, where you can assign duties to another Facebook user. What I like about this is that you can let someone else manage your page without giving them your password or full control over the page. For example, you can opt to only put someone on to look at your insights (an analyzer) or someone who can only delete and respond to comments (a moderator). This page is good to know about when it comes time to expand your page.

Under the Apps page, you can link together other social media platforms such as Twitter, Pinterest, and Youtube. You can also take advantage of apps that are built into Facebook, such as the video option, the notepad (good for blogs or long status updates) or the events calendar (good for marketing). Under Settings, you will also be able to manage any banned users.

Finally, you can view your activity log. This log shows you everything that's occurred on your page, from whether you commented on your own post or if you added a photo or shared a link. This log can be helpful if you want to do some of your own analyzing. You can see how often you like, comment, or share things as well as upload content.

Before you read on... get to know Facebook and your Facebook page. Make sure you have everything written up and displayed the way you want it. Before you can move on to really building your business and making money, everything on your page has to be pristine. You can always go back and make edits/updates later but it is important to have the best presentation possible. Try to put yourself in the shoes of your audience and look at your page to make sure it is the way you want it. If you want to be taken seriously, time to be a pro and put in the extra work to make yourself come off as a professional. As we all know... First impressions are very important!

Chapter 2: The Best Ways To Use Facebook for Business

Attracting New and Current Clients. Facebook pages serves as a great way to attract new and current clients. Using this platform, you can connect with the people you already know (your current clients) and use your marketing skills to multiply your leads using the Rule of 52. This theory states that for each person you know, they have 52 connections. If you can reach new clients through your current clients, you'll certainty be in good business.

Stir Up Clients. Your Facebook business page will also be a great way to stir up clients. In the next chapter, you will discover some awesome marketing techniques that can help you engage your audience, thus making the buzz around your business bigger. Once you have mastered that, you will have a great advantage in the world of Facebook.

Build Sales. By following the first two steps above, you can ultimately build sales for your business. Again, you will be able to learn more on how to do this with the marketing techniques in the next chapter. The more people you can reach on Facebook, the more potential sales you have in front of you.

Access Your Audience Any Time. Having a Facebook page for your business means that you can access your audience from anywhere with an internet connection and at the time of your choosing. Even if you're not in your business or office, you can easily check in with your audience on your phone while you're sitting on your couch. Establishing a sense of mobility allows you to be more in touch with your clients.

Generate More Reviews. If you register your page as a local business, there will be an option for your fans to leave you a review. This can be hugely helpful to the success of your business because other people tend to follow the crowd. The more 5-star reviews and compliments you can get, the more likely your audience will be to trust you and use you.

Private Communication. Not everybody uses email these days and it can be hard to find out your contact information if you're a busy business owner. Facebook pages has a great messaging function which allows people to message you right through your page. This makes you more accessible (especially if you download the FB Page app to your phone) and your chances of driving sales increases more with better communication.

Better Customer Service. I have noticed some big companies use their Facebook page to their advantage when it comes to customer service. If a fan leaves a complaint or bad review, you will have their contact information right in front of you, meaning that you can quickly and actively address their concerns.

This can save you from losing a lot of customers, especially if they see you respond to them in a quick manner.

Personalize Your Company. By being able to type directly into your status update box, you can convey your voice to your audience. This makes your business much more personable and increases the likelihood of clients being able to relate with you.

Remotely Control Your Team. Since you can assign multiple users limited access to your page, you can remotely control your team. They can work from home as well and be able to access the page at any time. If you break up the task of managing your page among a few people on your team, it can greatly reduce the stress of your social media management responsibility. Two great places to get great virtual help are Odesk and Elance.

Keep Your Audience Informed. Having page for your business is a great way to keep your audience informed. Think of it like a newspaper that is specific to your business. As soon as you come out with a special deal, you can let your audience know right away as opposed to sending out snail mail.

Save Money on Marketing. Marketing these days can be pretty costly. Sending out mailers requires printing costs plus the costs of envelopes, stamps, delivery, etc. Radio and TV advertisements can be even more expensive. One of the best things about Facebook is that it is FREE! No gimmicks here, just a really great, free tool that is easy to use and that allows you to access billions of people.

Good Cold Call Replacement. If you're an introvert and not very good at making cold calls, use Facebook! You can still contact people by messaging them instead of calling them directly. This can also take the pressure off cold calls for both you and prospective clients. It can also ensure that you're not interrupting anyone's day.

Connects You Around the Globe. Facebook is an international platform, so anyone from anywhere in the world can access your page (if you allow it). This can be especially helpful for making international connections—who knows, you might end up opening a few branches or getting some new customers in another country.

Chapter 3: The Best Ways To Use Facebook for Marketing

Not only is Facebook a powerful platform for business but it is also an effective marketing tool.

Set Marketing Goals. Before you start marketing on Facebook, the most important thing to do is set goals. Some of the most common goals when it comes to marketing on Facebok include getting more likes, more engagements, more website conversions, or something along those lines. If you try to market your business on Facebook without having a specific goal in mind, you will likely not get too far.

Don't Buy Likes. On that note, don't buy likes. You may see freelancers or people on websites such as Fiverr claiming they can get you 100k fans overnight, but the truth is that most of those "fans" are just bots. That means you'll have 100k likes but no engagement or leads. You're better off putting in the hard work to get real, live fans on your page.

Use Facebook Offers. Facebook offers is a program that offers virtual coupons to your fans. You can easily set it up on your timeline. Since it is through the Facebook ad application, you can target it to certain audiences and set your budget. You can also upload the picture of the coupon yourself so that people can print it out and use it.

Optimize Your Page For Mobility. Over half of all Facebook users access the website on their phone. Mobility has an advantage because it means you can reach more people at almost any time of the day. You can optimize your page for mobility by going under settings, clicking on mobile, and then checking out the offerings. You will find an email address that you can use to upload content to your page via your phone.

Plaster Your Call To Action Everywhere. Inspire your audience to get moving and take action in terms of your business. You can put your call to action anywhere, including in your cover picture, at the end of your statuses, and in your paid ads.

Use Sponsored Stories. I mentioned earlier that when a person interacts with the content of your page, their friends may see it on their own newsfeed. However, this update can quickly get lost in the depths of everyone else's status updates. You can use sponsored stories to help these posts stay at the top. You can get to this option in the Facebook ads application.

Use Customized Heading in Paid Ad. When you set up a paid ad, the headline will default to the name of your page. However, your audience may already be used to your page's name and may not notice. Not many people are aware of this but you can create your own headline. Make it catchy and appealing to stand out and increase the chances of getting more engagement.

Hire a Professional to Help You With An Ad. It may be that you're great at running your business but not experienced at all with marketing. It may be worth hiring a professional freelancer with marketing experience to step in. You can grant them limited access to your page through the page role function under settings. Work closely with your marketer to get the best results.

Experiment With Ad Budgets. It may not be a good idea to be cheap and only set your daily ad budget for $10, but at the same time it also may not be worth it to max it out when nobody knows who you are. Experiment with your daily ad budget and see which one gets you the most results. You may find it changing the more you grow. Try not to spend too much, but at the same time, don't short yourself.

Use Visuals. Whether in your paid ads or status updates, use as many visuals as you can. Research shows that graphics are more appealing to the eye than text and are more likely to stimulate audience engagement. Put yourself in your audience's shoes—would you be more likely to get captured by text or graphics?

Experiment With Visuals. Use multiple visuals for the same type of posts and see which ones stimulate the most audience engagement. Try infographics, inspirational quotes, and stock images that relate to the content. You can find some really good, free to use stock images. If you don't mind spending money on images, then Shutterstock.com is my favorite place to go.

Watch Your Potential Audience Meter. Your potential audience meter shows up once you've ran some paid ads to a target market. Facebook will then give you a forecast of how many more people you can reach. This tool is helpful for making sure that you're not aiming too broad or too low when it comes to your audience. Once you have a good forecast (usually around 1,000), you can tweak the settings in your paid ads to narrow your focus to the best audience possible.

Target Locals. If you run a business that has a physical store, you can focus on targeting people in the local area, which will help bring in more foot traffic. Combine this strategy with the Facebook Offers tool for the best burst of traffic.

Launch a Contest. Contests are a great way to engage your audience, boost likes, and get more foot traffic if you have a physical location. In the past, it was complicated to have a contest on Facebook, but the website has recently changed the rules to make it easier. You can do something like hold a caption contest or do a free giveaway for whoever shares your content.

Make Valuable Content Hard to Get. Don't give away your most valuable content for free—tease your audience and then give it away under the condition that they give you something in return. This is a good way to build an email list, get referrals, or get more page fans. Top the offer off with a nice visual and call to action to make sure it works well.

Don't Put Links Straight Into Status. When you put a link straight into your status, a picture related to the website usually comes up in a little box. Instead, use a larger picture in the actual status and then add the link later. Your audience is bound to be more engaged by the big picture rather than the little picture in the link.

Recognize Milestones. One cool thing about Facebook pages is that it lets you highlight milestones in your business. One good example is to celebrate when you reach 100 likes, then 1,000 likes, and more when you get higher than that. This also calls for audience engagement, as you're likely to stir them up with a lot of "congratulations" posts and the like. You could even offer special deals and discounts in honor of your milestones. You can create a milestone by clicking on it in your status box.

Pin Significant Posts to the Top of Your Page. When you pin a post to your page, it stays at the top forever, instead of getting lost in your sea of statuses. This means your audience will see this post right away when they click on your page. Some ideas of things to pin are event reminders, special deals, policy changes, etc. You can pin a post by clicking in the top right hand corner and selecting "pin."

Highlight Significant Posts. Alternatively, you can highlight a post instead of pinning it, meaning the post will take up half of your page, making it very noticeable. This is a good option if you have a special announcement but you don't want it stuck at the top of your page for a long time. You can highlight a post by clicking the top right hand corner and selecting "highlight."

Make Separate Business Cards. Don't forget to incorporate your Facebook link into your business cards. This further helps spread the word to clients who may not be as tech-savy. I've found that printing a separate business card that is Facebook themed is best, but some printing companies give you the option of making a backside to your card, another good spot to place your link.

Add a Link to Your Email Signature. Be sure to also add your link to the bottom of your email signature. If you use Gmail, you can do this by going into your settings. Make it something simple and appealing. A good strategy is to put your name, then title, then link to your Facebook. This is helpful if you deal with a lot of clients through email.

Use Other People's Facebook Accounts For Advertising. This is a great way to increase your exposure. There are a lot of people who have gone to incredible lengths to build up their own Facebook fans and who are willing to advertise your product or services to their fan base very cheaply. I have personally used www.Fiverr.com to advertise my books successfully to several of these people for just $5. Do a little bit of research and try to outsource your product or service to those who do a great job at the best price with the least amount of hassle.

Chapter 4: The Best Ways To Make Money With Facebook

Showcase Your Inventory. The photo albums feature on Facebook allows you to upload photos and organize them in separate albums. This is great for when you have lots of different items for sale. You can divide each category into a Facebook album and show what you're selling. I know of a family-owned video game store who posts pictures of all their merchandise. People on their page instantly start flooding in with comments asking about price, condition, etc. Remember how important visuals are—if you can show your audience what you're offering them, they are more likely to buy when they see it.

Post Your Blogs, Drive More Traffic, Make More Money. If you have a blog for your business (which I highly recommend because it qualifies as shareable content and drives traffic), you can generate paid-per-click ads on it. When you post these blogs to your Facebook page, you can increase the likelihood of more clicks, thus bringing in more income. You could also start a blog in the form of articles on paid-per-click article websites such as Examiner.com.

Network With Other Businesses. Networking is powerful, especially when it's business to business networking. Depending on what your business is, you can connect with similar or related industries to build rapport and further build your client base. It kind of works like this: you meet someone in a similar industry and they happen to know someone who can use your services. The more connections you can get, the more likely you are to get leads and sales.

Hand Out Exclusive Facebook Offers. A really good idea to increase the money flow from your fan base is to make offers and deals that are exclusive to your Facebook fans. This means that you will be more likely to get more likes, engagement, and more fans will want to take advantage of what they see as a "special" offer.

Sell Your Ebook. If you have an ebook that correlates with your business, you can sell it by advertising it on Facebook. One post about your ebook can stir up engagement and increase the chances of other people catching on as well. The more exposure you can get the better. A good strategy would be to make it an offer that is exclusive to Facebook.

Start a YouTube Channel. If you are good in front of a camera, start a Youtube channel and link your videos to your Facebook page. If you can rack up thousands of views a month, Youtube will allow you to generate income from your videos whenever a person clicks on them and watches.

Business Ideas For Facebook

If you're not already in business and you're looking to get started, there are a few industries that have an upper edge when it comes to making money on Facebook. Here are a few business ideas to consider:

1) Selling Gently Used Items
2) Remote Tutoring Services
3) Freelance Artwork
4) Freelance Writing
5) Freelance Web Design
6) Freelance IT and Tech
7) Selling Arts and Crafts
8) Food or Catering Services
9) Selling T-Shirts or Custom Clothes
10) Photography or Videography Services

Chapter 5: How To Integrate Facebook With Other Platforms

You can make your Facebook page more powerful and more accessible by integrating it with other social media platforms. This can extend your audience reach by far and bring in new clients that you may have not been able to get otherwise.

Youtube. I mentioned in an earlier chapter that having a Youtube account in addition to a Facebook page for your business can serve to be helpful and lucrative. Instead of constantly linking to your Youtube videos on your page manually, you can connect your Facebook page to Youtube for automated sharing. This means that whenever you upload a video to Youtube, it will automatically go out on your Facebook page. To do this, go under your settings in your Youtube Account and then click Activity Sharing in the left column. You'll come to a screen that lists several social media accounts such as Facebook and Twitter. You can then follow the directions on the screen to connect each account. This YouTube video by Joseph Bison, How To Connect Youtube to Facebook & Twitter, shows a good example of this.

Twitter. Twitter is another very powerful social media platform that connects many people around the world. Some people prefer Facebook over Twitter but without Twitter, you can lose out on a wide audience. To ensure that all of your Facebook updates go to Twitter, you can easily connect the two platforms and never have to worry about both at the same time. All you have to do is go to Facebook.com/Twitter and then click on the words Link to Twitter that are next to the name of your page. This YouTube video, How to Connect Your Facebook Profile or Page to Your Twitter Account by Christian Karasiewicz, shows this well. If you are looking to really get the most out of Twitter, be sure to check out my book: Twitter: How To Market And Make Money With Twitter.

Google +. Although Google + is not widely used, it is still a great platform and connects you with most of the people you email back and forth with. Like Twitter, *not* utilizing Google+ can also be a loss. You can easily connect your Facebook and Google+ account by downloading an app called Start Google Plus for your web browser. Once you download it, it will install into your web browser and take you through a set up. Once it is set up, you will see an orange icon in the top right hand corner of your web browser. If you click on it, you can sign in with your Facebook and Twitter ID and then make all your posts directly from this app. They will go out on all three platforms. This YouTube video, How to Link Google+, Facebook and Twitter Together by Christian Karasiewicz, shows how to do this.

Instagram. Some businesses can benefit from photo-sharing, which is exactly what Instagram is designed to do. Instagram has many users and can serve as a great platform. It also comes in handy for photo-sharing contests. To link your

Facebook and Instagram account, just go to apps.facebook.com/instagram_feed/ and follow the steps as you did when linking Facebook and Twitter. This YouTube video by Ali Rittenhouse, How to Easily Add Instagram to Your Facebook Page, shows you how to do it. Note that Facebook pages changed since this video was made. You can now access Instagram by looking in the Apps section, which is on the lower left hand side of your page.

LinkedIn. LinkedIn is the best business networking website around so it may be a good idea to make your Facebook page available on it. Although you can't actually integrate the two platforms, you can put the link to your page in your profile. To see how to link your Facebook page to LinkedIn, check out this YouTube video by RayRay Murphy : How to Connect Facebook to LinkedIn.

Using Facebook on Your Smart Phone

If you have a smart phone, you will have an even better edge when it comes to using Facebook for business. This means you will be able to access Facebook from anywhere, anytime and there are also some free, useful apps that you can use to help keep yourself organized. Here are some ideas on how to use Facebook on your smart phone for the best results:

Download the Facebook Page Manager App. The Facebook Page Manager App allows you to instantly access your entire Facebook fan page from the tips of your fingers. If you enable push notifications, you will instantly be notified of any messages that clients send directly to your phone. You can also easily upload content that you already have saved on your phone. If you have multiple pages, you can manage all of them at once.

Download a Quotes App. If you plan on including some inspirational quotes on your Facebook page (which is never a bad idea for audience engagement), a great and easy idea is to download a quotes app in which you can save the quotes and upload them directly to your Facebook page.

Download Buffer. Buffer is a social media automation tool that is free for the most part and works cross-platform, so you can manage it from a computer or from a mobile device. You can schedule posts to your Facebook as well as any of your other social media accounts (Twitter, LinkedIn, Google +, etc). This is useful for entrepreneurs who travel a lot and may not have access to an actual computer.

Email Apps. If possible, see if you can connect your email account that is registered with your Facebook to your smart phone. This way, you will never miss a notification and you can respond to your clients in a more efficient manner.

Upload Videos Directly. If you don't want to use Youtube, you can upload videos taken on your phone directly to your Facebook page using the Page Manager App.

Chapter 6: Putting It All Together

Now that you know all the awesome ways to put your business and Facebook together as well as how to market and make money with it, it is time to discover how to put it all together for the best results. This chapter will take you step by step on how to do this, from square one to the end.

Gather Your Materials. Gather up all the materials you have that you could use as content for your page. Go through any fliers, bulletins, pictures and logos that you have. Other material can be inspirational quotes, pictures of your team, pictures of your physical store and inventory, etc. Be as creative as possible. A good idea to organize yourself on your computer is to make a folder that is labeled "Facebook page" and then make sub-folders of all the categories to keep your materials in for easy reference.

Create Your Facebook Page If You Haven't Already. See Chapter 1 for more information on how to complete this step.

Fully Fill Out Your Page. Make sure your entire page is filled out with the correct information, including your description, biography, contact information, address, etc.

Set Goals. Without setting goals, it will be very difficult to achieve success on Facebook. The best way to set goals is to set one long term goal, followed by three to five short term goals that will help you get there. Here are some great ideas on goals and milestones to set for yourself when working with Facebook (note, these are just some common examples, see if you can get creative and come up with your own):

Reach 100 likes

Reach 500 likes

Reach 1,000 likes

Reach 1,000+ likes

Sell x amount of products using marketing strategies.

Reach x amount of new clients through x amount of your current clients.

Follow a consistent marketing strategy for one year and carry it into the rest of your career.

Reach other countries other than the one you're living in.

Create a buzz on all social media websites using Facebook as your base.

Get your audience talking and participating.

Create Your Marketing Strategy

Make consistent yet unique posts each day. Don't post the same material over and over again or else you may look like a spam bot. The best formula for posting content is to follow this trend:

One self-promotion item.

One inspirational quote.

One entertaining item (for example a buzzfeed article or YouTube video related to your business.)

One How-To item created by you.

Pay attention to any upcoming holidays and theme your marketing strategy on that, it is bound to get more buzz because everyone enjoys celebrating holidays.

Pay attention to all and any holidays.

Set up an automation program like Buffer and reload it each Sunday.

Research SEO keywords and hashtags related to your business and include them in your content to make yourself more likely to pop up in searches.

Start building your collection of stock photos to supplement your content.

Link All Social Media Sites Together. Go back to Chapter 5 and learn how to link all of your social media websites together to get the biggest reach possible. Even if you don't regularly use those websites, you would be cheating yourself to skip them.

Download and Install the Facebook Pages Manager on All of Your Mobile Devices to Become Fully Accessible. Put them on anything you have: iPad, tablet, smart phones, etc.

Watch and Analyze Your Insights. Keep an eye on your page stats each week or even every day if you get enough engagement and see what's working and what's not. This can help you tweak your marketing strategy until you get it just right.

Market Your Facebook Page. While it is up to you to market your business on your Facebook page, you may still want to market your Facebook page to people who are not yet a part of it. Remember the Rule of 52!

Never Give Up! To become and stay successful, the most important thing to do is never give up! It is much harder to keep up in the business world today, especially due to online trends and the ever-changing digital technology age. Always try to keep yourself ahead of the game and stay on top of trends so that you will have the upper edge.

Conclusion

I hope this book was able to help you to better understand how to use Facebook for business. Facebook is a powerful platform that has the potential to reach billions of people around the world. Mastering Facebook as well as pairing it with other social media websites can help drive traffic to your business and boost sales. Whether you use an actual computer, a mobile device, or both, your business Facebook page can help you drive your business to success when paired with a good marketing strategy.

The next step is to make your Facebook page, if you haven't already, and then start planning out your marketing strategy. Take it one day at a time and really focus on each step. The better you focus on your marketing plan, the more likely you are to develop a bigger presence on Facebook. The bigger your presence on Facebook, the more likely your chances are for success. Start by setting up your Buffer account and be sure to post consistently. You will not get results overnight but as long as you give it a good effort and stay consistent, you will slowly begin to see results. It's also a good idea to stay in touch with your customers. Ask them what they like and don't like and then change your strategy accordingly.

Finally, if you discovered at least one thing that has helped you or that you think would be beneficial to someone else, be sure to take a few seconds to easily post a quick positive review. As an author, your positive feedback is desperately needed. Your highly valuable five star reviews are like a river of golden joy flowing through a sunny forest of mighty trees and beautiful flowers! *To do your good deed in making the world a better place by helping others with your valuable insight, just leave a nice review.*

My Other Books and Audio Books
www.AcesEbooks.com

Business & Finance Books

LEADERSHIP
THE TOP 100 BEST WAYS
TO BE A GREAT LEADER
Ace McCloud

MARKETING
The Top 100 Best Things That You
Can Do In Order To Make Money &
Be Successful With Marketing
Ace McCloud

FACEBOOK
THE TOP 100 BEST WAYS
TO USE FACEBOOK FOR BUSINESS,
MARKETING & MAKING MONEY
Ace McCloud

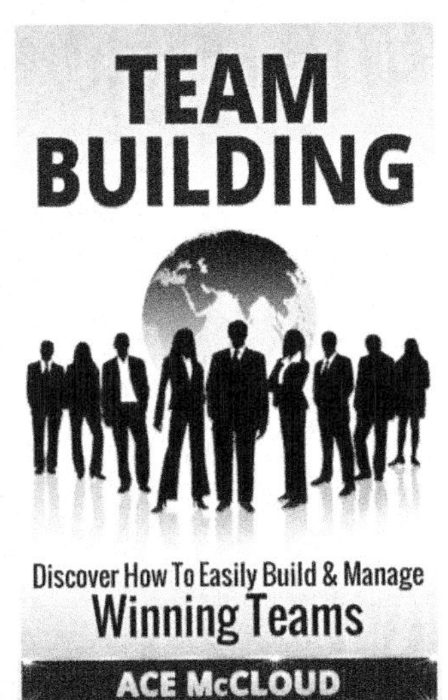
TEAM
BUILDING
Discover How To Easily Build & Manage
Winning Teams
ACE McCLOUD

MONEY
THE TOP 100 BEST WAYS
TO MAKE AND MANAGE MONEY
Ace McCloud

TWITTER
HOW TO MARKET & MAKE
MONEY WITH TWITTER
Ace McCloud

COMMUNICATION SKILLS

Discover The Best Ways To Communicate, Be Charismatic, Use Body Language, Persuade & Be A Great Conversationalist

Peak Performance Books

SUCCESS STRATEGIES

THE TOP 100 BEST WAYS TO BE SUCCESSFUL

Ace McCloud

Be sure to check out my audio books as well!

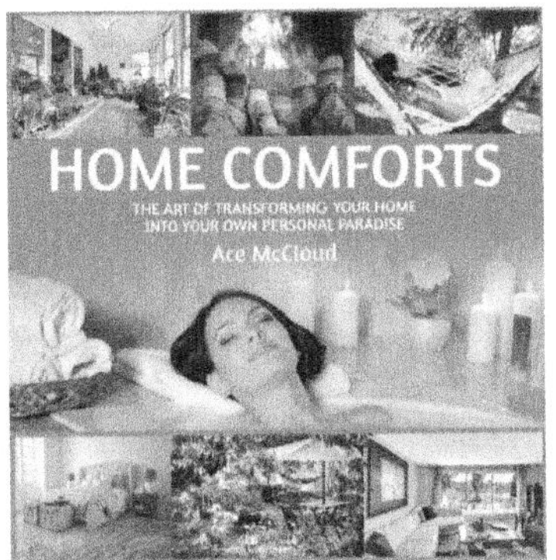

Check out my website at: www.AcesEbooks.com for a complete list of all of my books and high quality audio books. I enjoy bringing you the best knowledge in the world and wish you the best in using this information to make your journey through life better and more enjoyable! **Best of luck to you!**

CPSIA information can be obtained
at www.ICGtesting.com
Printed in the USA
LVOW04*0144041217
558539LV00005B/8/P

9 781640 48274